Nunavut

Nunavut:
Rethinking Political Culture

...... Ailsa Henderson

UBCPress · Vancouver · Toronto

© UBC Press 2007

All rights reserved. No part of this publication may be reproduced, stored in a retrieval system, or transmitted, in any form or by any means, without prior written permission of the publisher, or, in Canada, in the case of photocopying or other reprographic copying, a licence from Access Copyright (Canadian Copyright Licensing Agency), www.accesscopyright.ca.

16 15 14 13 12 11 10 09 08 07   5 4 3 2 1

Printed in Canada on ancient-forest-free paper (100% post-consumer recycled) that is processed chlorine- and acid-free, with vegetable-based inks.

Library and Archives Canada Cataloguing in Publication

Henderson, Ailsa
    Nunavut : rethinking political culture / Ailsa Henderson.

Includes bibliographical references and index.
ISBN 978-0-7748-1423-2

    1. Political culture – Nunavut. 2. Politics and culture – Nunavut. 3. Inuit – Nunavut – Politics and government. 4. Political participation – Nunavut. 5. Nunavut – Politics and government. I. Title.

FC4324.2.H46 2007   320.9719′5   C2007-904415-8

Canada

UBC Press gratefully acknowledges the financial support for our publishing program of the Government of Canada through the Book Publishing Industry Development Program (BPIDP), and of the Canada Council for the Arts, and the British Columbia Arts Council.

This book has been published with the help of a grant from the Canadian Federation for the Humanities and Social Sciences, through the Aid to Scholarly Publications Programme, using funds provided by the Social Sciences and Humanities Research Council of Canada.

UBC Press
The University of British Columbia
2029 West Mall
Vancouver, BC V6T 1Z2
604-822-5959 / Fax: 604-822-6083
www.ubcpress.ca

Contents

Tables and Illustrations	vii
Acknowledgments	ix
Abbreviations	xiii
1 Introduction	1
2 Politics in Nunavut	18
3 Inuit Political Culture	37
4 Political Integration in the Eastern Arctic	56
5 Institutional Design in the Eastern Arctic	85
6 Consensus Politics	112
7 Political Participation in Nunavut	138
8 Ideological Diversity in Nunavut	168
9 Transforming Political Culture in Nunavut	190
10 Cultural Pluralism and Political Culture	213
Appendix	221
Notes	223
References	228
Index	244

# Tables and Illustrations

Tables

2.1	Regions and communities in Nunavut	26
2.2	Proportions of households living in poverty	27
2.3	Measures of health and employability	30
5.1	Administration of political development in the NWT, 1936-99	110
6.1	Candidate reasons for running in the 2004 Nunavut election	122
6.2	Issues identified by voters and candidates	124
7.1	Turnout in land-claim–related plebiscites, 1982-97	146
7.2	Turnout in federal elections, 1979-2006	147
7.3	Turnout in Nunavut communities and constituencies, 1995-2006	148
7.4	Adjusted turnout rates for Nunavut elections, 2004	150
7.5	Turnout for NTI executive positions, 1999-2006	151
7.6	Primary identity attachments among Nunavut residents	156
7.7	Aggregate predictors of turnout in elections	157
7.8	Individual predictors of turnout in 2004	161
7.9	Competition for elected office in Nunavut, 1999-2006	165
7.10	Current employment of territorial candidates and MLAs, 1995-2004, in percent	166
8.1	Political attitudes in Nunavut and Canadian provinces, percent agreeing	171
8.2	Postmaterialism in Nunavut, in percent	174
8.3	Predictors of political attitudes	184

8.4 Political and demographic components of political clusters   186
9.1 Expectations of Nunavut   202
9.2 Support for the NLCA and Nunavut, percent agreeing   203
9.3 Support for the NLCA and Nunavut by ethnicity, percent agreeing   204
9.4 Impact of NLCA on individual, 2001 and 2004   207
9.5 Impact of Nunavut on individual, 2001 and 2004   208
9.6 Impact of Nunavut on ability to govern better, 2001 and 2004   209
9.7 Nunavut will face financial troubles, 2001 and 2004   210

Illustrations

Map of Nunavut   facing page 1
Postmaterialism by ethnicity and age   176

Acknowledgments

The community of scholars studying politics in the Canadian Arctic is a small but supportive one. I am particularly indebted to several individuals who provided their collective insights into political developments in Nunavut. Graham White and Annis May Timpson have endured most of the chapters in their initial incarnation as conference presentations, and I have benefited tremendously from their insights and support. Their company at conferences has been a delightful constant and an important source of advice. As Annis May will note, I have not grown out of my numbers phase, despite her predictions. Alex Baldwin at the Legislative Assembly of Nunavut has provided thoughtful and very thorough comments on various chapters and ideas and has facilitated access to public documents. His initial three-hour legislative tour was the most comprehensive introduction to politics in Nunavut I could have enjoyed, and I am grateful for the kindness he has extended to my undergraduate and graduate research assistants. Jack Hicks, formerly of the Nunavut Implementation Committee and Nunavut Bureau of Statistics, operates as a one-man Nunavut archive and has been unfailingly generous with his institutional memory, time, and energy. I am indebted to Emily Andrew and Ann Macklem at UBC Press for their enthusiastic support and professionalism.

Much of the research for this manuscript was conducted while I was an assistant professor in the Department of Political Science at Wilfrid Laurier University. The department provided tangible assistance in the form of a one-semester research leave and top-up funding for travel and research assistants, and this, in turn, provided me with the time and resources to conduct my work. I also benefited tremendously from the research community that the department fostered, and the book is much improved thanks to their support. Funding for initial fieldwork in Iqaluit was made possible by a SSHRC post-doctoral fellowship and a Victoria College George Metcalfe fellowship.

A Wilfrid Laurier post-doctoral fellowship funded additional research trips to Iqaluit, Pangnirtung, Igloolik, and Yellowknife. Additional funding for research assistance was facilitated through the Northern Scientific Training Program, and research assistance was provided by former Wilfrid Laurier students Stephanie Blenkiron and Jenny Tierney. Thanks to their resourcefulness, work ethic, and professionalism, they were both very valuable assets. Their time in the north was facilitated greatly by those who provided house-sits to unknown (but thankfully reliable) students: Terry Rogers and Amanda Ford, Rita Anilniliak and Shawn Strickland, Judy Anilniliak and Howard Chislett, Levinia and Ron Brown, Jack Hicks, Nancy Campbell and John Walsh, and Kim Cummings.

The quantitative analysis in this work would not have been possible without access to survey data. I would like to thank the Nunavut Bureau of Statistics and its directors Jack Hicks and Paul Harris for access to the Nunavut household surveys as well as Lucy Magee at the Department of Community, Government and Transportation for access to community voting data. I would also like to thank Pat Nagle and Fiona Christensen at the CBC and Doug Workman at the Nunavut Employees Union. The qualitative analysis would not have been possible without the interview subjects who generously took time out of busy work schedules to meet with me. This data collection was covered by a research licence issued by the Nunavut Research Institute in 2002. Those interviewed included Alex Baldwin, Jack Hicks, David Akeeagok, Simon Awa, Okalik Curley, Rebekah Wiliams, Jim Bell, Hunter Tootoo, David Omilgoitok, Wilf Atwood, Lee Selleck, and Rick Bargery. My Inuktitut teacher Papatsi Kublu-Hill showed considerable patience with my awkward if earnest efforts. For those who provided more informal opportunities to discuss political events, I am indebted for their hospitality and company. These include Nancy Campbell and John Walsh, Mary Cousins, Michael Bravo, Alison Rogan, Eva Aariak, Lena Eviq, Kenn Harper and Lynn Cousins, Jonah Kelly, Hunter Tootoo, Victor Tootoo, Nora Sanders, Jimi Onalik, Don Ellis, Ken Lovely, John MacDonald, Sousan Abadian, Chris Aquino, and Marianne Demmer. Mary-Ellen Thomas at the Nunavut Research Institute has been a useful sounding board for ideas, as have Gabrielle Slowey and David Brock. Birger and Marie Poppel in Nuuk, Karo Thomsen and Ono Fleischer in Illulisaat, Susan Soule in Anchorage, and Susan Woodley and Sheila Watt Cloutier in Iqaluit generously shared their homes and insights with me during my visits, and my stays with them are among the highlights of my research time in the North. Still others have provided company and support during successive research trips and have become valued friends. These include Maria Inês Monteiro and Claude Beauchamp, Gillian Corless, Matt Corless, Letia Cousins, Chris Douglas and Neida Gonzalez, Sandra Inutiq and Walter Oliver, Gavin Nesbitt, Shawna O'Hearn, Mitch Taylor, David Veniot, and Kathrine Wessendorf. I am particularly thankful to my Apex neighbours Philippe Lavallée, Terry Rogers, and Amanda Ford, who provided wonderful company, countless shared meals, and a much welcome diversion, often in the form of iced coffee, net cleaning, a short kayak trip, or a sewing lesson when the research process began to wear me down. Terry and Amanda's three brilliant children – Thomas, Sivu, and Matthew Ford-Rogers – and my regular house visitor Seepoola Shoo helped to provide an essential sense of perspective and reminded me often of the duty owed by the territory to its younger generation.

Previous versions of chapters were presented at the Nordic Association of Canadian Studies conference in Reykjavik (1999); the International Congress of Arctic Social Scientists in Fairbanks (2004); the First Nations First Thoughts conference organized by the Centre of Canadian Studies at the University of Edinburgh (2005); the Scott Polar Research Institute at Cambridge (2003); the Home Rule Government in Nuuk, Greenland (2004); and at the Toronto (2002), Halifax (2003), Winnipeg (2004), and London (2005) meetings of the Canadian Political Science Association (CPSA). The CPSA provided a welcome travel grant to the 2003 meetings. A previous version of Chapter 6 appeared as "Politics without Parties: Citizen Integration and Interest Articulation in Consensus Politics," in *Canadian Parties in Transition*, 3rd ed., edited by Alain-G. Gagnon and A. Brian Tanguay (Peterborough: Broadview, 2007). The updated chapter is reprinted by permission of Broadview. Sections of Chapter 7 appeared in 2004 as "Northern Political Culture: Political Behaviour in Nunavut," *Études/Inuit/Studies* 28 (1): 133-53. Sections of Chapter 8 appeared in 2007 as "Cultural Renaissance or Economic Emancipation: Predictors of Support for Devolution in Nunavut," *Journal of Canadian Studies* 41 (2): 1-23, and are reprinted with permission. Every effort has been made to contact copyright holders of material. If there are errors or omissions, they are unintentional and the publisher would be grateful to learn of them.

I was able to complete the book while serving as a visiting professor in Canadian Studies and Politics at the University of Edinburgh. Canadian Studies director Annis May Timpson and the centre's administrative assistant Anna Doherty provided the essential resources and welcoming environment for me to recreate an office-away-from-home, as did my colleagues in the politics department, Nicola McEwen, Annika Bergman, Wilfried Swenden, and Charlie Jeffery.

A final thank you to my friends and my family. My sister Kirsty's visit to Iqaluit and her Arctic swimming experience are particularly memorable. I am, as ever, indebted to my husband Stephen Tierney, whose continued enthusiasm and support I cherish and whose kindness and good humour I adore.

Abbreviations

ANOVA	analysis of variancce
APS	Aboriginal Peoples Survey
BRIA	Baffin Regional Inuit Association
CEO	chief electoral officer
CES	Canadian Election Study
CLEY	Department of Culture, Language, Elders and Youth
COPE	Committee for Original Peoples' Entitlement
CORA	Canadian Opinion Research Archive
CPSA	Canadian Political Science Association
CRIC	Centre for Research and Information on Canada
DEW	Distant Early Warning
DIAND	Department of Indian Affairs and Northern Development
DNANR	Department of Northern Affairs and Natural Resources
DV	dependent variable
GN	Government of Nunavut
GNWT	Government of the Northwest Territories
ILCC	Inuit Land Claims Commission
IQ	Inuit Qaujimajatuqangit
ITC	Inuit Tapirisat of Canada
LISPOP	Laurier Institute for the Study of Public Opinion and Policy
NIC	Nunavut Implementation Commission
NLCA	Nunavut Land Claims Agreement
NNI	Nunavummi Nangminiqaqtunik Ikajuuti
NRI	Nunavut Research Institute
NSDC	Nunavut Social Development Council
NSO	Northern Service Officer
NTI	Nunavut Tunngavik Incorporated
NuHS	Nunavut Household Survey

NWT	Northwest Territories
OLS	ordinary least squares
OSR	Office of the Special Representative
PCs	Progressive Conservatives
QIA	Qikiqtani Inuit Association
RCAP	Royal Commission on Aboriginal Peoples
SLiCA	Survey of Living Conditions in the Arctic
TFN	Tungavik Federation of Nunavut

Nunavut

North Pole
0
400 miles
0
400 kilometres
ARCTIC OCEAN
Ellesmere Island
GREENLAND
Magnetic North Pole
Grise Fiord
Baffin Bay
Melville Island
Devon Island
Resolute
Davis Strait
Lancaster Sound
Pond Inlet
Arctic Bay
Nanisivik
Clyde River
Victoria Island
NUNAVUT
Baffin Island
Qikiqtarjuaq
Cambridge Bay
Taloyoak
Igloolik
Kugluktuk
Hall Beach
Pangnirtung
Great Bear Lake
Umingmaktok
Gjoa Haven
Kugaaruk
Arctic Circle
Repulse Bay
Foxe Basin
Iqaluit
Cape Dorset
Back River
NORTHWEST TERRITORIES
Coral Harbour
Kimmirut
Hudson Strait
Baker Lake
Yellowknife
Chesterfield Inlet
Great Slave Lake
Rankin Inlet
Ungava Bay
Whale Cove
Arviat
Hudson Bay
Sanikiluaq
SASKATCH-EWAN
MANITOBA
QUEBEC
James Bay
ONTARIO

1
Introduction

In 1993, Inuit in the eastern Arctic of Canada signed a comprehensive land claim agreement with two other signatories: the federal government of Canada and the territorial government of the Northwest Territories (NWT). Stretching from Greenland in the east to the Yukon territory in the West, the NWT was at the time the largest political jurisdiction in Canada and home to a diverse blend of indigenous groups, including Dene, Métis, Cree, Inuvialuit, and Inuit. With their land claim, Inuit gained title to 350,000 square kilometres of land, including subsurface mineral rights to 35,000 square kilometres, over $1.1 billion in federal money to be transferred over a period of fourteen years; royalties from oil, gas, and mineral development on Crown land; hunting and fishing rights; and participation in land and resource management decisions through co-management boards. The Nunavut Land Claims Agreement (NLCA) also outlined provisions for a political accord, which provided for the creation in 1999 of a new territory in the Canadian Arctic. Meaning "our land" in Inuktitut, Nunavut is currently home to 30,000 residents, 85 percent of whom are Inuit beneficiaries of the Nunavut land claim.

This book explores the emergence of a distinct political culture in Nunavut, the norms of political behaviour, political values, and institutions that structure political relationships within the territory. It would be understandable for such a work to begin its description in 1999, with the first elections to the Nunavut Legislative Assembly, the opening of its doors, and the creation of a separate Nunavut bureaucracy. Such an approach would locate the birth of Nunavut political culture in the establishment of a distinct polity in the eastern Arctic. Political culture in Nunavut, however, bears the legacy of its past and, as such, is influenced by three separate cultures:

1 the culture of its precontact and contact Inuit population;
2 the culture of the Canadian political system into which this population was integrated; and
3 the territorial culture of the pre-division NWT.

Although these might seem linked to institutions rather than cultures, they are the product of, and agents in, a wider approach to political life. Each of these three cultures contains discrete approaches to political life and has influenced the achievement of the NLCA, the institutions established under the Nunavut Political Accord, and the attitudes, beliefs, values, and behaviours of the Nunavut electorate. These three cultures might be considered Inuit, southern, and northern, respectively, although these are only approximate labels. The federal government, for example, was undeniably a presence grounded in southern political practice, but it did, to different degrees, adapt to northern realities. The territorial government of the NWT, while based since 1967 in the north, also bears the imprint of southern political institutions. Neither of these is a monolithic, homogeneous, or pure example of "southern" or "northern" influence. Inuit varied in their reactions to the increasing contact with traders, missionaries, and government officials. Indeed, contact for different areas occurred at different times, and the method of contact itself structured reaction. By consulting diverse historical and contemporary sources drafted by both Inuit and non-Inuit, it is possible to identify general cultural approaches to political relationships that seem typical of these three influences. Political culture in Nunavut, then, bears the influence of these three cultures, each of which has been marked by adaptation to the other. Whether or not the end result is a unified, distinct political culture bearing the marks of both a Westminster political tradition and an Inuit approach to community decision making is the focus of this book.

Our traditional understandings of political culture suggest that political institutions both spring from and influence the behaviour of the citizenry. This organic relationship between the act of institutional creation and the continuing influence of institutions should not suggest that all members of the electorate have an equal say in the creation of institutions. More often than not, political institutions have been created by political elites with vested interests in certain outcomes or certain patterns of stability within the polity. In polities where elites share the same goals as the electorate, or in polities where non-elites possess the capacity to influence the design of institutions, the result can be a unified political culture. In polities where political elites represent a distinct subgroup within the population – a subgroup whose members have little in common, either economically or culturally, with the rest of the population – the result can be an uneasy grafting of one group's institutions onto another's. Political culture research certainly provides us with examples of institutions selected by state elites and grafted onto polities whose economic or ideological realities provided them with a hostile home.

The process of institutional creation helps us to understand political culture in Nunavut. Here we have a population that had its own decision-making practices, if not formal institutions as we traditionally understand them. The institutions of Nunavut, however, bear a decidedly British influence. These institutions were not created by elites, leaders, decision makers, or power brokers within Inuit or northern society but by elites within the Canadian political system. Since the redrawing of territorial boundaries in 1905, we have seen two processes of adaptation in the north: one that occurs among institutions, which have only slowly and recently started to bear the mark of the population for which they were created, and one that occurs among residents. This second process of adaptation has occurred much faster than the first. Until now, however, we have not paid very much attention to the political adaptation of northerners. This is not to say that there is little research on the north. On the contrary, both southern academics and northern residents have addressed the Christianization of the population, the transition to a wage economy, relocation, and the establishment of settlements. What we have lacked until now, however, is research that focuses on the collision of different political cultures within the north.[1] Relying on a wealth of primary and secondary sources, *Nunavut: Rethinking Political Culture* addresses three key research questions: (1) how has the pre-existing model of Inuit governance and the process by which Inuit were integrated into the Canadian political system influenced the current operation of political life in Nunavut? (2) to what extent does the institutional structure of political life affect the political behaviour of its citizens? and (3) is there a distinct political culture within Nunavut? Throughout this book, I track the emergence of a variant political culture within Canada, one in which opportunities for participation are plentiful but in which the costs of involvement – in time and money – are far higher than they are in southern Canada and in the two other territories.

Although sparsely populated, Nunavut has proven a fertile ground for researchers. The physical environment has attracted the attentions of scientists interested in species variation, glaciology, climate change, and mineral deposits. Inhabitants of the eastern Arctic have also received considerable attention from social scientists. Typical research addresses kinship patterns, naming conventions, food sharing, knowledge transfer, taboos, games, songs, myths, and the material culture of Inuit. Such research is supplemented by the diaries and biographies of the explorers, traders, missionaries, nurses, teachers, miners, construction workers, and government employees who have travelled to the eastern Arctic for adventure or job prospects and who, upon returning home, decided to put their experiences to paper. Rarely has so much been written about so few. Given the wealth of information, one might wonder why an examination of political culture in Nunavut is useful or even necessary. This books fills a gap in existing political research on Nunavut, and there are three rather obvious reasons for the need to do so.

First, the creation of Nunavut is the result of the largest settled land claim in Canadian history. Considered as one of a number of experiments in quasi self-government for Aboriginal peoples, it holds obvious lessons for political scientists. How individuals adapt to institutional change, the sources of tension between public government and Aboriginal organizations, and whether citizens develop a greater sense of trust in political institutions are all issues that arise from a serious consideration of political life in Nunavut. In this approach to the study of Nunavut, residents of the north are viewed primarily as citizens in a contemporary polity rather than as members of a particular cultural group.

Second, the establishment of new public institutions provided an opportunity to create a new political culture. Inuit claims negotiators viewed the creation of a territory not just as a way to improve resource access but as a means to secure greater attention to Inuit values and culture. Coupled with the land claim, it provided the route to political and economic self-determination. The new territory could not only effect a cultural renaissance for eastern Arctic Inuit but it could also change the culture of political institutions. For members of the Nunavut Implementation Commission, the establishment of a decentralized bureaucracy provided the chief deviation from the structure of NWT political institutions. Positions with the Nunavut public service were to be distributed among the ten largest communities, spreading expertise and wealth throughout the territory. A second key deviation, articulated primarily since 1999, would see the improved integration of Inuit ways of thinking and problem-solving and of approaches to life. Has such an integration produced the intended rewards? In order to answer this question, I identify various institutional approaches to political culture, indicate how they are shaped by individuals, and discuss how, in turn, they shape the rules of political life.

Third, Nunavut is something of an anomaly within the Canadian federation. It contains the fewest residents spread among the largest geographic area. It is the only jurisdiction in which Aboriginal people form more than three-quarters of the electorate. Indicators of health and education, however, point to worrying trends. The sheer dominance of government in people's lives – as an employer and a provider of housing, education, or income – must be acknowledged. These differences are useful for they highlight the multiple and overlapping influences on political life in Nunavut, and it is not always easy to determine whether events or patterns may be attributed to the predominantly Inuit population, to its territorial status, or to the fact that we are dealing with a sparsely populated Arctic environment. In addition, the markers that serve to distinguish Nunavut are not zero sum. The territory contains a predominantly Inuit population, but it is not ethnically homogeneous. Its institutions reflect the considerable influence of the NWT, but there are important distinctions. As the product of a land claim and political accord, this distinct polity provides an opportunity to examine the multiple influences on contemporary political culture.

Research linking Aboriginal politics to a wider theoretical political literature appears in two general groups. The first group approaches Aboriginal politics from a political economy perspective and, in so doing, explores inequalities of resources and power (Abele 1997; Wotherspoon and Satzewich 2000). Topics include the real and metaphorical processes of colonization (Green 2003), the integration of First Nations workers into a capitalist system (Kellough 1980), the impact of globalization (Slowey 2001), the position of First Nations women (Green 2003), and the internal colonialism that results from a fundamental inequality of access to resources and power (Hicks 2004). Research in this vein views self-government as a way, often imperfect, to correct for past injustices by providing access to the very things that Aboriginal groups have traditionally lacked in the political sphere; namely, resources and economic development (Alfred 1999; Billson 2001; Ladner 2001; Macdonald 2000; Russell 2000; Rynard 2000; Stabler 1989). A second group employs Aboriginal peoples (or Aboriginal culture) as an empirical example in a normative discussion of rights, citizenship, or belonging in contemporary liberal society (Kernerman 2005; Kymlicka 1995; Tully 1995a, 1995b, 1999). Viewed as national minorities, Aboriginal peoples are deemed worthy of certain collective rights. Self-government, in this research, is viewed as a welcome component of multicultural approaches to constitutional recognition and as the moral motor for a system of differentiated citizenship, described by one political scientist as "citizens plus" (Cairns 2000). The position of culture within such research varies. The political economy literature integrates culture into a larger discussion of power, while the normative literature assumes that Aboriginal peoples have a specific and different cultural approach to political life from that of Euro-Canadians. Although it sees this approach as one worthy of recognition, it frequently fails to catalogue either the extent to which it exists or how it has matured.

Nunavut: Rethinking Political Culture grounds itself in cultural explanations of political attitudes, behaviour, and institutions. If culture functions as a toolkit, informing individuals about the dominant beliefs, values, and approaches of a particular society, then political culture includes the dominant political beliefs, values, and approaches to political life that define a particular polity. Political culture has both a theoretical and practical significance. In practical terms, it is worth identifying the ideal cluster of attitudes and behaviour that allows democracy to flourish in some states while ensuring that it will flounder in others. This was certainly the interest of early studies of political cultures, from the more sociological approaches of Tocqueville to the more quantitative approach of political scientists writing in the 1960s (Almond and Verba 1963; Pye and Verba 1965). Political culture also helps us to understand the way individuals interact with the institutions that structure their daily lives, why certain modes of interaction are favoured over others, and why particular models of institutional design recur over time. Such insights are not necessarily immediately relevant from a policy perspective, but they help social scientists to better understand how individuals acquire certain beliefs and why they act the way they do.

Political culture is the product of empirical fact and perception. What citizens think of the state is, in part, a function of the way the state treats them through its rules and institutions. In part, though, attitudes toward the state are a function of perception divorced from fact. While Tocqueville was concerned with the quality of political representatives, contemporary political culture researchers are more likely to explore what individuals *think* of their political representatives – whether they trust them or think them worthy of deference, whether they find that they foster a sense of efficacy, whether they, as individuals, are satisfied with them – rather than the extent to which their representatives are performing effectively.

Research on political culture also addresses the relationship between institutions and values, including the capacity of institutions to create or sustain attitudinal and behavioural norms and the fit between externally imposed or internally developed institutions and citizen expectations. Although evidence has been mixed, much research argues that political cultures prove themselves resistant to change. In some cases, this is because the behavioural norms are so powerful that institutional reform provides an insufficient influence (Putnam 1993). In others, the attitudes provide a hostile environment for new institutions, producing the political equivalent of organ rejection. Within Canada, political culture research has focused on an earlier stage, on the establishment of political institutions in nascent cultures and their capacity to influence contemporary political culture. Fragment theorists argued for the impact of settlers from New France (Hartz 1964; Horowitz 1966) or of United Empire Loyalists (Bell 1970; Lipset 1968; Lipset 1990) on the Tory-tinged liberalism of Canadian political culture. More recently, the Charter is attributed with transforming Canadian political culture, engendering among its citizens (and political scientists) a rights-based approach to citizenship (Howe and Fletcher 2001). Here, institutions are both the product of one coherent political culture and a variable in the creation of another. If much of the comparative research on political culture suggests a certain skepticism about the capacity of institutions to shape attitudes and behaviour, Canadian research has tended to stress the ways in which coherent cultural fragments and the institutions they develop can have a long-lasting effect. Both Horowitz and Lipset warned that cultural influence was not automatic. Settlers must appear before the point at which political institutions congeal in order to exert influence on political culture. The only problem with these explanations – so tightly woven into our understandings of Canadian political culture – is that empirical research has shown influence to be overstated, if apparent at all (Stewart 1994).

The creation of Nunavut provides an opportunity to test three aspects of political culture. First, it allows us to examine the interaction of what we might identify as distinct cultural fragments in the eastern Arctic. We can identify the fundamental precepts of Inuit, federal, and territorial political cultures, the points on which they disagree, and how they have influenced and been marked by contact with each other. In the collision of cultures we can identify values that remained and became dominant as well as those that disappeared over time. By exploring the political culture of Nunavut, we can test whether earlier cultural fragments provide an inheritance for the contemporary polity.

Second, the creation of Nunavut enables us to explore the relationships among different aspects of political culture. Nunavut provides a useful context within which to study the fit between institutions, on the one hand, and citizen attitudes and behaviours, on the other, precisely because its political institutions were so obviously grafted from one culture onto another. The state is, of course, a non-neutral agent, and research on Canadian politics has shown how the state at times validates a system that discriminates against Aboriginal people (Frideres 1991). Not only does the state act in the interests of certain groups within the polity but it also reflects particular visions of the ideal relationship between itself and its citizens. Within Nunavut, these views are evident both in the way the state sought to integrate Inuit and in the successive and conscious efforts to create political institutions that altered the relationship between citizen and state. Times of institutional change provide particularly fruitful opportunities to examine political culture for they show how different groups of individuals exert an uneven influence on the development of political institutions, allow for a before-and-after vision of the dominant political attitudes, and test for the capacity of reform to produce meaningful change in the aggregate attitudes and behaviours of the electorate.

Third, we can test for the capacity of federal systems to house variant political cultures. The state could be considered a homogenizing influence on political culture. If citizens are subject to similar laws or rules of participation, if policy seeks to make uniform access to education, health care, or social and economic rights, the result can be a state with few political cleavages. And yet, in their investigation of Canadian political culture, Simeon and Elkins (1974) identified significant regional variations in attitudes and behaviours. They attributed these to the unique activities of provincial governments and variations in the way the federal government treats its citizens. Both of these culture generators are evident in Nunavut. We can hardly find a better example of federal exceptionalism than the treatment of Inuit in the eastern Arctic, and much of the existing research on the north chronicles the extent and effect of institutional anomalies such as consensus politics. We also know that socio-economic realities serve as predictors of political attitudes and behaviour. If we know that economic situation, language, religion, and urban-rural environment can have an impact on people's political views; and if we know that the economic, linguistic, religious, and urban profile of the north is different from that of the south, that the federal government has treated its citizens differently and that the territorial political institutions contain anomalous features; then we have an ideal opportunity to test for the generation of cultural boundaries. I contribute to each of these debates by exploring the generation and operation of political culture in Nunavut.

I also offer an opportunity to test the boundaries of cultural pluralism. In Canada, multiculturalism is the most obvious example of normative support for cultural pluralism. Culture, in this sense, is often linked to private expressions of difference; multiculturalism thus allows individuals to remain connected within an ethnic culture while enjoying full rights as Canadian citizens and full integration within Canadian society. It is decidedly pluralist in that it welcomes the existence and expression of multiple cultures. If governments can display positive support for cultures, or can abide by a policy of negative non-interference, then Canadian multiculturalism clearly supports cultural pluralism (Kymlicka 1995; Requejo 2005; Tierney 2004; Tully 1995b). This seems relatively straightforward when we associate culture with food, customs, or even visions of the good life. In a liberal state, all visions of the good life are considered fair game so long as they do not run afoul of the law. If we adopt a different definition of culture, if we see it as a political culture, concerned with public interactions between the state and citizens, then the management of cultural pluralism is rather more difficult because it involves rival visions of the role of the state.

There are, of course, different ways to embrace the pluralism of political cultures. In one scenario, we might decide that one political culture should take priority over others without infringing upon the ability of a particular group to express itself. This is possible in a federal state, where the state possesses one political culture while substate units, whether nations or not, possess their own political cultures, each of which is sustained and nurtured by domestic political institutions. Within a unitary polity, however, it is not immediately clear how these dominant and subordinate political cultures might interact. We might detect the existence of rival political cultures, each vying for supremacy. For Wildavsky and others this situation is entirely normal, the eventual political culture of any state formed by a jostling among its constituent cultures, whether public or institutional, mass or elite (Wildavsky 1987; see also Smith 1993; Mamadouh 1997). If we think of cultural pluralism not in terms of private cultural expression but, rather, in terms of political cultures – with each culture having a different vision of the role of the state, the interaction of citizens, citizens' rights, decision making, and the goals of public institutions – then we begin to see how a polity might become marked by rivalries between different political cultures.

An investigation of political culture in Nunavut is relevant, therefore, not only because of what it tells us about Inuit, northerners, or particular types of elections but also for what it tells us about cultures, about how one culture comes to dominate others. Those interested in the political cultures of advanced industrial democracies must deal with the fact that the period during which radical change occurred, during which the political culture settled, is far removed. In Nunavut, however, this is not the case: the process of cultural change is far more recent. As a result, it affords us an opportunity to understand the process by which cultures attempt to supplant one another, the challenges that they face, and the uneasy accommodation that exists when a population attempts to replace the dominant political culture with another one, however hesitant or contested those efforts may seem.

Methodology

Research on Canadian political attitudes and behaviours relies almost exclusively on the analysis of quantitative data taken from large surveys, data that are not readily available for the territories. Typical data sources include the Canadian Election Study (CES), the World Values Survey, and, occasionally, private polling data made available through data archives such as those housed at the Canadian Opinion Research Archive (CORA) at Queen's University or the Laurier Institute for the Study of Public Opinion and Policy (LISPOP) at Wilfrid Laurier University. Territorial residents are typically absent from these datasets.

The World Values Survey, by far the most comprehensive comparative study of public opinion, and one now conducted in over seventy countries worldwide, contains no northern respondents in any of the three surveys (1981, 1990, 2000) conducted in Canada. The CES, begun in 1964 to study political attitudes and behaviours during and after federal election campaigns, contained northern respondents in only one of its versions; for the 1997 election the CES team included ninety-seven respondents from the NWT out of a total sample of 3,949. We cannot distinguish between eastern and western residents of the territory, and only twenty-two out of ninety-seven indicated their ethnicity as Native or Inuit, far short of the 52 percent recorded for the general NWT population. Of the private firms, only two, the Centre for Research and Information on Canada (CRIC) and Environics, have regularly included northern respondents in their surveys. In its latest Portraits of

Canada survey, CRIC included three hundred northern respondents, one-third of whom were from Nunavut, in its sample of 3,204. Environics routinely runs a North of 60 monitor, composed entirely of northern respondents. This includes a more developed series of questions on voting and key issues facing voters. Although Environics archives its Focus Ontario and Focus Canada reports with CORA, it does not release its North of 60 monitor because it can continue to sell these data for profit. The paucity of available northern data no doubt facilitates its sale. If southern-based surveys rarely include northern respondents, northern surveys do not necessarily fill the gap for those interested in political attitudes and behaviour.

The 2001 Aboriginal Peoples Survey (APS) conducted by Statistics Canada contains very few attitudinal questions and none related to political attitudes and behaviour. The APS was the vehicle used to distribute the Canadian component of the Survey of Living Conditions in the Arctic (SLiCA), a comparative survey of demographic data, behaviours, and social attitudes in the circumpolar world. Because Canadian investigators went into the field before the comparative survey was fully developed, the Canadian instrument lacks the attitudinal questions included in the Greenlandic, American, Swedish, Finnish, and Russian surveys (Andersen and Poppel 2002; Andersen, Kruse, and Poppel 2002). Between them, SLiCA and APS provide reliable data on why a respondent would leave his or her hometown, harvesting activities, and degree of satisfaction with language retention. They do not contain data on the degree of satisfaction with politics nor do they address a range of social and political behaviours.

Government surveys are often a useful source of information. The federal government commissions polls of Aboriginal Canadians, but these focus on the on-reserve First Nations population to the exclusion of Inuit and Métis respondents. Inuit organizations in particular have criticized the Department of Indian and Northern Affairs for equating Aboriginal issues with First Nations issues (Inuit Tapiriit Kanatami 2004). Each of the territories conducts its own surveys, but only one includes more than a few attitudinal questions about politics. In the 2001 Nunavut Household Survey (NuHS), this is limited to whether one voted in the last election, how one feels about the NLCA, and whether one is satisfied with the progress of the territorial government. The absence of attitudinal data is not surprising as citizens might view government-commissioned surveys on past voting behaviour, views of the state, and satisfaction with the government as an intrusion. Within this general paucity of data, the 2004 Nunavut Household Survey is unique in its coverage of political and social topics. Questions probe political interest, democratic satisfaction, voter turnout, efficacy, cynicism, deference, and postmaterialism. The survey replicates questions employed in the Canadian Election Survey and the World Values Survey and, therefore, makes it possible to draw a comparison between Nunavummiut and other Canadians. The 2004 NuHS thus enables the type of political culture research that is already common in southern Canada.

And yet Nunavut is unlike other Canadian jurisdictions. Before the arrival of missionaries or government officials, its predominantly Inuit population possessed distinct approaches to social relations, power, and leadership. The manner in which Inuit were integrated into the Canadian political system established avenues of participation and set up a system of goals and benefits that structured not only the process by which a claim was achieved but also the dominant patterns of political interaction throughout the 1970s and 1980s. The territorial institutions of the NWT have had an obvious impact on the post-division institutional framework of Nunavut. Each of these is integral to political culture in Nunavut and helps to explain contemporary attitudes and behaviour. For this reason, I rely on a range of evidence – historical and contemporary, qualitative and quantitative, aggregate and individual – that allows for both a thick and thin description of political culture in Nunavut.

The first half of *Nunavut: Rethinking Political Culture*, which establishes the patterns of political culture prior to and during the establishment of a new territory, relies almost exclusively on qualitative data. These include material from the NWT archives at the Prince of Wales Heritage Centre in Yellowknife and semi-structured interviews with elders, transcripts of which are housed at the Igloolik office of the Nunavut Research Institute (NRI). The archival material covers the period from 1950 to 1982 and draws on the files of the Office of the Administrator of the Arctic, government departments such as the Northern Administrative Branch, religious organizations, the Carrothers Commission, and the previously classified files of the Drury Commission. The more than four hundred interviews conducted by the NRI, which often include repeated sessions with particular individuals, address topics such as childhood memories, myths, hunting practices, mobility patterns, exposure to religious authorities, and perceptions of social, economic, and cultural change. Conducted since the early 1990s, the interviews provide a comprehensive account of life among Inuit hunting camps and settled communities since the middle of the twentieth century. The majority of elders interviewed would have spent much of their adolescence and early adulthood on a swath of land bound roughly by Repulse Bay to the southwest and Pond Inlet to the northeast, with hunting areas around present-day Igloolik and Hall Beach in the middle. As such, their experiences should be seen as an accurate reflection of life among the *Amitturmiut* and *Tununirmiut*. Exposure to *Uqqurmiut* Inuit in the south Baffin area and to inland groups in the Kivalliq was relatively limited. For this reason, the interviews have been supplemented by a wider range of primary sources, some of which are available through elders conferences or are published in collections of oral histories such as *Uqalurait* (Bennett and Rowley 2004). Secondary sources include personal memoirs and the research of academics and social commentators, primarily anthropologists, who have for decades travelled to the north in an effort to better understand Inuit society. These sources were supplemented by information acquired through semi-structured interviews that I conducted with territorial, federal, and local officials, MLAs, and journalists in Iqaluit and Yellowknife.

The second half of *Nunavut: Rethinking Political Culture* relies on quantitative data covering attitudes and behaviours in Nunavut. These include surveys I conducted for the CBC and Nunavut Employees Union during the 2004 territorial election campaign as well as two databases that I created: the first on community demographic and electoral behaviour from 1995 to 2006 and the second on constituency political behaviour for 2004. My analysis also draws on three territorial datasets: the Nunavut add-on to the 1999 NWT Labour Force Survey and the Nunavut household surveys for 2001 and 2004, respectively. Together these datasets enable me to analyze the goals and previous employment of political candidates, predictors of voter turnout, dominant attitudes and behaviour, and evaluations of political development in Nunavut. These qualitative and quantitative data were acquired on ten research trips to Nunavut from 2002 to 2005 and an eight-month research leave in Iqaluit, with side trips to Pangnirtung and Igloolik, from January to August 2003. I gathered comparative information during a two-week visit to Greenland in August 2004.

This triangulated research design contains both strengths and weaknesses. It is tied inherently to definitions of political culture as the property of the aggregate rather than as something contained within individuals. Individual behaviour is treated as a symptom of political culture and merely directs us toward general themes within any given polity. This definition of political culture could be perceived as a potential weakness, as could the focus on cultural explanations in general. My analysis assumes that rational or economic motivations of voter behaviour, for example, occur within a general cultural context that establishes the parameters of acceptable behaviour, the goals and benefits identified by citizens, and the dominant modes of their expression. Researchers more sympathetic to rational choice or economic explanations might find fault with this approach, preferring a purer calculus based primarily on cost-benefit analysis. In my analysis of political developments in Nunavut I rely upon a canon of comparative political science. In doing this I am aware that I am imposing a Western, scientific lens on political life in the territory. I do not give voice to an over-studied indigenous population but attempt to map and explain the competing cultural influences that have helped to shape political culture in Nunavut.

The methodologies employed have certain reliability concerns. I conducted my research either in English or through the lens of interpretation or translation. This trusts, for example, that the terminology employed by those translating the NRI interviews accurately reflects the intentions of the interview subjects. Qualitative and quantitative approaches each raise different concerns. Quantitative research is often thought to provide, at best, thin interpretations of culture. Questions designed by other researchers for other purposes cannot always contribute meaningful evidence to different research questions. For these reasons, I supplement statistics with more qualitative information. And yet here too we should exercise caution.

Anyone hoping to impute political values based on primary documents faces certain challenges. With interviews, imperfect recall is an obvious concern. In the case of the elder interviews in Igloolik, the cohort of interview subjects was asked to provide information about events that happened half a century ago. For any sample of subjects this would pose certain problems, but for this cohort, the fifty-year period in question covered the oft-quoted "stone age to space age" transformation of Inuit life. Comments about how young people no longer behave as they used to are influenced both by the same steady cultural transformation we find in other societies and by an unrelenting series of cultural transformations far greater than that experienced elsewhere in Canada. Teasing out which comments can be attributed to which transformation is not always easy. At the same time, we are dealing with a cohort of interview subjects whose role in society has been considerably diminished from what it would have been in a more traditional era. It would be reasonable in such a situation to emphasize the positive elements of traditional life and attach less importance to trials or difficulties.

Still other pitfalls relate primarily to the nature of the case study. We must avoid the temptation to reify Inuit culture and, thus, to assume a static interpretation. Practices among Inuit varied over time. Many of these accounts stem from the postcontact period, when interactions with traders were regular and exposure to missionaries was increasing. We must avoid using easy stereotypes, which are usually informed by an incomplete vision of various aspects of social life. As Trott (2001) notes, much that was written about Inuit in the mid-twentieth century portrayed them as rather happy and simple, a view reinforced by the staged photographs of smiling Inuit made available by missionaries. The stereotype of the adaptable Inuk is based primarily on how quickly Inuit took to improvements in hunting implements rather than, for example, to transformations in gender relations or child rearing. Reductionism masks considerable variations among both regions and individuals. Not all Inuit reacted to Christianity, the incursion of government officials, and the imposition of formalized education in the same way.

Structure of Nunavut: Rethinking Political Culture

The first half of the book analyzes influences on contemporary political culture in Nunavut, while the second half analyzes the constituent elements of that culture. Chapter 2 identifies the dominant approaches to power, leadership, and social control in contact and postcontact Inuit society. Because Inuit society did not require public institutions of governance, I explore how decisions about resources and mechanisms for ensuring social control help us to understand Inuit political culture. I distinguish between spiritual and temporal agents of social control and chronicle the impact of Christianization on each of those agents. Chapter 3 explores the process by which Inuit were integrated into the political system. It addresses both the opportunities for Inuit involvement in the existing structures and the manner in which their participation was courted. That Inuit were treated not as though they were subject to the rules but as exceptions to them can be seen in the operation of elections, in differing visions of representation, and in the encouragement of democracy at the local level. At certain times, federal and territorial approaches to Inuit served to exclude them from further participation; at other times, governments courted and encouraged their participation. The integration process was twofold, in that state elites designed methods they thought would aid the integration of Inuit, but Inuit themselves had goals and plans on how best to become active Canadian citizens. At times these efforts were at cross purposes. I argue that federal and territorial officials were unprepared for the speed with which Inuit adapted to the norms of political life; benevolent paternalism was replaced with surprise and frustration in light of often aggressive attempts on the part of Inuit to secure full political rights. While Chapter 3 addresses government decisions about people, Chapter 4 explores government decisions regarding the institutions structuring political life. It tracks the changing cast of characters who made decisions about institutional design, from federal administrators and territorial bureaucrats to legislative members and Inuit land claims negotiators. It focuses on disagreements among these actors not only with regard to the ideal institutional components of political life but also to the process by which an ideal institutional framework might emerge. I conclude the chapter by examining disagreements about institutional design during and after the 1993 land claim. Together, Chapters 2, 3, and 4 analyze an overlapping chronology of events in an effort to detect different cultural approaches and their potential influence on political culture.

The second half of the book systematically examines contemporary political culture in Nunavut. Chapter 5 addresses consensus politics, tracking its origins and impact on the behaviour of legislators both during campaigns and legislative sessions. It explores the subsequent costs to citizens of staying informed and becoming involved, and it identifies how, in the absence of political parties, political elites mirror behaviour in other political jurisdictions. Chapter 6 examines the behaviour of voters, focusing primarily on voter turnout in federal and territorial elections. It argues that the measurement of territorial turnout exaggerates levels of activity among political "spectators," but demonstrates that opportunities for gladiatorial activity are far greater in Nunavut than elsewhere in Canada. Chapter 7 begins by measuring the extent of the north-south attitudinal divide before mapping the separate issue publics that exist within Nunavut political culture. It identifies the demographic foundations for political cleavages and then locates five attitudinal clusters within the territory, each of which appears to have integrated the discrete cultural fragments in Nunavut in different ways. Chapter 8 evaluates political developments in Nunavut. After discussing current academic and government assessments of the territory, I turn to the sole conscious effort to significantly modify political culture in Nunavut through the promotion and integration of Inuit Qaujimajatuqangit, or that which Inuit have long known. This raises the possibility of two success stories in Nunavut. Economic gains made by Nunavummiut could affirm that branch of political economy research that argues that land claims and treaties offer a fundamental shift in power relations by providing resources to those long denied them. Rival explanations view the territory as an opportunity for cultural change. Using quantitative data, Chapter 8 concludes by identifying predictors of support for the NLCA and the new territory, whether economic or cultural. Each of the chapters in the second half of the book contributes to our understanding of political developments in Nunavut while offering a nuanced interpretation of how political culture operates.

Finally, the terminology employed in *Nunavut: Rethinking Political Culture* reflects northern conventions. The book subscribes to English naming conventions for place names, and thus uses "Igloolik" rather than "Iglulik" and "Pangnirtung" rather than "Paniktuuq." Communities that have changed names, such as Iqaluit, Kimmirut, Qikiqtarjuaq, Kugluktuk, and Kugaaruk, are referred to by their current rather than by their former appellations of Frobisher Bay, Lake Harbour, Broughton Island, Coppermine, and Pelly Bay. The exception occurs when archival material contains quotations referring to original place names. For the sake of precision, references to people are given in Inuktitut. "Inuit" is used consistently as the plural of "Inuk." Two people of Inuit ethnicity are referred to as "Inuuk." The terms "Qallunaat" and "non-Inuit" are used interchangeably. The singular term is "Qallunaq," while "Qallunaak" refers to two non-Inuit. "Nunavummiut" refers to residents of the territory and includes both Inuit and non-Inuit. Direct quotations from the interview material, particularly from the elder interviews, have not been corrected; quotations from written material, however, have been corrected for style or grammar. Where relevant, square brackets indicate editorial changes.

2
Politics in Nunavut

Most descriptions of Nunavut begin with an acknowledgment that its population is composed primarily of Inuit beneficiaries of a comprehensive land claim. Any analysis of political life in Nunavut must acknowledge the rapidly changing social, economic, and political environment of its Inuit population. Research on Inuit in the nineteenth and twentieth centuries often employs categories of contact, adhering to roughly chronological periods, such as precontact or contact-traditional. In part, this helps to distinguish among groups that at the same point in time enjoyed different patterns of interaction with Europeans. At a time when Inuit around Pangnirtung or Pond Inlet would have enjoyed sustained and frequent contact with whalers, Inuit in the Keewatin interior would have led lives far less influenced by European capitalism. Outlining the different waves of cultural exposure helps us to better understand both the considerable diversity of the contact experience for Inuit and its potential impact on the north as a whole.

Inuit in the eastern Arctic are part of a wider ethnic group found in Alaska, Russia, and Greenland. Linguistically, they are distinct from Inuvialuit in the western Canadian Arctic and Y'upik in northern Alaska. Although practices varied, Inuit in the eastern Arctic travelled in small social units made up of extended family members, their movement tied to seasons and the availability of food. The result was a life that was very much dependent on the resources available from the land, lived in rhythm with the seasons, where surviving and living to become an elder were signs of land-based skills.

The land on which Canadian Inuit live has been described as barren and inhospitable, but this mistakes temperature for resources. Certainly it is cold, with winter temperatures regularly varying between -20 and -30 degrees Celsius. Snowfall also varies, but by January and February the frozen waterways and sea allow transportation by dog team or snowmobile. Viewed in this way, ice is not inhospitable but life-sustaining, providing an environment where animals can hunt and a means of transportation for a population so dependent on the land. Contemporary concern about climate change attempts to make this link between ice and livelihood explicit, evocatively expressed by the Inuit Circumpolar Conference as the right to be cold.

The northern diet includes caribou, seal, walrus, polar bear, muskox, whale, Arctic char, clams, and mussels; some of these are eaten raw, some are air dried, and some are usually cooked. Non-protein sources include seaweed and berries. The availability of food varies by season and region. In general, the term "country food" is used to refer not just to the food itself but also to its method of acquisition.

Commercial shipping and airborne pollution are blamed for elevated toxin levels, particularly in those animals higher up the food chain who acquire the accumulated toxins of the animals they eat in addition to those found in vegetation. Heavy metals such as mercury, lead, and cadmium, along with organic chlorine compounds such as PCBs, make their way to those who eat seal, polar bear, or walrus, resulting in critically high toxin levels in northern populations. Although the land and country food provide a constant in both precontact and postcontact life, these elevated toxins levels point to the challenges faced by those attempting to lead more traditional lives.

Precontact Inuit society was not homogeneous. Inuit social networks varied, as did linguistic dialects and food sources. Identifying the boundaries of groups, then, depends on the criteria that one uses. Typically, geographic groupings are identified by the suffix "-miut," which means "people of." Iglulingmiut, therefore, refers to those who originally lived near present-day Igloolik, while Qairnirmiut refers to those who lived near present-day Baker Lake and Rankin Inlet. Such distinctions are grounded in territorial occupation and thus reflect types of food sources as well as linguistic differences. Other approaches identify broader cultural groups that vary in their internal organization. In Nunavut this would distinguish among Copper Inuit, Caribou Inuit, and Inuit from Netsilik, Iglulik, and Baffin Island. These groups are all part of the Central Inuit, which is itself part of the circumpolar Inuit population, bounded by Alaska Inuit to the west and Greenland Inuit to the east. Each of these groups possessed distinct features. Caribou Inuit occupied the Keewatin interior, while Netsilik Inuit lived in the area now occupied by the Kitikmeot communities of Taloyoak, Kugaaruk, and Gjoa Haven. The two types of groupings – territorial and cultural – are related, so that the

"-miut" groups reflect a greater variation within the Copper, Caribou, and Baffin Island Inuit. Chapter 3 examines the variations in decision making and social control among these groups.

The arrival of Europeans occurred in three waves and, in the words of one observer, brought both "the joys and pitfalls of cross-cultural contact" (Merritt 1993a, 2). The first wave included Norse and, much later, English explorers searching for resource-rich land or routes to the Orient such as the Northwest Passage. This group spent little time among Inuit, wintering among them only when forced to by fickle ice conditions or navigational mishaps. Diary accounts suggest that they tended to acknowledge their own inferiority in the Arctic environment and saw Inuit as an obvious resource upon whom their survival depended (Mocellin and Suedfeld 1991).

The second wave brought those seeking economic opportunities. This period of contact began with the arrival of whalers from Scotland, the Netherlands, and Norway. The most significant economic presence in the eastern Arctic in the twentieth century, however, were traders, chief among them the predominantly Scottish employees of the Hudson's Bay Company (HBC).[1] Although HBC employees could be found north of urban settlement since the seventeenth century, activity in the Arctic occurred predominantly after the company ceded Rupert's Land to Canada. At the height of its activity, the HBC operated a network of trading posts far more extensive than the network of communities that now exists within Nunavut. The amount of time those seeking economic opportunities spent among Inuit varied. Whalers had far greater contact with Inuit than did earlier explorers, making repeat voyages to areas now known as Pangnirtung and Pond Inlet and, on occasion, having children with Inuit women. The HBC traders spent even more time with Inuit as they lived throughout the year at their trading posts. It was not unusual for a post to employ an Inuit family, the husband to help with the dogs and the wife to assist with cooking.[2] For the earlier arrivals economic success depended on the extent to which Inuit could be convinced to alter their hunting practices and trap animals for pelts. For later employees of the HBC Inuit were merely customers like any other.

The third wave of arrivals included Roman Catholic and Anglican missionaries hoping to convert the Inuit population to Christianity (Laugrand 1997; Oosten and Laugrand 2000; Remie and Oosten 2002). This group perceived itself as having the greatest contact with Inuit, adopting their material culture while advocating the transformation of their beliefs and practices (Trott 2001). These last two groups, traders and missionaries, overlapped.

The result was an Inuit population living in contact with a decidedly cosmopolitan grab bag of Europeans long before southern Canadians began arriving in great numbers. In some cases, this did not change until the latter half of the twentieth century. As late as 1964, a member of the Advisory Committee on Northern Development noted that the non-Inuit population of Baker Lake included an RCMP sergeant born in Ireland, his American wife and their daughter, a Scottish trader from Dundee, an Anglican missionary from Wales, and two Roman Catholic missionaries, one from France and one from Belgium (Rowley 1969).

Southern Canadians arrived in the north in similar waves. Teachers, construction workers, and government officials arrived primarily in the 1960s. One might be tempted to distinguish between the economic motivations of construction workers and the more altruistic concerns of teachers or government officials, but reliable employment in the north has long been a source of internal migration, as the current number of Newfoundlanders and Quebecers in the larger communities of Nunavut can attest. It would be more appropriate to distinguish between those who lived among Inuit in settlements and those whose contact with Inuit was sporadic or limited to building sites located away from Inuit social activity. Increased exposure to southern Canada occurred as Inuit became the focus of government policy. Excluded from the first Indian Act in 1876, Inuit were not acknowledged to be a federal responsibility until the Supreme Court declared them to be so in 1939 (*Re Eskimos* [1939] S.C.R. 104). Before they were acknowledged to have specific rights as citizens, Inuit were objects in a political world that was not of their making.

At the start of the 1950s, news that Inuit in the eastern Arctic were enduring conditions of near starvation prompted the Canadian government to offer them an opportunity to relocate.[3] RCMP officers were used to deliver the news and, upon arriving in camp, informed any adults present that the government was going to help them by moving them away from the land for two years to a place where there would be lots of animals to hunt. The officers added that Inuit would be able to return to their former lands if they did not like the new environment. Primary accounts suggest a certain reticence on the part of Inuit to go against the wishes of a perceived agent of the state. Between 1953 and 1955, the government relocated eleven families from Inukjuak (Port Harrison) in northern Quebec to two communities in the High Arctic: Resolute and Grise Fiord. This first group was joined by four families from Pond Inlet. To residents of southern Canada, northern Quebec and southern Ellesmere Island might seem to have similar environments. Northern Quebec, however, has shrubs and plants (which feed larger game) as well as sunlight during the winter months. This was not the case in Resolute and Grise Fiord. If federal policy had truly been motivated by a desire to alleviate starvation (Jull 1994), then more proximate locations would certainly have been less disruptive. If one interprets government action as a particularly craven attempt to secure Canadian sovereignty in the north, such efforts were only rewarded with new security concerns. Fear that the Soviet Union would dispatch weapons across the Arctic prompted Canada and the United States to establish a series of satellite stations that would provide an early warning system in the event of Soviet attack. Between 1955 and 1957, construction workers from southern Canada erected sixty-three stations as part of the Distant Early Warning (DEW) line. The project involved 1.6 million workers in Canada and the United States, including 20,000 in the Arctic alone. Although Inuit had been exposed to a nascent form of capitalism in the north, where pelts were exchanged for goods or money, construction on the DEW line marked the arrival of a large-scale system of wage labour. These two examples are instructive for two reasons. First, they show us that the federal government viewed the Arctic environment as something that could be owned and, later, as something that could be controlled. Second, they show that Inuit enjoyed federal attention first as objects of policy and second as incidental participants in megaprojects that would mark a profound transformation in their way of life.

Since the arrival of state agents in the Arctic, the relationship between Inuit and the federal government has attracted scrutiny. The most contentious period involves the behaviour of RCMP officers and the slaughter of dogs in the 1950s and '60s. Organizations such as the Qikiqtani Inuit Association (QIA) and Makivik Corporation contend that the RCMP engaged in a systematic campaign to slaughter dogs (QIA and Makivik Corporation 2006). These organizations argue that, by denying Inuit the means to procure food or goods that could later be exchanged, the government hoped to encourage their entry into the labour market. Researchers attempting to get to the bottom of the problem have failed to uncover RCMP records that indicate any kind of systematic campaign. For its part, the RCMP has maintained that the scale of the dog slaughter was far less than has been assumed and that it was conducted primarily to contain an outbreak of distemper. Archival records suggest that dogs were killed at times to control distemper, at times to protect white children living in settlements, and, on isolated occasions, as a punitive measure. The dispute is an evocative one and forms part of a series of events that appears to highlight a federal policy that vacillated between well-meaning if ill-judged paternalism and outright cultural assimilation. Three further examples prove useful.

First, as already mentioned, between 1953 and 1955 the Canadian government relocated eleven families from northern Quebec and four families from Pond Inlet on the north coast of Baffin Island to Resolute and Grise Fiord in the High Arctic. Inuit were left without housing and had to make their way in an unfamiliar land. Two interpretations of the High Arctic relocations are common. The favourable one notes that the federal government believed that, without relocation, Inuit would have starved and that the move guaranteed their survival. The less favourable one notes that the Canadian government, which was preoccupied with sovereignty in the Arctic, saw an obvious benefit in creating communities of indigenous inhabitants in the High Arctic. The relocations became the focus of discussions within the context of the Royal Commission on Aboriginal Peoples (Canada, RCAP 1996), and its report on the matter noted that the relocations had been "poorly planned and executed." It called on the federal government to acknowledge that what it had done was wrong. An apology has not been forthcoming, although the government provided a compensation package in 1996.

Second, residential schools, which were designed to provide Inuit with the skills to participate in a pan-Canadian job market and political society, removed children from their communities and severed familial and cultural ties. Located in Chesterfield Inlet, Yellowknife, Churchill, and Inuvik, the schools varied in their administration. The Chesterfield school was run by the Roman Catholic Church, others were run by the Anglican Church, and still others were run by the federal government directly. The experiences of students varied as well. For some, it was a horror that entailed various forms of physical and sexual abuse; for others, it appears to have been a happy socialization experience that produced future leaders of northern society. For all, it was a period of forced separation from family. A 2006 settlement between Inuit and Inuvialuit organizations and the federal government is estimated to cover 4,000 Inuit and 2,500 Inuivialuit in the eastern and western Arctic. The compensation package includes a uniform amount for all participants (a sign, perhaps, of the cultural damage perpetrated by the schools) and specific amounts for individuals to reflect differing levels of abuse.

Additional changes attempted to improve service delivery while at the same time "Canadianizing" the Inuit population. As the welfare state expanded in the twentieth century, and as the Canadian government started to provide education and health services to a northern population, the government decided that it needed a method to enumerate Inuit and to keep track of service delivery. In the absence of last names, Inuit were provided with numbers: E numbers for those in the east and W numbers for those in the west. These numbers sat awkwardly with Inuit naming practices that reflected a deeply personal approach to names and kinship, names holding the character of the previous bearer and embedding individuals within a wider social network. The numbers were eventually replaced with surnames traditionally passed down the male line. Surnames were selected by each family in an endeavour organized by Abe Okpik and dubbed Project Surname (Alia 1994).

It was in this environment that, in 1971, Inuit created a pan-Canadian organization, the Inuit Tapirisat of Canada (ITC), and began agitating for a land claim in the eastern Arctic (see, for example, ITC 1974, ITC 1977, ITC n.d., ITC 1979). This was not a bolt from the blue as Inuit political activity had begun twenty years earlier with the establishment of various government and community committees in which Inuit could become involved. It can also be seen as part of a wider interest in collective identity within advanced industrial democracies.[4] Efforts to secure an Inuit land claim were helped by the Supreme Court's *Calder* decision in 1973, which recognized unextinguished Aboriginal title to land. Federal reaction to the decision led to the creation of the Office of Native Claims and outlined two types of land claims: (1) specific claims, for those who had previously signed treaties and who had a grievance with the Crown, and (2) comprehensive claims, for those who had not signed away title to their land. In 1976, the ITC issued a proposal calling for the division of the Northwest Territories and a land claim for Inuit (ITC 1976). The campaign, from 1976 to 1993, involved an expected number of twists and turns. One group that had initially been part of the claim withdrew to cut its own deal, another sought a solution to the delayed claim in federal court; the chief task of negotiating for Inuit was transferred from one body to another and yet another before resting with the Tungavik Federation of Nunavut (TFN). Throughout this period federal administrations alternated between Liberal and Conservative governments, each with its own approach to Aboriginal policy. Efforts to secure a final draft agreement in 1990 were initially delayed by Inuit insistence on a separate territory in addition to a land claim (Dacks 1993; Merritt 1993a). The process also involved several trips to the polls, including a 1982 plebiscite on the principle of division, a 1992 plebiscite for all within the NWT on a confirmed boundary, and a 1992 vote among Inuit on the text of the agreement. Ratified in 1993, the claim provided those in the Arctic six years to divide the NWT and to create a bureaucracy, legislature, and judiciary for Nunavut. In 1999, the new territory separated from the NWT and the new legislature in Iqaluit opened its doors.

Reactions to the claim have been mixed. Before 1999, many researchers heralded it as an important experiment in Aboriginal self-government. The claim, according to one observer, provided the chance to "sustain Inuit cultural distinctiveness while equipping residents with the political and bureaucratic levers needed to assert northern priorities against the competing claims of the South" (Merritt 1993a, 4). Not all accounts have been rosy. The weekly newspaper *Nunatsiaq News*, the territory's main source of print news, has criticized various aspects of the claim's implementation. By far the most damning criticism, however, has come from those who suggest the territory is unviable as an economic unit (Howard and Widdowson 1999), its creation a sop to a "parasitic 'aboriginal industry' of legal advisers, consultants and accountants" (Widdowson and Howard 1999a)[5] that now props up a culture that has little to offer to the rest of the world: "The function of the Nunavut government is to maintain Inuit culture in the Neolithic period, preserving it as a museum piece for the rest of the world to observe" (Howard and Widdowson 1999, 60).

Although political life in Nunavut unfolds differently than it does in the provinces or in the two other territories, the key distinction between this jurisdiction and other parts of Canada is demographic. The size of the population is far smaller than is that in other jurisdictions, and Nunavut's geography introduces a diseconomy of scale to most policy decisions. The territory contains twenty-five communities spread among three regions: the Qikiqtaaluk, Kivalliq, and Kitikmeot, details of which are contained in Table 2.1. No two communities in Nunavut are joined by roads, although until the mine closed the now-abandoned community of Nanisivik was linked to Arctic Bay, and, for a few years, the hamlets operated a winter ice road between Rankin Inlet and Whale Cove. Composed predominantly of the communities on Baffin Island, the Qikiqtaaluk, or Baffin, region contains over half of the territory's population as well as the capital, Iqaluit. Iqaluit is something

TABLE 2.1

Regions and communities in Nunavut

Communities	Former names	Population
Qikiqtaaluk	(Baffin)	
Iqaluit	(Frobisher Bay)	6,184*
Igloolik		1,538
Pangnirtung		1,325
Pond Inlet		1,315
Cape Dorset		1,236
Clyde River		820
Sanikiluaq	(Belcher Islands)	744
Arctic Bay		690
Hall Beach		654
Qikiqtarjuaq	(Broughton Island)	473
Kimmirut	(Lake Harbour)	411
Resolute		229
Grise Fiord		141
Total		**15,765**
Kivalliq	(Keewatin)	
Rankin Inlet		2,358
Arviat	(Eskimo Point)	2,060
Baker Lake		1,728
Coral Harbour		769
Repulse Bay		748
Whale Cove		353
Chesterfield Inlet		332
Total		**8,348**
Kitikmeot		
Cambridge Bay		1,477
Kugluktuk	(Coppermine)	1,302
Gjoa Haven		1,064
Taloyoak	(Spence Bay)	809
Kugaaruk	(Pelly Bay)	688
Total		**5,361**

NOTES: Population data are from the 2006 Statistics Canada census. Names in bold are decentralized communities. Totals might not add up because of individuals not attributed to communities (e.g., in hunting camps or smaller settlements).
* = Capital of Nunavut.

of an anomaly in Nunavut. With more than six thousand residents, it is by far the largest community in the territory, approximately three times larger than Rankin Inlet, the administrative capital of the Kivalliq region. Largely due to the predominance of government jobs, the non-Inuit, or Qallunaat, population in Iqaluit represents a far higher proportion of the inhabitants than is the case in other communities. The Kitikmeot contains the communities that are closest to the NWT border, such as Kugluktuk and the regional administrative capital Cambridge Bay. The western portions of the region contain the bulk of the territory's Inuinnaqtun speakers. An official language of Nunavut and part of the language family that includes Inuktitut, Inuinnaqtun uses Roman orthography rather than syllabics. In the Kivalliq region, above Manitoba, use of Inuktitut is far lower than it is in the Baffin region. Most of the communities in the Kivalliq (or Keewatin, as it was formerly known) are situated on the western coast of Hudson Bay. The three regions are distinct in patterns of contact, patterns of language use, levels of traditionalism, and approaches to religion. While the selection of Iqaluit as a capital for the territory improved the proximity of government for people in the Baffin region, for some residents in the Kivalliq and Kitikmeot regions the capital is now further away than were the centres of political power in the pre-division NWT.

Measures of economic and social well-being emphasize differences between Nunavut and the rest of Canada, as Table 2.2 makes clear. In many cases, such indicators also serve to distinguish Nunavut from the two other territories. Identifying the single factor that most distinguishes Nunavut from the rest of the country is difficult. Broadly speaking, though, we can distinguish among economic, health-related, and employment-related indicators.

The cost of living in Nunavut is high. Although wages are only slightly lower than the national average ($28,215 versus $31,757 per year), the market

TABLE 2.2

Proportions of households living in poverty

	Canada	Nunavut
Low-income cut-off	10.9	16.8
Low-income measure	11.1	28.4
Market basket measure	13.1	33.1

SOURCE: All data are from Survey of Household Spending, based on after-tax income in 2001 (Henderson 2004a, 23).

basket measure of poverty, which identifies the cost of typical items for a typical family, reports that one-third of Nunavummiut are living in low-income households. By comparison, just over 10 percent of Canadian households are similarly defined. Alternative measures produce similar results. The low-income cut-off, which provides an absolute measure of poverty, indicates that 16.8 percent of Nunavut households are below the cut-off, while the relative indicator provided by the low-income measure captures 28.4 percent of Nunavut households (Henderson 2004a, 23). Such measures ignore foods acquired directly from the land, which are seen to somewhat alleviate levels of poverty. As Usher, Duhaime, and Searles (2003) note, on the one hand, the ability to secure food through hunting provides a greater measure of security than one might experience in market-based southern communities; on the other hand, the ability to procure meat cannot be seen as an automatic corollary of economic well-being.

The high cost of living is, in part, a function of a very limited private rental market, so that monthly rents for available units far exceed those in southern urban centres. In part it is tied to the cost of goods, whose prices reflect the added costs of shipping to the Arctic. Heavy items such as milk, or bulky items such as diapers, are particularly expensive. Essential items and healthy food qualify for government subsidies to reduce the gap between prices in northern and southern stores, but northern costs remain high. In October 2005, *Nunatsiaq News* reported that orange juice was selling for $21.99 per litre in Pond Inlet, although the paper also noted that the juice had been eligible for subsidized shipping and should therefore have been on sale for less. The same article noted that, in 2003, a "typical basket of food to feed a family of four" for one week varied in cost throughout the territory, from $244 in Iqaluit to $274 in the Kitikmeot and $315 in the Kivalliq (Minogue 2005). The Canadian average for weekly food expenditure, by contrast, is $123 (Statistics Canada 2001). As one report noted: "Poverty, when examined in southern Canada, can point to factors such as a lack of employment to explain financial difficulty. In Nunavut, however, the numbers of working poor suggest that even for those who opt to work within the wage economy the costs of living are outstripping financial resources" (Henderson 2004a, 18).

Levels of literacy, in both English and Inuktitut, are low, as are high school completion rates. Less than 2 percent of Inuit hold university degrees. Mobility within a wider Canadian job market is obviously impaired by such figures. The ability to secure employment within the territory varies widely, depending on community of residence. The underdeveloped private sector makes government employment the only game in town for some communities, and public-sector jobs represent half of all employment opportunities in the territory as a whole (White 1999a, 5). In some of the smaller communities, the number of adults of employable age far exceeds the number of job opportunities. In other communities, particularly those with decentralized government positions, the number of unfilled jobs points to different concerns. High unemployment limits the available tax base for a population that places high demands on social services such as school construction, public housing, and welfare support (White 2006). Unemployment varies not only by region but also by ethnicity. Among Inuit, the unemployment rate is high; but among the "largely transient" non-Inuit population, it is among the lowest in the country (Merritt 1993c, 7), as the 1999 Nunavut Labour Force Survey confirms.

In his assessment of the NLCA for the Royal Commission on Aboriginal Peoples, Gurston Dacks (1993, 49) summarized the social and economic environment of the territory:

> The present high level of unemployment there is one strand of a tightly woven pathology of low educational attainment and social dysfunction which takes such forms as family violence, substance abuse and conflict with the law. High rates of unemployment burden government with the heavy costs of responding to these problems as well as to the widespread need for housing and social assistance, and limit the tax revenues which can be put to these purposes. A rapidly expanding, young population base will intensify these problems; by substantially increasing the Nunavut labour force in the coming years, it will increase the need for new jobs.

Dacks refers to yet another unique feature of Nunavut: it is the youngest jurisdiction in Canada. The median age in the territory is twenty-two, as opposed to thirty-seven for the rest of Canada. This places obvious financial burdens on the community. As this younger generation ages, it will have an obvious effect on policy costs for housing, education, and health, not to mention on competition for government employment.

As Table 2.3 demonstrates, key indicators of health are poor in Nunavut, and life expectancy is approximately ten years lower than the Canadian average (sixty-eight versus seventy-eight). Infant mortality rates are 16.9 per 1,000 live births, versus 5.2 per 1,000 in the rest of Canada. Mortality rates from

TABLE 2.3

Measures of health and employability

	Canada	Nunavut
Population under 14	17.6	34.7
Infant mortality	5.3	19.8
Life expectancy	78.3	69.8
Lung cancer	57.8	261.7
Smoking	22.9	64.8
% less than high school	31.3	50.2
% university degree	25.8	12.0
% below average literacy	19.9	47.2
% below average numeracy	25.5	55.7
Crimes of violence	946.1	7,883.6
Suicide rate	12.0	80.0

NOTES: Rates for data are as follows: infant mortality rates by province and territory, calculated per 1,000 live births (2003); disability-free life expectancy by province and territory (1996); lung cancer incidence per 100,000 (2000); smoking status age 12+ (2005); population 15 years and over by highest level of schooling (2005); crimes by offences per 100,000 population (2004); suicide rates per 100,000 (2004). Literacy was tested in either English or French, not in Inuktitut (2003).
SOURCES: Henderson (2004a); Statistics Canada, Canadian Institute for Health Information (2005); International Audit Literacy and Skills Survey (2003).

lung cancer are three times the Canadian average, and for women they are five times the Canadian average (Henderson 2004a, 19). Stout and Kipling (1999) report that alcohol consumption among pregnant women is higher in Nunavut than in the rest of Canada and that there is a high incidence of middle ear infections (with a concomitant detrimental effect on hearing) as well as high levels of dental decay and clinical depression, all of which create a state of generalized physical stress. On a more positive note, rates for asthma, arthritis, and rheumatism are lower in Nunavut than in the rest of Canada, as are rates of contracting and dying from breast cancer.

Rates of suicide present by far the most worrying health indicators. Calculated on the basis of political jurisdictions, Nunavut has the highest suicide rate in Canada, with 80 suicides per 100,000. The Canadian rate, by contrast, is 12 per 100,000 (Langlois and Morrison 2002). This represents in excess of two suicides per month in the territory. Most of these suicides are committed by young men between the ages of 15 and 24 in the Baffin region. If we calculate the suicide rate for this group it is 824 per 100,000 (Henderson 2003a, 2).

Various theories have been put forth to explain these suicides, most of which are contested by advocates of rival theories. Psychiatric explanations point to higher-than-average rates of depression. Cultural explanations point to the disastrous consequences of the imposition of Christianity, residential schools, and the practice of adoption, as well as economic disruption brought by the introduction of capitalism and a sedentary lifestyle. Each of these changes has been seen as sufficiently disruptive to account for the sense of despair experienced by young people in Nunavut. Stevenson (1996), for example, argues that the economic consequences of the end of the seal hunt had a disastrous effect on communities such as Qikitarjuaq and Pangnirtung. The Inuit women's organization Pauktuutit (1991) argues that residential schools destroyed the social fabric of Inuit society and created docile, obedient, "unthinking followers" whose sense of despair is understandable.

Efforts to account for the high suicide rate in Nunavut sometimes rely on theories of social well-being. This approach to the problem identifies not only risk factors that might make individuals more prone to suicidal ideation but also protective factors that might lower the risk of suicide. Such an approach grounds itself in social psychology, identifying stresses within an individual's social environment that might affect mental health. We can distinguish between specific risk factors, which affect only Inuit, and general risk factors, which affect all individuals but predominantly those living in Nunavut. General risk factors would include spousal abuse, drug abuse, and alcoholism, for which there is considerable anecdotal evidence of high incidence in Nunavut. We know that families prone to alcohol abuse, substance abuse, and violence are more likely to produce teenagers who think about suicide (Henderson 2003b; Rossow 2000), and sexual abuse has been identified as a strong predictor of suicidal behaviour (Macaulay 2002; Macaulay et al. 2003), particularly among young Inuit women (Kirmayer 1994).[6] Specific risk factors include rapid cultural change. In this case, the introduction of Christianity, residential schools, and a wage-earning economy are thought to have so altered Inuit society that its members find themselves less able to effectively socialize successive generations and to protect them from the various stresses of contemporary life. Viewed in this light, the current suicide rate is the result of accumulated transgenerational grief (Abadian 1999).[7]

Analyses of the high suicide rate among young Inuit reveal more than a distressing tale of life in the north. The tangle of intervening variables points to multiple and converging influences on individuals and groups. While many of the cultural theories about suicide in the north are untested, they are useful because they attempt to map the competing cultural pressures faced by individuals and because they note that factors affecting entire societies can have very real effects on individuals. Political culture in Nunavut has been shaped by a similar series of multiple and overlapping influences.

INSTITUTIONAL CONTEXT

The NLCA contains provisions for a political accord, and it is this latter document that outlines the creation of a new territory. Eighty-five percent of those living in Nunavut are Inuit, most of them beneficiaries of the Nunavut land claim.[8] Because the new territory grew out of the negotiation of the land claim, and because a majority of the population is Inuit, Nunavut can be seen as an example of de facto self-government in Canada. Government in Nunavut is public; it is elected by voters regardless of their ethnicity and it governs for all. A clear Inuit majority ensures, however, that Inuit perspectives and preferences inform political decision making in Nunavut.

The political settlement bears the marks of both demography and geography. The unified judiciary does away with the distinction between the Territorial Courts and the territorial Supreme Court that existed in the pre-division NWT. The Nunavut Court of Justice also operates as a circuit court, travelling to communities on a regular basis, though the periods between visits vary. The Legislative Assembly is small, with nineteen members, and operates without political parties as the basis of its organization. Despite this deviation from the norm, the legislature reflects its institutional origins. Operating according to a Westminster system of government, cabinet ministers are responsible to the legislature as a whole, which, in turn, is responsible to the electorate. It is a unicameral system and so lacks an upper house that may alter or delay legislation. As in other parliamentary systems, the executive sits within the legislature and is responsible for introducing legislation and for administering government. Non-executive "regular" members not only participate in the creation of legislation but perform a scrutiny role as well. The legislative process in Nunavut would be familiar to observers of politics in other Canadian legislatures. Notice of a bill occurs in a first reading, which is followed by a second reading, where members debate the principles of the bill. From there it is sent to one of the standing committees of the Legislative Assembly and then is returned to the entire legislature for a discussion with the Committee of the Whole.[9] This is followed by a third reading and, finally, by assent.

The most distinctive feature of the Nunavut Legislative Assembly is the absence of political parties. In this system of "consensus politics," candidates hoping to become MLAs present themselves to the electorate as independents. Elections operate according to single-member plurality, so that each constituency sends the individual receiving the most votes to sit in the legislature. Upon election, members of the legislature elect from among themselves a speaker, a premier, and a cabinet. Portfolios are then assigned to cabinet ministers by the premier. As in the other two territories, political life in Nunavut is governed by a legislature that has jurisdiction over areas such as education, health, social services, transportation, community government, justice, language, and culture. The legislature is supported by a bureaucracy that is distributed among ten departments.

Public government in Nunavut co-exists with a number of public bodies directly and indirectly related to the NLCA. Charged with negotiating the land claim for Inuit, the Tungavik Federation of Nunavut (TFN) has, since 1999, become Nunavut Tunngavik Incorporated (NTI), the body that represents all Inuit beneficiaries in Nunavut. NTI manages federal funding resulting from the claim and offers services and programs, some operating in conjunction with public programs run by the Government of Nunavut. In addition, each region within Nunavut has its own regional Inuit association: the Qikiqtani Inuit Association in the Baffin/Qikiqtaaluk region, the Kitikmeot Inuit Association in the High Arctic, and the Kivalliq Inuit Association in the Keewatin. The land claim also mandated the creation of co-management bodies such as the Nunavut Planning Commission, the Nunavut Wildlife Management Board, the Nunavut Water Board, and the Nunavut Impact Review Board, each of which provides opportunities for nominees of Inuit organizations and the government to realize, together, policy decisions relating to particular sectors of the economy and environment. Although the Government of Nunavut provides the territory with its sole public political institution, it operates within what might be considered a dizzying array of bodies, each with distinct policy roles. Predictably, public understanding of the relationship among these bodies, of the considerable political pluralism that exists within Nunavut, varies.

The creation of a new territory provided an opportunity for institutional reform. The chief agent of innovation was the Nunavut Implementation Commission (NIC), an advisory body whose remit allowed it to determine a timetable for service delivery, the legislative election process, the design of training programs, the selection of a capital, the method by which assets and liabilities would be divided, the identification of necessary public works, and the administrative design of the bureaucracy. Faced with such an expansive mandate, the NIC recommended two significant departures from politics as usual in the NWT, one of which was adopted, another that was ultimately rejected. Public desire for radical reform was almost non-existent. In public consultation meetings voters called for a continuation of democracy and party-free politics. The single change that voters desired was an improvement in the proximity of politicians and policy making to the electorate. In the midst of what must be considered a tepid appetite for change, the NIC proposed two key reforms. First, it recommended setting up a decentralized bureaucracy within the territory. Within the pre-division NWT there was considerable concern, particularly among residents of the eastern Arctic, that the capital of Yellowknife effectively insulated policy makers from the realities of life throughout the territory. In response, the Political Accord called for "an equitable distribution of government Activities among Nunavut communities" (s. 7.3.i) and referred to a "decentralized and efficient government delivery system" (s. 7.3.ii). In an effort to ground decision making in the communities that were to benefit from policy, and in an effort to share the considerable economic rewards brought by government jobs, the NIC suggested that mid-sized communities within the new territory should house coherent units of the government bureaucracy. By December 2004, 459 positions had been decentralized to the ten largest communities outside the capital, although fully one-third of these were vacant. Decentralization has been a controversial policy (Hicks and White 2005), its implementation marred by high costs, high staff turnover, and a high number of unfilled positions. A rather intemperate editorial declared that government departments had been "carpet-bombed into near-total dysfunction by the GN's badly-implemented decentralization policy" (*Nunatsiaq News* 2004b).

The second reform proposed by the NIC was not adopted. Based on the belief that a new institution should better reflect the population of Nunavut, the NIC promoted an electoral system based on gender parity, with one male and one female politician elected from each constituency (Young 1997; Minor 2002). Although it failed in a public referendum, the proposal demonstrates the extent to which the new territory was seen as an opportunity for the conscious creation of a new political culture.

The most significant deviation from "politics as usual" surfaced after 1999. Although the NIC had some suggestions for how the new institutional arrangements could bridge the gap between public government and the electorate, the extent to which the Nunavut government is run by a predominantly Inuit political elite for a predominantly Inuit population provides the clearest example of a new political culture. In 1998 and 1999, various departments hosted retreats and conferences on cultural sensitivity and Inuit traditional knowledge, the result of which was a gradually emerging consensus on the terminology of heightened Inuit influence if not on the process by which that influence might be attained (Nunavut, CLEY 2000; Nunavut Social Development Council 1998). Inuit traditional knowledge and practices came to be summarized by the term "Inuit Qaujimajatuqangit" (IQ). The integration of IQ has proved something of a tricky task. Eschewing easy definition, the term has become a catch-all benchmark by which some observers judge the success of devolution in Nunavut (see Chapter 9 for an examination of the success with which IQ has been implemented).

Closely related to IQ is the success of components in the NLCA and Political Accord designed to encourage Inuit participation in the political settlement. The two most common are (1) requirements for a territorial and Nunavut-based federal bureaucracy that reflects the ethnic composition of the electorate, described in Article 23 of the NLCA, and (2) the NNI (Nunavummi Nangminiqaqtunik Ikajuuti) policy to give priority to businesses that hire northern employees, and Inuit employees in particular, when assigning government contracts. Far easier to measure than the integration of IQ, the implementation of Article 23 falls short of the target of 85 percent Inuit employment in the territorial bureaucracy. As of June 2006, over 90 percent of administrative or clerical positions and half of all executive positions were staffed by Inuit. Inuit staffing levels for middle and senior management and for professional positions are far lower, ranging between one-fifth and one-quarter of occupied posts (Nunavut, Department of Human Resources 2006; see also Timpson 2006b). These proportions are slightly below levels attained in 1999. High levels of mobility among employees of the GN, NTI, and other Inuit organizations might account for these fluctuations. It is also worth noting that there are high vacancy levels for some posts. Almost one-fifth of the paraprofessional posts were unstaffed as of June 2006, as were 17 percent of both professional and administrative positions.

The empirical reality of Nunavut, its political history and its demographic and institutional context, confirms that it is a polity unlike any other in Canada and that it is one whose development warrants a thorough account. More important, though, it provides an opportunity to test theories about the establishment of polities, the way institutions and individuals interact, and the capacity for cultural variation within a single state. The seismic transformation in the economic, social, and political lives of residents in the eastern Arctic provides a rare chance to determine whether the explanations we use to describe a general political reality – whether regarding voter turnout, social capital, or the acquisition of postmaterialist attitudes – can also account for political culture in a system so dissimilar to the rest of Canada.

3
Inuit Political Culture

Before they were integrated into the Canadian political system, Inuit did not have a parliament that provided legislation, nor did Inuit from different regions gather together in a central location so that they might divide resources, plan for the future, or discuss common troubles. This is not to say that Inuit did not divide resources, plan for the future, or react to troubling behaviour, only that they did not do so within a pan-Arctic forum among chosen representatives. Although the venue of Inuit decision making may have been different, many of the issues discussed in legislatures as we have come to understand them were, indeed, the focus of discussion. The following chapter highlights what we know of Inuit governance during and after the contact period, as well as the salient features of Inuit political culture.

I focus primarily on the area covered by present-day Nunavut. Inuit are, however, spread throughout the circumpolar Arctic, and their daily practices have always reflected both the varying environmental circumstances in which they found themselves and, later, the distinct colonial systems into which they were integrated. Focusing on the geographic territory covered by Nunavut offers something of an artificial distinction among Inuit. At the same time, the newest territory contains a variety of regional groupings whose separate senses of identity are reinforced by variations in dialect, clothing, and, at times, values. I seek to draw broad lessons about values and practices that might be considered political, while highlighting any regional diversity that might exist. My purpose is not, however, to survey existing scholarship on all elements of Inuit culture, and I exclude topics such as kinship, social organization, and material culture; rather, I focus on the distribution of power in society, the values prized in precontact and contact Inuit society, and the mechanisms for ensuring adherence to those values.

After the ratification of the NLCA, academic assessments suggested that the settlement would provide a long-overdue opportunity for the territory's government to reflect the values of Inuit: "The people of Nunavut deserve to have a government that, within the general constitutional principles of Canada, they can recognize as embodying their values" (Dacks 1993, 36). In the same document, for example, Dacks notes the Inuit reputation for pragmatism (45). In general, though, there has been little scholarship on Inuit values as they relate to the political process, and what little there is must be teased out of more general accounts of Inuit social organization: "The high premium Inuit place on consensual decision making, for example, directly reflects the importance of maintaining harmony in small nomadic groups where disunity could literally threaten survival" (White 2006, 10). If Nunavut is to reflect the values of its predominantly Inuit population, we might identify what those values might be. To so do, we must investigate Inuit attitudes toward governance. The following account identifies Inuit values and practices not in an effort to fit them into a larger comparative typology of social units but to identify within precontact and contact Inuit life a coherent approach that might affect political life in Nunavut. It seeks parallels for Inuit values and behaviour not in the anthropology of other cultures but in the considerable research on the political cultures of other polities.

Identifying an Inuit Political Culture

Contemporary research on political culture often refers to the results of surveys. Such datasets allow us to determine, for example, how often people vote or whether they are satisfied with democracy or their current political leaders. Other approaches to the study of political culture ground themselves in political institutions and, in so doing, might explore the rules governing the behaviour of politicians or the topics to which they devote their time. If we want to explore the political culture of precontact or contact-traditional Inuit, we have neither of these means at our disposal. We have no census of adult attitudes about group leadership, nor were there formal political institutions. And yet in the absence of a pan-Inuit legislature or annual surveys of hunters, we can still identify themes within the political culture of Inuit. The chief data source for this chapter is the database of elder interviews housed at the Igloolik NRI office. Interview subjects are identified by the NRI number, expressed as IE followed by a three-digit interview code. The geographic focus of the interview subjects has been supplemented by oral histories and academic research covering Inuit collective decision making or legal concepts across the eastern Arctic. Some of these secondary sources were written just as missionaries, explorers, or government employees arrived (Jenness 1922; Rasmussen 1929, 1931; Steenhoven 1956, 1959, 1962), while others draw on contemporary accounts of earlier practices (Briggs 1982; Stevenson 1993). Together these sources make possible three separate analyses of Inuit approaches to political life. First, we can identify Inuit visions of the good life and, thus, identify ideal behaviour and valued resources. Second, we can explore preferred methods of resource distribution within Inuit society. This helps us to understand the relative importance of individualist or collectivist approaches as well as the relationship between egalitarianism and equitable treatment. Third, we can examine collective decision making both for its emphasis on particular patterns of leadership and for its preferred mechanisms of social control. This enables us to identify the rules of behaviour so central to political culture. These three approaches to Inuit political life rely on three different definitions of politics as: (1) the interaction of competing visions for society, (2) the distribution of resources within a community, and (3) a method for identifying, distributing, and sharing power. Taken together, these approaches provide us with an opportunity to explore the themes of Inuit political culture.

Visions of the good life stem from the social and material conditions of daily life. Inuit in the eastern Arctic led a generally nomadic life, though geographic footprints varied.[1] The basis for social groups was the family unit (but not usually the contemporary notion of nuclear families). The boundaries of social units varied from those whose imagined communities included only the restricted nuclear family, such as the Copper Inuit (Condon, Ogina, and Holman Elders 1996), to those whose imagined communities would have included extended family members, such as the *Netsilingmiut* (Rasmussen 1931; Steenhoven 1959). Still more expansive definitions, such as those held by the *Igluingmiut*, would have included all Inuit within a wider region (Rasmussen 1929; Stevenson 1993). The composition of social groups varied according to region. Family could be defined by relationships on the male side, with married daughters relocating to the husband's social unit. Or it could be structured around an elder, with the social group extended to include unmarried sons, married daughters, and their husbands and offspring (Briggs 1982, 111). Nor were family units static. With the exception of the Copper Inuit, family groups provided a fluid basis for social organization, the nuclear family fleshed out by grandparents, single adults, orphaned children, loaned, exchanged, or multiple spouses, and more transient individuals on their way from one destination to the next. These social units travelled, their itineraries a function of environmental conditions and the anticipated availability of resources.

Given the social environment in which Inuit spent most of their time, it is not surprising that their interpersonal relations dominate our understanding of ideal human interaction. There are valuable lessons here as the treatment of different generations, different genders, and different children or siblings helps to form a template for social interaction on a larger scale. Perhaps the first thing to note, then, is that, in many ways, values obvious in eastern Arctic social groups were not particularly different from those prioritized by other social groups, whether Inuit or non-Inuit, Christian, Muslim, or secular. We find an emphasis on what might be considered universal values: the desire to avoid suffering, the desire to survive, an emphasis on sharing, concern, and respect for others. The environment within which Inuit found themselves ensured that the manifestations of those values – storing meat for the future, sharing certain sections of a catch with particular members of the community – are less familiar to southern Canadians. An Arctic environment also ensured that the consequences of eschewing such values, of pursuing a life of selfishness, would be disastrous for the social unit as a whole. As a result, Inuit precontact culture not only prioritized values related to the distribution of resources but also identified clear methods for ensuring compliance with those values.

Political Values

In 1943, Abraham Maslow (1943) published a typology of development for different societies. According to Maslow, each society could be characterized by the dominant needs of its citizens. The needs to survive and to procure food and shelter were considered lower-order needs. Higher-order needs included the need to belong, to feel love, a sense of self-esteem, and self-actualization. The resulting hierarchy of needs suggested that, once a society was finished completing lower-order needs, then and only then would it become preoccupied with higher-order needs. At the time Maslow was writing, the predominant preoccupation of most Inuit would have been the acquisition of food and shelter, and so one might assume that Inuit society would be placed at the lower end of his hierarchy. Maslow's hierarchy is imperfect, however, for it suggests that societies must be defined by a preoccupation with one type of need rather than with several simultaneously; the search for food and shelter does not preclude a life that values happiness, social networks, or the search for knowledge. Much of the writing on twentieth-century Inuit society emphasizes the lower-order needs of Inuit, perhaps because these are the needs that most contrast with those of southern Canadian society. Inuit society is remarkable, however, for the way in which it blends the acquisition of food and shelter with the need to belong and the need to acquire knowledge. Data on precontact and contact-traditional Inuit society suggest that dominant Inuit values reflect the simultaneous importance of belonging and survival.

Both belonging and survival were made possible by the acquisition and distribution of resources. Inuit society had two chief resources: material and human. Material resources included food, skins, and hunting equipment, while human resources involved the skills necessary to acquire material goods. For men, this meant the ability to hunt; for women it meant the ability to produce clothing that would keep hunters warm and safe. Skill and knowledge were linked. In this context, political values governed the acquisition of food and shelter in the Arctic environment as well as the relations among individuals within the social unit.

Resource Values

Human relationships and the acquisition of resources were both governed by utilitarianism. All other values, along with the mechanisms to ensure their adherence and the structure of leadership, are designed to maximize the efficiency of human and environmental resources. Waste, whether in the form of material, food, or energy, was abhorred as everything and everyone in traditional Inuit society had a role and a purpose. Gender roles were equitable (rather than equal) and marked. Children's games were designed to teach skills as much as to expend boisterous energies. String games for girls taught them manual dexterity that would benefit their sewing. Games for boys sought to develop speed, hand-eye co-ordination, and agility that would improve hunting ability. Seen in this light, the easy adoption of improvements in technology has less to do with a now-heralded ability to adapt and has more to do with an eagerness to employ the most efficient methods for securing resources. The same could be said of trading, the entry into wage labour, and early support for the necessity of formal education. All were perceived to be the most expedient method of securing resources.

Human relationships were also governed by a considerable degree of utility, as can be seen in the practice of lending individuals to other social units for a variety of purposes. Absence from loved ones was seen as an ordinary, necessary component of life. This is not to say, however, that such practices were without emotional consequences. Separation from loved ones who had joined other social groups or who were away hunting prompted a considerable degree of anxiety. The primary documents suggest constant low levels of anxiety concerning those absent. Disquiet about those not heard from or those rumoured to be ill features far more prominently in interviews than do concerns over hunger, threats of starvation, or danger from the physical environment. Inuit utilitarianism did not imply an absence of emotion but was tied instead to the importance of work.

Cooperation may be seen as the bedrock of Inuit society, but it was not meant to replace self-reliance made possible by sheer hard graft. The comments of parents suggest that they particularly feared laziness in their children; pampered children would feel little drive to acquire skills central to the survival and productivity of the collective. Myths and legends emphasize the dangers of laziness. One particular tale recounts the fate of a lazy hunter whose dismembered arm was skinned and served to his wife as a polar bear leg (IE 100).

The value of work extended beyond survival. Despite incidents of desperate privation, the most catalogued of which occurred at Ennadai Lake (Karetak 2000; Kreelak 2002; Mowat 1959; *Regina v. Kikkik* 1958; Tester and Kulchyski 1994), the goal of hunters was not mere survival but the provision of the means for the collective survival of the larger social group. The Inuit work ethic did not see signs of salvation in the acquisition of goods, and so here the value placed on work differs from that identified by Weber. For Inuit, the importance of work was clearly tied to notions of self-reliance and providing for others. Food sharing was motivated less by the benefits of altruism than by pragmatism. It was in one's best interests to be kind to others so that one might rely on them should resources prove difficult to acquire, a virtuous cycle that could only be possible if one typically had resources to contribute. Sharing was tied far more to pragmatism and work than to a normative philanthropic ideal. It was, however, clearly tied to nurturing, or *nallik*, which was seen as the opposite of dependence (Briggs 1982). As Briggs comments: "They [Inuit] behave self sufficiently partly because they feel intensely dependent, and they are nurturant partly because they wish not to be" (129). Treatment of the elderly clearly fell under this theme: "We used to be told that we should always help the elderly whenever possible. During the time when the only means of survival was through subsistence hunting, we were constantly reminded that should I catch an animal or someone in my family caught some animal I should always give even a small piece to an elderly" (IE 174).

The notion of private property, which is at the heart of so many approaches to governance, is less clear in Inuit society. Discussions of rights, collective interaction, or power were not approached through the lens of life, liberty, and the pursuit of property. Certainly there was no concept of private land ownership.

> They never even consider land ownership, whenever they reached a land they would use it, land did not belong to no one. If they went to a place that they had never occupied before they will start to call it their home *(nunaga)* [my land] ... In those days on serious note, no one ever never considered the land that they are on to be theirs nor have they ever thought that certain land belonged to certain persons. If this visitor lacked something that he would need these people would make certain that his needs are met, at least that was the custom of the people that resided in these parts as well as those of *Tununirmiut* [around Pond Inlet]. No one ever thought of "their own." (IE 253)

This is not to say that individuals lacked personal possessions or that borrowing did not rely on the acknowledged necessity of seeking permission first. Skins and meat were shared among individuals: "They all lived cooperatively. The thought of paying for service never existed. The family had supplies and other things which belonged to everyone. If one had none someone else would have it" (IE 146). Dogs were similarly viewed as a communal asset, although eventually they came to be seen as something of a status symbol. The paucity of resources meant that certain materials were treated very carefully. Bullets, for example, were reused or saved for particular circumstances. Food was by far the most plentiful resource to be shared among a social unit, and here practices varied both by region and within camps. If acquisition can be viewed along a spectrum, from collective acquisition to individual acquisition, then Inuit social groups tended to value the former rather than the latter.[2] Individuals within the social unit would also have been spread along the same spectrum, more or less dedicated to surrendering individual resources to the collective. One interviewee remembered with amazement the first time he saw an elder receive food and retreat to his shelter without sharing it among the group: "This was the first time that I had ever seen someone taking a meat and did not bother to share it with everyone in the camp in a customary manner which is to *turlulaujaq* [to call everyone in the camp to come and eat]" (IE 129). Related to this is the notion of obligation. Without a formal partnership, food sharing brought no automatic promise of reciprocation. Having shared food with another hunter did not guarantee, then, that this person could be relied upon for future resources; rather, food sharing was viewed as an obligation to the social group, reciprocity a collective ideal rather than a contract among individuals.

SOCIAL INTERACTION

Values related not just to the distribution of resources but to the position of individuals within the social group. Respect for authority, both spiritual and temporal, was a key trait. Children were expected to obey parents, and disobedient children could receive a smack to ensure future compliance. Although strong vertical relationships characterized Inuit interaction across generations (Kral et al. 1998), this should not obscure the fact that there were rigid boundaries between child and adult behaviour. Children were often excluded from adult conversations. It is not clear whether this was due to the subject matter – for example whether adults felt it best to exclude children from conversations about shamanism, Christianity, or government officials that might distress them – or whether adults genuinely identified a clear distinction between the roles of adult and child. Wives were expected to obey husbands, their "separate-but-equal" roles characterized by what might be considered by contemporary Western standards to be an inferior position to that of men. This is not to say that the creation of clothing was considered to be inferior to hunting – if anything, the work of women was valued as equal to that of men – but that wives were expected to accept the decisions of their husbands. This is not a vision of Margaret Mead's genderless society, and accounts of women hunting tend to be regionally specific exceptions to the general rule of gendered behaviour. Men, however, were expected not to abuse their position by doing anything "reprehensible" or "humiliating" "to domineer [or] bully their wives" (IE 154). This notion of equity, as opposed to equality, across gender, age, or status differed by region, as can be seen with regard to the process of meat distribution. In some areas, better parts of the catch would be distributed based on who the hunter was, on whether he had a food-sharing partner, on whether he was taboo or not taboo, and on whether the social group in question contained elders or particular relatives.

In other regions, meat was divided into equal portions and distributed among all individuals. Referring to the equitable distribution of skins, one interviewee noted: "No one ever made any attempts to get more than the others, everyone tried to get their fair share according to their needs" (IE 113). We see similar variations with regard to deference. The Copper Inuit emphasis on egalitarianism and individual autonomy (Jenness 1922; Stevenson 1993, 1997) stands in sharp contrast to the eastern Arctic emphasis on deference to leaders - a deference that, although voluntary, was equated with loyalty and was an ever-present feature of social life (Briggs 1982, 112).

Those to whom deference and loyalty were owed were distinguished by their skill, which was equated with knowledge. Leaders within camps were deemed to be expert hunters, elders were seen to be experts on how to lead a good life, and shamans possessed unrivalled knowledge of the spirit world. Within an environment in which material and human resources were prized, those with knowledge were seen as those whose demonstrated skill with regard to resource acquisition was most evident. Information acquired through a lifetime of experiences on the land had, for the Inuit, the same foundation of experiential knowledge regarded as "scientific" in post-Englightenment culture. For this reason, elders were seen as valued repositories of knowledge. This meant, of course, that it was impossible for individuals to procure knowledge immediately. Certain individuals were believed to be repositories of information and others were not. A good hunter could *eventually* become a leader or an elder, but until that time he was expected to defer to others. Knowledge, then, can be seen as a resource that was distributed unevenly within the Inuit social group. It was neither instantly nor easily acquired but was linked to experience, which, in turn, was linked to age.

In many respects, Inuit possessed an Enlightenment vision of the world: that it could be known, understood, and explained. Inuit sought to explain the world around them. The primary difference is not the method used to acquire knowledge. Research on Inuit astronomy demonstrates that Inuit followed a scientific process in their quest for knowledge (MacDonald 1998). A life spent on the land provided a sound understanding of biology, weather patterns, and the environment. The primary difference between Inuit and Enlightenment explanations is that the former were not merely temporal but were also spiritual. This included the belief in an animate universe inhabited by spirits of various forms, and a belief that future events and personal qualities could be affected by current behaviour. Giving children amulets, for example, could encourage hunting prowess or speed; if a pregnant woman exited the igloo or tent quickly, she could ensure an easier birth. This, then, was the chief deviation from an Enlightenment ethos. In some respects, this could have made the transition to Christianity almost seamless, at least in terms of values.

Mechanisms of Control

Described as one of the harshest environments on the planet, the Arctic would seem satisfy Hobbes' contention that life is "nasty, brutish, and short." And yet it is Hobbes' vision of human nature that is most applicable to Inuit political culture. Inuit believed human nature to be fallible, and this fallibility was viewed as innate rather than the product of poor socialization. Adults and children had instincts and urges and passions that at times could get the better of them, impairing their judgment and imperilling their dependents or relatives. Values prized within Inuit society reflected the importance of keeping such base instincts in check. There was, however, little expectation that individuals would, on their own, be able to exercise adequate control, and so Inuit society developed a series of mechanisms that sought to guarantee acceptable behaviour. Some of these functioned at an interpersonal level, and so individuals conformed to accepted codes of behaviour out of fear that deviance would be met with abandonment, either figuratively or literally. The chief mechanism of control involved a labyrinthine system of taboos enforced by self-policing and by shamans.

Spiritual mechanisms

Inuit society identified different types of taboos, some clearly designed with health and safety in mind. The best method of storing meat, for example, was considered sufficiently important that imperfectly cached meat was seen as taboo. Behaviour that could be seen as wasting resources, such as setting fire to objects or throwing them in the water, was also declared taboo.[3] Breaking the wooden tent rafter was seen as taboo (IE 113) for obvious reasons. Other taboos reinforced desired values and customs. The sharing of food, in particular, was subject to a series of taboos. A third set of taboos might seem more whimsical, but we should view it as part of a network of beliefs motivated by a desire to lead a good and healthy life. Individuals travelling to different regions, defined often as regions where inhabitants wore different clothing, were subject to food taboos. Within any given social unit, different hunters would be declared taboo or non-taboo, and this affected who could eat what they provided. Many taboos pertained to pregnant or menstruating women as well as to those who had recently miscarried. Such women, at times, stayed in separate igloos, wore different clothing from other women, and could only eat meat provided by non-taboo hunters.

We should distinguish between behaviour that involved breaking taboos and behaviour that was merely seen as being ill-advised or impolite, more likely to incur the wrath of a parent or concerned elder than the involvement of a shaman. Elders recalled parental warnings that using kelp as a whip while playing was taboo because it would cause the wind to blow (IE 210). Children playing with kelp no doubt also ran the risk of having the whip end fly into their faces or eyes. We know from elder interviews that children were kept out of adult conversations, and much of the information we have is from individuals who, now elders, lived in traditional settings primarily as children. It is not always easy to distinguish between behaviour that adults believed among themselves to be genuinely taboo and behaviour that they presented to children as taboo in an effort to secure their obedience, a variant of "don't screw up your face like that or when the wind changes it will freeze that way." Children were subject to a number of different rules. They were expected to leave the igloo or tent quickly each morning, were discouraged from wearing dog harnesses while playing, and were expected not to address adults by their names. Sarcasm, particularly directed toward leaders or elders, was frowned upon, as was abusing animals and staying up all night getting up to no good. Some of these rules would appear familiar to southern Canadian parents, others were animated clearly by Inuit values, informed as they were by their environment.

Those who broke taboos were believed to face considerable risk. Any individual who ran afoul of a taboo was supposed to confess to the group immediately. Failing that, the only hope to prevent illness, sickness of a loved one, difficulty procuring animals, or even death was to confess the breached taboo to a shaman. Informed of the need to cure the offending individual and upon receipt of an offering, the shaman would attempt to appease the offended spirits and correct the wrong. An individual could improve her or his chances of avoiding misfortune if she or he confessed to a shaman, but there was no guarantee of this. Individuals who refused to confess, even when urged to do so by a shaman, were perceived to be in the gravest circumstances. Denying that a taboo had been broken was seen as disastrous, lying to a shaman seen as futile. In other words, it was not enough simply to declare an act taboo: the breaking of a taboo had to be seen to have negative consequences. The regulation of Inuit behaviour relied on a self-policing approach to conduct and, failing that, a system of punishment for inappropriate behaviour. Such a system depended on a complicit population, one that believed the punishments meted out by shamans were a real and direct result of poor behaviour.

Temporal mechanisms

If shamans provided spiritual leadership within the camp, elders and leaders offered temporal leadership. Social units could have more than one elder, but they usually had only one leader. The line between these positions was fluid, so that an individual could be both a leader and an elder. As Stevenson (1993) argues, the difference was between roles rather than individuals, between *isumataq*, one who thinks, and *angajuqqaq*, one who is listened to or obeyed. Some elders point to a division between men who hunted and men who adopted a more active role in settlement life (IE 070). Camp leaders would have been chosen from the former rather than the latter group.

Leaders were deemed to be those best able to provide for the group, possessing a skill set that could cope with such phenomena as weather patterns, ice conditions, and hunting grounds and techniques as well as the butchering of animals and the caching of meat. Leaders had little involvement in the policing of social behaviour but were seen instead as those most likely to guarantee a reliable supply of food and shelter:

> At that time that people saw that I was more able than others ... they started to encourage me to lead them. I never had the desire to become a leader, but it was the people that looked up to me to lead them ... It appears as if I helped them to secure food with my hunting, I led the community ... At the time when I started to lead my people, I found myself having to pay much closer attention to the weather conditions. (IE 315)

Camp leaders were usually selected by group consensus, although leadership selection and the relationship between leaders and other adults varied according to region. Around Igloolik and the north Baffin region, the eldest hunter would have assumed the role of *isumataq*, while among the Netsilingmiut, near, for example, Taloyoak, the leader would have sought the counsel of various peers before making decisions (Stevenson 1993). Among the

Utkuhikhalingmiut, the head of each household served a similar purpose, with the result that the extended social unit lacked a singular group leader (Briggs 1982, 112).

The chief role of elders, by contrast, was maintaining the moral and social standards of the social group: "It is the responsibility of the elders to correct the wrong being done" (IE 090). Interviews with elders suggest that they viewed "moralizing" to be their main role, explaining and cautioning against inappropriate behaviour without attributing blame. Typically, elders focused on inappropriate behaviour that was not covered by taboos. Such behaviour would have included getting too attached to someone else's wife, breaking things, being sarcastic, or staying up all night. Humility was prized, so anyone who bragged of his own hunting prowess or who made it clear that he was jealous of another hunter would find himself subject to moralizing. At times, moralizing did encompass taboo behaviour, such as bestiality, or behaviour that was taboo in some regions but not in others, such as marrying a blood relative. At first, the act of moralizing usually occurred in private; on subsequent occasions it occurred in public. Inuit stressed the importance of early intervention as individuals were believed to be more remorseful after a first instance of poor judgment than they were after any that might follow. Individuals would be confronted with an account of their inappropriate behaviour and then told why it was detrimental to themselves or to the group. Elders readily acknowledged that not all individuals were equally affected by the act of moralizing. Some appeared contrite, while others clearly required more blunt tactics. One interviewee explained the logic of elder behaviour:

> When the elders start to hear of rumors that activities are being carried out that is something contrary to acceptable standards, and the individual had been identified, he will start to preach him, usually with the wife of the individual, this happens in a private setting in order to tell him things not allowed and the reason why he must not act in a way that might be harmful to other people, to respect elders and the importance of treating them in dignity. The elder will moralize the individual on these grounds usually alone with the person at fault, the elder will not censure the individual. The main task would be to preach the individual so that he understands about the morality and what is expected of the individual.

> When one is preached without being censured one feel obligated to follow the preaching of an elder, as well, his words are implanted within, not to be forgotten easily for years to come. (IE 090)

Elders who immediately censured individuals were seen to be less effective than those who subjected such individuals to a quieter approach. The act of moralizing provided an opportunity for those who had behaved inappropriately to air their grievances and then move on. Mentioning events that had been discussed during a moralizing session was seen as inappropriate and contrary to the general goal of restoring social balance within the group. Moralizing was not seen as a form of punishment, punishment being associated with the spiritual realm of taboos and shamans. Temporal mechanisms of social control, then, emphasized positive reinforcement, while spiritual mechanisms of social control emphasized punishment:

> No one ever thought of punishment, the only concern they had was to restore peace among themselves and to strengthened their relationships. For example, I would have to talk about the things that I would rather not talk about, something that I was shy to discuss with anyone, by so doing we would confess to the gathering to what might be considered wrong, it was in this manner that they use to be able to restore relationship. Nothing was hidden, no one would mention it after the gathering as it is common for someone having confessed to a priest ... This was a form of cleansing oneself from conscience and guilt. (IE 214)

One might wonder whether such tactics were effective. Certainly, there is evidence that young people claimed to heed the word of their elders: "The word of an elder is something that one does not forget too easily, especially when one is lectured not scolded. There will be times when you will be able to remember certain things that you once heard from an elder no matter how late in life it may be" (IE 183). That moralizing appeared to achieve its intended purpose of ensuring social harmony guaranteed its continued use.

Venal behaviour for which moralizing was not deemed appropriate was subject to a more ad hoc method of social control: retribution. The frequency with which violence was employed as a mechanism of social control is difficult to gauge, and violence has rarely been presented as an ideal solution. We can distinguish between two types of violence. The first type involved disputes between males that were settled through fights that had clear rules. Such events were structured more as competitions than as dangerous brawls (IE 097). The second type of violence was reserved for extreme cases of unacceptable behaviour and could involve a severe beating or even death (Steenhoven 1959). Often, such violence was reserved for behaviour that imperilled the survival of the group. Clearly, these acts of violence differ from those prompted by individual jealousy, whether over hunting prowess or a partner, meted out by more impetuous individuals.

Given the spiritual and temporal mechanisms used for social control, and the various individuals associated with them, one might wonder which roles most easily graft themselves onto contemporary leadership positions such as those occupied by businesspeople and politicians. The deference shown to shamans can be seen to explain, in part, the deference Inuit initially offered to priests, ministers, and Roman Catholic and Anglican missionaries upon their arrival in the eastern Arctic. In some ways, Christianity offered not so much a radical break from traditional Inuit beliefs as a different venue within which to practise them.

The Introduction of Christianity

The twentieth-century transformation of Inuit culture from one lived predominantly outside the influence of southern Canada to one integrated within a global media environment may be attributed to several phenomena. Certainly, for example, the introduction of capitalism and a wage economy served to distance Inuit from lives spent on the land. The advent of Christianity rivals this transformation for four reasons: first, by identifying similarities between traditional Inuit practices and Christianity, missionaries facilitated the process of conversion; second, conversion had an obvious and immediate impact on behaviour (if not on values); third, the similarities between shamanism and Christianity served to reinforce a rule-based culture in the eastern Arctic; and fourth, Christianity, by transforming the agents of social conformity, for the first time placed a significant leadership role beyond the reach of Inuit, thus denying Inuit society spiritual leaders from their own social group.

Missionaries in the eastern Arctic were of two varieties: (1) Roman Catholic missionaries from the Oblates of Mary Immaculate and (2) Anglican missionaries from the Church Missionary Society of the Church of England (Trott

2001, 174). The chief goal of both was to convert Inuit to Christianity. The speed with which Inuit took to Christianity could be seen as an example of their reputed ability to adapt. Instead, the values present in Christianity – the universe is animate, one must atone for one's sins, one benefits from good behaviour – required remarkably little transformation on the part of Inuit. The two belief systems were sufficiently similar to ensure their easy cohabitation. Placing a rosary and a cross on the wall of an igloo in order to thwart a spirit that looked like a polar bear offers one typical example (IE 111). Nor was it difficult to explain the relationship among key figures in these respective belief systems: "*Saataanasi* [Satan] is like a bad tempered spirit that can kill you without warning" (IE 150); "The shamans were the authoritative power in the community as if he was a God to the people in the community, even though it is said that he is lesser than that of God ... It is just like *takanna* [spirit below] is the law enforcement officer, once the offender confesses she no longer care about him" (IE 235).

In their efforts to convert Inuit, missionaries exploited this similarity between certain aspects of Christianity and Inuit beliefs regarding taboos and shamans. Inuit were told that the Christian system of taboos and atonement was far simpler than the Inuit system. Rather than the catalogue of errors that could occur, Christian sins were far simpler than Inuit transgressions, and one could atone for them in one day rather than the five or four or three recommended by shamans. That Christian rules for leading a good life were much simpler than Inuit rules appears to have been the chief motivation for conversion: "My parents were grateful for having been introduced to Christianity as they found that it was so much easier from the old custom where taboos ruled the behaviour of ... almost ... everything" (IE 214). For those encountering Roman Catholic missionaries, the act of confession appeared similar to traditional practices: "It [confession] is much better and will make you happier. If you are doing something that is embarrassing but you disclose it to a confidant who makes you welcome and encourages you to confess then you can mingle among your peers in their daily activities without secluding yourself from the rest of your peers" (IE 275). This individual is referring to confession in church, but he could just as easily be describing the after-effects of interactions with a shaman or moralizing from an elder.

The streamlined nature of Christian atonement made conversion a more appealing option than might otherwise have been the case. One by-product of this, though, was the need to keep track of days so that the day of atonement,

Sunday, could be identified. This had an obvious effect on the importance of time, and Inuit devised methods for tracking the days, acknowledging that, when hunting, the rhythm of the day made this difficult. Homemade calendars began to appear in Inuit camps. Patterns of migration also changed. Christmas and Easter were marked on the Inuit calendar, and their social celebration replaced events associated with good weather or the return of the sun. The establishment of churches in settled areas also served to transform patterns of migration, eventually drawing people into emerging communities on Sundays.

Rules for behaviour, and atoning for inappropriate behaviour, were the primary source of continuity between traditional Inuit beliefs and Christianity. In an environment already very respectful of rules, the conversion to Christianity only served to heighten their potential influence. The act of conversion itself, *siqitiqtut*, focused on the changed rules governing behaviour (Laugrand 1997). Inuit were invited to consume previously taboo food, such as a piece of seal heart, to symbolize that taboos had been replaced by prayer (IE 155). Since then, each new cultural influence has been integrated primarily by the identification of new or changing rules:

> Today with laws imposed on the people by the government a person is deemed to have gain an independence from his parents when they reached the age of sixteen or nineteen. On account of this we find that we no longer have the access to our children to moralize them or take disciplinary action against them otherwise we will be charged and will have to go to court on account of having to take physical disciplinary actions against our own children. This makes it so much easier for our children to behave the way they wish to behave as the law is on their side so they can act in any way they so wish no mater how damaging it may be morally, because the courts are on their side. This I know for certain makes it that much easier for our own children to live a life that is damaging to one's moral standards. (IE 097)

If traditional Inuit spiritual mechanisms of social control were initially supplanted by those associated with Christianity, temporal mechanisms were supplanted by southern Canadian government employees, including the RCMP and various bureaucrats. If we recall the initial distinction between positive reinforcement and punishment employed by temporal and spiritual mechanisms of social control, the arrival of RCMP officers would have muddied the waters considerably as they replaced positive temporal reinforcement with temporal punishment. The links between contemporary rules governing moral behaviour and Inuit leadership were obviously clear to one elder, who, within a larger explanation of elders and moralizing, told a story about the local alcohol education committee (IE 226). Both the elders and the committee were seen to be concerned with moral behaviour, using public discussion as a means of achieving it.

Without underestimating how bewildering it would have been to assimilate a new set of beliefs about creation and codes of behaviour, it is important to see that the primary relevance of the advent of Christianity has to do with how it altered Inuit mechanisms of social control. If a belief in shamanism initially ensured compliance with a strict set of behavioural rules, conversion to Christianity kept the focus on behaviour but altered the source of the rules. The taboos enforced by shamans were created by a society that found them relevant to the lived environment. If rules can emerge from within a culture or be imposed from the outside, Christian morality was clearly exogeneous to Inuit culture. The arrival of traders changed Inuit behaviour in that individuals began to supplement hunting with trapping as a method of securing goods or money. This change was significant, but it did not prevent Inuit from performing traditional tasks. Indeed, traders depended on the ability of Inuit to procure resources from the land. The conversion to Christianity, however, provides the first instance where Inuit were urged to abandon a significant element of their culture. That Inuit and Christian values were not particularly different from one another should not lead one to underestimate the profound effect of Christianity on Inuit culture. Ironically, value congruence led missionaries to perceive themselves as being closer to Inuit than were other European or southern Canadian arrivals, and to defend a Christianized Inuit culture against further cultural transformation, particularly in the form of wage labour and relocation to settlements: "Those who originally moved to transform Inuit traditions through the direct attack on their belief system become the guardians of that same tradition in the face of increasing government pressures towards change" (Trott 2001, 186). Minor alterations in behaviour, particularly in terms of spending more time near settled communities, slowly transformed social bonds from those in which kinship hierarchy was paramount to more horizontal relationships among peers. In this light, the advent of a wage economy and the transition to settlements merely completed a process that began with the Christianization of the Inuit population. If the short hand of the clock became relevant with the arrival of missionaries, the long hand became relevant with the transition to wage labour.

Inuit culture identified a moral code to govern ideal behaviour, which in turn was informed by a life led on the land. Christianity accepted many of the ideals governing Inuit life but altered fundamentally the mechanism for enforcing them. Accomplished hunters were still able to be effective leaders, but shamans found their role as spiritual arbiters supplanted by religious figures from England, France, Belgium, and southern Canada. Just as the nature of spiritual leadership changed with the advent of Christianity, so the acquisition of resources altered under capitalism. Capitalism was about more than taking power away from those who hunted well and giving it to those best able to type or teach. It heralded a shift from the collective to the individual. Equally significant, the transition to capitalism and the move to settlements began to erase the social foundations upon which the dominant values of an Inuit moral code had been built. The source of a normative vision of the "good life" eroded, leaving behind a penchant for rule following but no clear rules to follow.

From this evidence, what might we make of a pre-institutional Inuit political culture? First, it was not homogeneous for it varied in its approach to resource distribution and decision making. Rigid social hierarchies among certain groups can be contrasted with an almost anarchic existence among others. Second, Inuit mechanisms for social control placed a heavy emphasis on rules, with clear punishment for deviation from those rules. Because it was seen as key to survival, social conformity was not rewarded but expected. Third, we can identify key values that would have been relevant to emerging political institutions. An attention to environmental stewardship can be paired with an inherent conservatism that emphasized survival. It was survival of the group, rather than survival of the individual, that mattered, and, from this, we can see obvious support for communitarian approaches to resource distribution. And yet these broad themes mask different approaches to change and, in particular, different approaches to the state. The following chapter charts Canadian government efforts to integrate Inuit into the Canadian political system, along with the differing reactions of those within Inuit political culture.

4
Political Integration in the Eastern Arctic

Excluded from the 1876 Indian Act, Inuit were spared formal government interference until the middle of the twentieth century. Traders and missionaries who lived among Inuit had an obvious impact on their behaviour, but it was not until the 1939 Supreme Court ruling (*Re Eskimos* [1939] S.C.R. 104) that the federal government saw Inuit as a federal responsibility and sought to integrate them as citizens within the Canadian political system. One of the current goals of the Government of Nunavut is to successfully integrate Inuit perspectives into the political system. Initially, however, Inuit were integrated into a Canadian political system that bore the marks of a British Westminster political tradition. In the 1960s, Inuit in the eastern Arctic were provided unprecedented opportunities to participate in elections – both federal and territorial – and local decision-making bodies. The rules of this participation structured the process through which Inuit would become political citizens, and they have had a profound influence on how Inuit later viewed the state. The arrival of peace, order, and good government in the eastern Arctic also highlighted the cultural distance between traditional Inuit life and Canadian political culture.

As of 1949 Canada had ten provinces and two territories, the Yukon in the western Arctic and the Northwest Territories in the central and eastern Arctic. The Northwest Territories has, throughout Canadian history, represented that vast area not occupied by the provinces, a rump of land from which successive entities have been carved. These include Manitoba in 1870, a short-lived Keewatin territory in 1876, the Yukon territory in 1898, and Alberta and Saskatchewan in 1905. The boundaries of Quebec extended into the NWT District of Ungava in 1905 and again in 1912. As outlined in sections 92 and 93 of the Constitution Act, 1867, Canadian provinces retain the right to legislate in areas such as education, health, municipal affairs, and non-renewable resources. Generally, territories legislate in similar areas and appear as provinces "writ small," their populations only a fraction of those found in the provinces, their areas of legislative competence more restricted. Territories differ from provinces in three additional ways. First, unlike provinces, whose sovereignty is derived from the Constitution Act, territories are created by federal statute and cannot amend their own constitutions. They could, as a result, be disbanded, or have their boundaries altered, by later federal acts. This formal sovereignty over the existence of territories extends to all territorial legislation, any piece of which could be overruled by the federal government. However unlikely either of these two scenarios might be, the legal status of the territories clearly differs from that enjoyed by the provinces.

Second, territories enjoy much less fiscal autonomy than do provinces. They do not have control over the management of Crown lands, and, although they maintain the right to collect provincial income tax, the diseconomies of scale created by a small and dispersed population mean that the bulk of their funding arrives in the form of block grants from the federal government in Ottawa. This dependence on federal funding affects the perceived viability of the territories (Howard and Widdowson 1999, 59) in addition to more mundane planning decisions about program funding. Put simply, territories lack the essential tax base to be anything other than wholly dependent on federal transfers for basic program delivery.

The third distinction between territories and provinces relates more to political development. Because of their size and their perceived dependence on federal coffers, territories have been treated as entities that are in the process of political development, their eventual end stage the attainment of provincial status. While provinces generally enjoyed elected legislative councils or cabinet governments at the time of their creation, the arrival of territorial elections or accountable executives – the arrival of responsible government – occurred only when deemed appropriate by federal administrators.

Politics at the provincial and federal levels operates according to a system of responsible government modelled on the Westminster parliamentary system. This system has several key features. Members of a legislature are elected by an electorate composed of all eligible adults within a set region. Voters retain the right not only to select the individuals who make legislation but also to chuck them out at election time if they have not been happy with their performance. The executive is composed of legislative members. Typically, the leader of the executive is the head of the largest political party in the legislature, and he or she selects executive colleagues to form the governing cabinet. In responsible systems, the executive is accountable to the legislature in the same way that the legislature is accountable to the electorate. This model differs from those practised in presidential systems, where the executive is not part of the legislature. Responsible government typically relies on the presence of political parties and strong party discipline, particularly among members of the cabinet. It is this model that operates in Ottawa and in the capitals of the ten provinces. This was not the model employed in the NWT at the start of the 1950s; instead, an unelected territorial council operated in place of a legislature, and its leader was a public servant appointed by the federal government. The selection methods associated with responsible government – legislative members being selected by the electorate, the head of the executive holding the confidence of the legislature – were absent in the NWT. When federal officials sought to integrate Inuit into the Canadian political system, the set of institutions governing their political lives were different from those affecting the lives of Manitobans, Albertans, and Quebecers. When we speak of federal attempts to integrate Inuit or other Arctic residents as citizens, it is accurate to refer to the efforts of the territorial council as part of a wider federal campaign of integration. Until 1951, all members of the council were appointed by the federal government, and their leader, the commissioner, was until 1980 an appointed federal bureaucrat. While the various bureaucrats may have perceived themselves to be serving different masters – federal public servants serving their political masters and council members and support staff serving residents of the territories – they were, in reality, all agents of the federal government.

In this chapter, I examine how Inuit were integrated into the Canadian political system in the 1960s and 1970s. I focus less on institutional development than on the desired cultural transformation of Inuit from hunters to what would have been considered more conventional citizens. I address three key elements of integration: (1) the operation of the first elections for residents in the eastern Arctic, (2) the conflicting messages about representation that would have been sent to Inuit residents, and (3) the flourishing of local democracy. Helped along by Northern Service Officers, communities in the eastern Arctic became hosts to a dizzying array of decision-making bodies, including community councils, Eskimo councils, housing associations, hunters and trappers associations, social welfare committees, and, eventually, regional Inuit associations and regional councils. The chapter ends by exploring the activities set in motion by federal and territorial administrators, their cautious efforts to ensure that the "appropriate" type of Inuk became active within politics, and their eventual bewilderment at Inuit appetites for involvement and activity. The seeds of integration, sown as they were in the 1960s, are evident in the political organization of Inuit and in Inuit campaigns for a land claim in the 1970s. It is this pattern of political participation, begun unwittingly by bureaucrats, that forms the bedrock of political culture in Nunavut.

Elections

From 1876 to 1960, the federal government did not always see Aboriginal identity and Canadian citizenship as obvious bedfellows, though access to political participation varied by region and Aboriginal group. Those registered as status Indians who wished to vote in federal elections were required to surrender their status and, in so doing, to signify their entry into the Canadian political settlement. This effectively disenfranchised those governed by the Indian Act until 1960, when the rules regarding suffrage changed. We know, of course, that Inuit were excluded from the Indian Act until a major revision of the legislation in 1951. As a result, there was no piece of legislation that served as an ethnic bar to Inuit participation in federal elections. In the territories, however, potential voters faced an additional hurdle. Throughout the development of the NWT, from the nineteenth century until 1966, constituencies in the north were created on the basis of sufficient representation. If there were sufficient numbers of voters in a relatively concentrated area – and indeed the notion of "concentration" was relative – then the government would create a constituency. Those areas where the population was too sparse, or the communications networks too underdeveloped, would be excluded from constituency boundaries, their residents denied the right to vote regardless of ethnicity. At every election, then, vast areas of the NWT were left out. In 1951, with the creation of the first elected seat on the NWT Council, the eastern Arctic was considered too sparsely populated to justify the creation of constituencies – a situation that continued to disenfranchise voters in the east, regardless of their ethnicity, until 1966.

As part of its mandate to be closer to the people, the territorial council travelled extensively. In 1957, for example, the council travelled to Frobisher Bay at a time when the community was not a part of a constituency electing members to the council. Council sessions were held in the local school, which cancelled lessons for the week. While in Frobisher, the council met with three representatives of the Inuit population and discussed proposals to create constituencies for the Keewatin and Franklin districts. Eventually rejected as unrealistic, the creation of eastern constituencies had less to do with the political sophistication of residents in the eastern Arctic, although certainly this formed a consistent theme in council discussions, than it did with practical problems. The sparseness of the population, along with poor transportation and communications networks, were seen to inhibit the usual campaign process so integral to proper elections. Infrastructure in the eastern Arctic was seen as a challenge both to candidates and to voters. If candidates were unable to travel to the outer reaches of their constituencies, how would they be able to identity the concerns of those in the region and represent those concerns to council? If voters were unable to meet their candidates, or hear about their ideas, on what basis would they cast their ballots? Territorial and federal officials believed that the structure of life in the eastern Arctic was, in a practical sense, unsuited to the operation of democracy (Dinsdale 1963). It is also true that some held a dim view of potential voters. A document prepared for the Northern Administrative Branch summarizing territorial council debates on political development notes, for example, that despite the "rudimentary forms of democratic government" in communities such as Baker Lake, Cambridge Bay, and Frobisher Bay, and despite the presence in these places of "some articulate Eskimos,"

> it is doubtful that it would be possible for them to cope with the sort of business dealt with by the Council. For the present, therefore, it is probably undesirable to encourage Eskimos to run for a seat on the council because their failure to cope with problems at this early stage might set them back seriously in their own minds as well as in the minds of others. (Northern Administrative Branch 1963)[1]

Here we find an example of what we have come to expect from federal bureaucrats of the 1940s and 1950s: well-meaning paternalism and a fear for the future development of those incapable of performing the tasks generally associated with contemporary Canadian life. The administration added, of course, that it would be no better to have elections just for the white settlers in the Arctic as they would not necessarily understand Inuit issues. Here, the concern was not with a violation of the principle of universal suffrage – that certain groups should be able to exercise the right to vote but not others – but whether the violation would meet the needs of the council. The best result, then, was to delay holding elections in the eastern Arctic. Speaking at the second session of the 1961 NWT Council meetings, the commissioner noted: "It would be doing the Eskimo people no service if they were rushed into political responsibility before at least a few of them were able to understand what it was all about and take part as equals with other elected or appointed representatives" (Northern Administrative Branch 1963).[2] Acknowledging that this policy denied it an understanding of Inuit concerns, the council arranged for the appointment of an administrator of the Arctic, who would keep tabs on developments in the eastern portion of the territory and report back to it.

The 1962 federal election saw the creation of a constituency in the Arctic, and it provided for those resident in the eastern Arctic the first opportunity to vote in federal or territorial elections. Concerned about an Inuit lack of political maturity, the federal government issued a pamphlet entitled *Voting* that outlined the task expected of individuals and the purpose of their enfranchisement. The introductory section of the pamphlet notes: "On June 18, 1962, we will be asked to choose one person who will speak for us. The person who will speak for us is one of the bosses in Ottawa. Everyone else in Canada will choose, just as we do, a person from their own land who will work for his people." The statement attempts to integrate the eastern Arctic population into a wider Canadian whole and, in so doing, implies that the rights of the former are identical to those exercised by other Canadians. It explicitly mentions a geographic basis for representation, but it does so in a way that could be interpreted as having ethnic connotations. Land determines representation, but reference to a group's "own land" could suggest a sense of homeland, or *patrie*. Perhaps most significant, the introductory section of the pamphlet identifies politicians not as representatives of the people, or as regular people, but as bosses. This suggests that politicians are above their electors, that they are in charge of them. It would be entirely reasonable to argue that the reverse is true: that voters are, in fact, in charge of their politicians, and can influence their behaviour by expressing their wishes. Instead, the pamphlet presents the political system in a way that suggests that voters are subservient to their politicians and, by extension, to the state. This view is in keeping with the rule-based social unit. In postcontact Inuit society, the state was viewed as the boss, in large part because for many years the state was represented in the Arctic either by the military or the church, each of which had a number of rules and regulations to be followed.

The right to vote in federal elections did not bring with it the automatic right to participate in territorial contests. The extension of voting rights to the east, although rejected in 1961, was, by 1964, obviously an issue of concern for the members of the NWT Council. That year, the council passed a motion calling on the commissioner to write to the federal government and request an extension of the franchise. Both elected and appointed members were sufficiently convinced that the "advancement" of the Inuit population justified their participation in elections. The council also had by this time its first Inuk member. Abe Okpik, originally from Aklavik, was appointed to the council in 1964. Speaking in the first session of 1966, he expressed a desire to establish constituencies in the eastern Arctic and suggested that practical considerations might not be the sole basis for their current exclusion:

> Although I am the newest member of this Council, I hope my term will be short. Nothing would give me greater pleasure than to have my place on this Council taken by a new elected member from Keewatin, Baffin Island or the Coronation Gulf area. The people of these areas have a right to representation on this Council. We of this Council make decisions which affect the lives of these people. We discuss splitting the Territories, their Territories, without giving them a voice in this decision. If we consider them too backward or ignorant for participation in this Council, let us say so. At least they will know that our reason for neglecting them is not indifference. (NWT Council 1966)

Then-deputy-commissioner Stuart Hodgson responded that it was better to do things properly than to do them quickly. When the Carrothers Commission reported on the issue of territorial division in 1966, it added its voice to those calling for the creation of constituencies in the eastern Arctic. This additional impetus led to the creation of three eastern Arctic constituencies and extended the right to vote to all eastern Arctic residents, providing they met the standard criteria of age (twenty-one) and residency.

In an effort to integrate the eastern Arctic into its workings before the next round of territorial elections, the NWT Council organized by-elections in 1966 in the three newly created eastern ridings: Keewatin, including communities such as Baker Lake and Rankin Inlet; Central Arctic, including communities such as Coppermine/Kugluktuk; and Eastern Arctic, which was composed largely of communities on Baffin Island. The territorial council issued a pamphlet similar to the one distributed by the federal government in 1962. This included a general version as well as three separate documents, one for each of the constituencies. The territorial document was hampered by the inability of translators to identify phrases in Inuktitut that adequately communicated the spirit of its contents. One staff officer lamented: "Despite the distribution of our excellent bi-lingual paper ... the Eskimo people are still largely unaware of the significance of elections, and more particularly, the bodies to which men are elected" (Jull 1966).

The document attempts to outline the differences between the federal government and the territorial government: "Four years ago for the first time the people of the Arctic chose a man to represent them in the Big Government, the parliament of Canada, at Ottawa ... Years ago this Parliament had created a small Council to govern the NWT." The Eastern Arctic document asks: "How do the people know who is willing to represent them? Not everybody wants to represent his people at the Council. It is much work and he must be away from home a lot." Territorial officials wondered whether the resulting document was not too simple and asked whether it might not be possible to produce a "shorter but perhaps more sophisticated paper for the non-Eskimo population" (Murphy 1966).

Aside from problems with the pamphlet, the campaign itself was plagued by a variety of difficulties. There were problems with the Inuk returning officer in Keewatin, who did not distribute forms or file reports with the speed, accuracy, or diligence expected by elections officials. Reports of his performance vary: some thought him developmentally and temperamentally unsuited to the job; some thought him overwhelmed, bewildered, and under-supported. At one point, the area administrator asked to be given duplicates of all the material destined for this returning officer in order to keep tabs on him. Administrative problems surfaced elsewhere. In the Eastern Arctic, none of the polls on the Belcher Islands received election material before the election date. These events, though no doubt exacerbated by the fact that it was the first territorial election in the eastern Arctic, are unrelated to the ethnicity of the electorate. Two further events suggest an uneasy accommodation of the Inuit population.

First, the deposit for candidates in the 1966 by-election was $200, at a time when the annual income for Inuit in the eastern Arctic was $426. By today's standards this would represent a candidate deposit of $6,191.[3] The perceived financial bar to participation prompted the commissioner to write to the chief electoral officer (CEO) in Ottawa, requesting that the deposit be lowered to $100. In his one-sentence response, the CEO wrote back that a lowering of deposits would not be entertained. Incidentally, the 1966 daily per diem for elected members was $100, with an annual maximum of $2,000.

If the deposit represented a significant obstacle, given the average annual salary of Inuit, the financial rewards upon election would have been nearly unfathomable. The event that best illustrates a culture clash between Westminster and Inuit political expectations, however, took place in the Central Arctic constituency.

After the elections, Coppermine resident Peter Kamingoak wrote a letter to the NWT commissioner criticizing the election procedures. In it he indicated not only that he had intended to run in the election but also that he had been unable to do so because his community had received insufficient information and guidance. In his list of concerns, Kamingoak noted, for example, that, with the exception of one sign posted in English, public information was not available, that the sign did not indicate how individuals might become candidates, that notices of the election were not posted, that nomination papers were not available, and that the returning officer failed to visit the community. Kamingoak ended his telegram to the commissioner by saying: "I protest apparent indifference in informing Eskimo and white population Coopermine [sic] and Holman Island about election which resulted in acclamation of individual unknown in this area" (Kamingoak 1966).

The telegram prompted two responses. In the first, Commissioner Hodgson, who clearly appeared to be frustrated by the situation, forwarded the letter to the regional administrator. Hodgson noted, in particular, that Kamingoak had made it clear to him, to the local MP, and to the returning officer that he intended to run, and that to Kamingoak, that expression of interest was likely seen as tantamount to a formal nomination. The returning officer later admitted that she had heard of Kamingoak's intention but, because he had not filed nomination papers, she assumed he had decided to withdraw. The second response, from the regional administrator to Kamingoak, outlines the array of jurisdictional responsibilities that Kamingoak should have known about in order to prevent this situation. Noting that the CEO, not the NWT commissioner, is in charge of elections, the regional director pointed out that Kamingoak should have written to other individuals and that only a formal inquiry would have prompted a response as government officials are forbidden from interfering in elections (Neve 1966). Since this was the first territorial election, it is not surprising that there was a considerable level of confusion concerning the right of individuals to stand as candidates and the process by which they might do so. More surprising is that we do not have more evidence of this sort of thing.

Indeed, the only reason we know about this particular event is likely the result of Kamingoak's ability to dictate a telegram in English.

This event is all the more telling because of correspondence between the commissioner and other would-be candidates. In June 1966, Simonie Michael, who was later elected for the Eastern Arctic constituency, wrote in English to Commissioner Hodgson, noting that when they had last met in Frobisher Bay: "You kindly suggested that I write to you if I decided to be a candidate for Representation of this area. This letter is to let you know that I want to be a candidate" (Michael 1966). Michael then asked whether there was funding available to visit the various communities within the constituency. In his response, the commissioner expressed pleasure that Michael had decided to run and directed him toward the returning officer. This shows that, for two Inuit would-be candidates, the NWT commissioner was seen as the first point-of-contact.

In the end, two Qallunaak – Duncan Pryde and Robert Williamson, born in Scotland and England, respectively – were acclaimed in the Central Arctic and the Keewatin. The three-candidate election in the Eastern Arctic pitted the successful Simonie Michael against two Qallunaak: Waldy Phipps, an aviation company president living in Resolute, and Gordon Rennie, manager of the Hudson's Bay Company Store in Frobisher. The terms for the candidates were short, though, as in 1967 the NWT Council resumed its normal election schedule.

The 1967 elections again produced problems in the east. Some of these were typical of electioneering anywhere. Incumbent candidate Williamson complained that the principal at the Rankin school was using the school photocopier to publish flyers for an opponent and that the principal in Whale Cove was displaying the offending flyer, which suggested that his opponent was being officially endorsed by the school and the education system at large. In addition, a teacher in Chesterfield Inlet was reported to be saying mean things about Williamson, who was offered equal access to the photocopier as compensation and eventually bested his opponent by a margin of four to one. Other problems speak to the uneasy process of integrating Inuit into the political system. Milton Freeman wrote multiple letters to the Northern Administration Branch to complain that the notices and forms that reached Iqaluit were entirely in English (Freeman 1967a, 1967b). The response he received was that it was "just not practical" to translate acts, regulations, forms, and smaller booklets into Inuktitut. In a May letter to Commissioner Hodgson,

Canon Whitbread indicated that a unilingual Inuk in the community was considering candidacy and wondered whether an interpreter would be available for his speeches to council (Whitbread 1967). The commissioner wrote back that, yes, interpretation was available, but under the same conditions that had been extended to Simonie Michael, namely, that the opening speech would be translated but all other comments would have to be made in English.

In the three eastern constituencies, all three incumbents regained their seats in two-candidate runoffs that saw wildly different turnout rates. Turnout in the Keewatin was over 90 percent, while rates in the central and eastern constituencies were lower, at above 50 percent and 60 percent, respectively. The 1967 election also saw the birth of typical electioneering in the north, with many western candidates publishing pledges in newspapers. In its analysis of the pledges made by the elected members, the Northern Administration Branch noted that Williamson had two handbills, no doubt produced by the photocopier in the Rankin school, and that Michael and Pryde had not published pledges in newspapers. Among the western representatives who did create campaign pledges, typical promises included the full implementation of the recommendations of the Advisory Commission on the Development of Government in the Northwest Territories, which included the relocation of territorial administration to the north and "the introduction of TV in any form at the earliest possible date" (Stewart 1967).

The operation of elections in the Eastern Arctic shows that an inflexible approach to the rules governing political behaviour was more exclusive to Inuit than it might have been. The electoral rules were neither modified nor sufficiently enunciated to meet the needs of a population unfamiliar with the complex web of requirements, forms, and deposits. The translation of materials into Inuktitut was, for many areas, limited to the bilingual pamphlet that summarized the process of voting. In this case, the equality of information produced an inequity of electoral participation. Inuit were not given information about the formal rules of participation, and their participation was hardly courted. As the next section shows, however, when Inuit were subject to different rules, the results communicated inconsistent messages about their intended participation in the political system.

Representation

The formal inclusion of Inuit in federal and territorial elections provided them with cues about the universal nature of their rights. Other political developments in the 1960s also gave them knowledge about the dominant constructions of representation. Western liberal democracy is grounded in the notion of universal access to rights, including political representation, which in Canada had a geographic foundation. There were considerable exceptions to universal access and geographic representation in the Northwest Territories, where representation on the basis of other characteristics would have been made apparent to Inuit.

Writing in 1962, then NWT commissioner Robertson (1962, 3) noted that Britain and its colonies had always distinguished between the rights of those whose lands were acquired by conquest and the rights of those whose lands were acquired by settlement. The latter group was owed an "inherent and inalienable" right to representation, while the former group could be bestowed rights at the discretion of the conquering power. Robertson argued that this distinction could be seen in Canada, and he cites the extension of specific and limited rights to the conquered population in New France. He notes, however, that this distinction operated everywhere but within Canada's own territories. As we know from the previous section, the right to vote for federal or territorial representation was not universal. This changed in 1962 and 1966, when all residents of the territory were entitled to vote. The notion of representation, then, was far from inherent or inalienable for those living in the eastern Arctic, although the grounds for their exclusion were portrayed as practical rather than ethnic. Individuals living in other parts of the country, and even in other parts of the territory, were able to participate in elections and, thus, had rights to representation that residents of the eastern Arctic did not.

One of the components of the Westminster system has long been its insistence on a geographic basis for representation. Those elected to the House of Commons, or to the NWT Council, represent geographic areas rather than ethnic or religious groups or genders. There is, of course, no automatic association between first-past-the-post electoral systems and responsible government, as national list proportional systems can attest. The geographic element surfaces not in the position of the executive but in the electoral system. The two, however, are paired in the British application of responsible government and can be compared to other alternatives, such as consociational systems. The Westminster system was grounded not in the representation of particular *types* of people but in the representation of geographic clusters of people. The integration of Inuit into the Canadian political system, however, would have provided confusing lessons about the universal application of this tenet. Nowhere is this more evident than in the election of delegates to the Eskimo Affairs Committee.

Formed in 1952, the Eskimo Affairs Committee met twice each year for two years, then annually after that. It provided an opportunity for federal officials and other vested interests to discuss development in the Arctic and the impact of changing conditions on Inuit. At first, the committee was concerned primarily with identifying a way to ensure a continued income for Inuit without making them dependent on the "relief economy" (Clancy 1987, 193). Rival proposals included the creation of a Crown corporation that would employ Inuit and greater Inuit dependence on the Hudson's Bay Company as a source of income. For the first seven years, the committee contained representatives from a variety of government departments, the RCMP, Roman Catholic and Anglican missions, and the HBC. Alexander Stevenson, the administrator of the Arctic, noted that the Eskimo Affairs Committee wanted to assist Inuit to live traditionally but that its ultimate goal was to enable those willing and able to relocate and to find employment, preferably within the north. This particular task was a difficult one, Stevenson added, because of the small white population in the north, limiting potential employers of Inuit. It was apparently unfathomable that Inuit might one day create employment opportunities for themselves and others, rather than rely on a white population for employment (Peter 1982).

In preparation for its tenth gathering, the Eskimo Affairs Committee decided that Inuit themselves should be present at these meetings. The process by which qualified Inuit were identified, and the criteria used to determine who was qualified and who was not, speaks volumes about how Inuit were viewed at the time (Honigmann and Honigmann 1965). The task of identifying suitable candidates was passed on to the field officers who lived in many of the communities, and their recommendations were to be passed on to the administrator of the Arctic. The list of criteria noted that those

> Eskimos selected should be able to speak English, be at least sufficiently acquainted with our southern ways so they will not be completely baffled by parliamentary procedures and adequately self-confident so they would be prepared to contribute their opinions and present the views of the Eskimo population on the various matters affecting Northern development and Eskimo affairs discussed at the committee meeting. (Stevenson 1959, 2)

Two Inuit delegates were invited to the committee meeting on 25 May 1959. The minutes include their names but identify them not as members of the committee but, rather, as "special delegates." Reports from the meeting note with surprise that the "interest of the Eskimo people to have their own delegates at the meeting surpassed anticipated demand" (Hamilton 1960). Apparently pleased with the outcome, the committee decided that the 1960 meeting should be attended by four Inuit, two of whom were to come from the Mackenzie district in the west and two from the Arctic district in the east. The choice of delegate was to be left to Inuit themselves. This in itself would have reinforced the geographic basis of representation, and had an election taken place, it would have provided those residents not yet active in community boards with their first opportunity to cast a ballot. In the end, though, the committee decided that the selection of the delegates, though still left to Inuit, should be more structured. From each of the two districts the committee wanted one representative from an area where hunting and trapping formed the primary means of livelihood, and one representative from an area in which wage employment dominated. Rather than hold elections within the districts, the committee decided that the best tactic would be to rotate the communities from which delegates would be selected, and picked Great Whale River, Baker Lake, Coppermine, and Tuktoyaktuk as the initial source of representatives.

It is interesting to see how far the Eskimo Affairs Committee departed from the principle of universal access and its concomitant tenet of geographic representation. The committee decided that four communities, rather than the territories as a whole, would provide it with representatives and, further, that these four communities would be selected according to economic profiles, with field officers on the spot to ensure that the representative from a wage-earning community would be a wage earner and that the representative from a hunting and trapping community would be a hunter or trapper. Thus, not only were Inuit who were invited to join the committee expected to be English-speaking, politically sophisticated, and self-confident, but they were also expected to have certain economic profiles. Committee members decided that the best way to tap the views of Inuit was to identify representatives in this decidedly consociational fashion. We should remember, of course, that Inuit were being sent not to a legislative body but to a committee, not that this distinction would have been clear to most northern residents, regardless of ethnicity, given their exclusion from federal and territorial elections and given the largely appointed nature of the NWT Council. Most northern residents would have had little sense of how the authority or jurisdiction of the NWT Council differed from that of the Eskimo Affairs Committee. Leaving this aside, the identification of members suggests that there were certain types of Inuit who were deemed suitable and prepared for political life and others who were not.

The actual method of selecting the delegate within each community was left to Inuit, with, in most cases, liberal influence from the field officers, a situation that produced marked variations in the operation of democracy across the four communities. In Great Whale, only one candidate responded to the notice for a representative. Inuit met in a group, decided that the candidate appeared to be the logical choice, and he was declared the representative. In Baker Lake, Inuit identified a period for nominations, held an election with "some little assistance in procedure" from the field officer, and identified a hunter as their representative. In Tuktoyaktuk, the field officer outlined the method to be followed when he attended a meeting of all Inuit men in the village. Voting was to take place at the local school one evening just before its weekly show. All Inuit who were over sixteen were entitled to vote in a secret ballot and were to print the name of their preferred representative. The process therefore lacked a nomination period. Qualifications for the position were described as "the ability to speak in a forthright and accurate manner, [and] good knowledge of local problems." In his notes the field officer suggested that by passing instructions on to men they would in turn be able to control the votes of their wives and children if they wished to do so, something that was not seen as detracting from the electoral process. On election day, ten names received votes, and the eventual choice seemed to surprise the local non-Inuit population, prompting the field officer to report that this "was a valuable reminder of the fact that the Eskimo, given a chance, will demonstrate refreshing non-conformity." Finally, in Coppermine, an election by secret ballot, open to all men and women over eighteen, produced a candidate who won by only one vote. The six candidates received sixty-four votes, which, according to the field officer, represented an approximately 90 percent turnout. The voters agreed that if the representative was ill or unable to meet his obligations then the second-place candidate should step in.

The simultaneous existence of appointed and elected members on the NWT Council further illustrates competing perspectives on representation. In 1969, Commissioner Stuart Hodgson wrote to the deputy minister of the Department of Indian Affairs and Northern Development (DIAND), John A.

MacDonald, and outlined potential divisions between the appointed and elected members:

> The elected members from the East have already given clear expression to their feeling that they represent the interests of the Eskimos and residents of the Keewatin and Baffin Districts. Any increase in elected representatives from the East will strengthen the point of view that elected members are the official representatives. (Hodgson 1969a)

Having written this in response to calls for an additional assistant commissioner to represent the east, it is not entirely clear what Hodgson means here, although the context of the letter shows that he was decidedly against such a prospect. On the one hand, it could mean that the assumed link between voting in a constituency and having a representative that speaks for that constituency had taken the commissioner by surprise. In this sense, the elections to the NWT Council could be nothing more than methods of selection, without the concomitant notion of constituency representation. This is certainly possible. If elected members were expected to represent the north in general, then the absence of constituencies in the east could not be seen as a denial of representation for eastern residents. Appointed members would represent the interests of Ottawa, and elected members would represent the interests of territorial residents, writ large, regardless of constituency. This would be possible without political parties, but it would also be possible in a system without responsible government. If the executive is not responsible to the legislature, then there can be no automatic assumption that the legislature is responsible to the people. In this scenario, then, the representatives in the newly created constituencies were not representatives of the residents in those constituencies but were merely three additional individuals among a group that represented the north. This view is confirmed by 1961 reports from then minister Dinsdale to a lawyer in Yellowknife. Dinsdale argued that appointees to the NWT Council could not be drawn from people able to gain seats in a democratic manner as this would interfere with the electoral process. The logic of including appointed representatives from southern Canada stemmed from the belief that "Canada as a whole takes responsibility for the development of the partially autonomous and exceedingly sparsely populated region" (Dinsdale 1961, 7). Dinsdale added that northerners, and particularly Inuit, could not be appointed to the council because they were eligible to compete for elected seats and that, after division, those Inuit not living in constituencies would be able to run once elected positions were created. Besides, said Dinsdale, the council travels precisely so that Eskimos can attend its sessions as observers. His views suggest that the role of appointed members was to ensure territorial development proceeded in Canada's interests, while elected members were to ensure that development proceeded in the interests of territorial residents. In this light, then, Hodgson's remarks could mean that the eastern elected members were not expected to represent only the residents of their particular constituencies.

A second possible interpretation of Hodgson's letter also stems from the difference between appointed and elected members. Here, the distinction is not between representing the territory as a whole and representing one particular constituency but between serving as a representative of the people and not. Certainly, the appointed members were not resident in the north. In its records for 1968, the NWT Council noted the addresses of appointed and elected members. Appointed members were living in Vancouver, Saskatoon, and in Rockliffe, Ottawa, although, for much of the session, one member provided an address in Yailuku, Hawaii. The elected members, by contrast, were northern residents. The exception was Robert Williamson, who lived in Saskatoon but spent much of the summer in Rankin Inlet. In this second interpretation, the division is between those who have the responsibility of representation and those who do not.

Representation in the NWT demonstrates that federal officials identified their own methods for including Inuit and that they felt free to pursue consociational methods of inclusion when they felt that this would best meet their needs. Exceptions to the principle of universal access to representation and, indeed, to the geographic basis of representation are evident. In the first northern elections, Inuit were included through an extension of the formal rules. With regard to representation, inclusion was extended to the right type of Inuk, and government officials saw to it that the process by which Inuit could exercise influence was highly structured. As a result, how Inuit concerns were represented within the decision-making process and on decision-making bodies was at the considerable discretion of the powers that be. Far from being an inherent and inalienable right, representation was conditional and controlled. The third avenue for Inuit integration, however, provides entirely different messages about participation.

Local Democracy

Although elections provided a structured opportunity for Inuit to participate within the wider political system, the day-to-day practice of democratic decision making was seen as integral to their political education. Deemed to be the main avenue for political development, participation in local affairs was considered likely to prompt discussions on issues more tangible to the lives of Inuit and, thus, easier for them to understand than the decisions taken by the NWT Council. The territorial policy statement on municipal development, for example, suggests that local matters are more concrete than territorial matters, and, thus, the locus provides a more useful training ground for democracy: "Here, [an Inuk] can develop a healthy scepticism which is his protection against political demagogues" (Northwest Territories n.d). The main agent of local political socialization was the Northern Service Officer (NSO). As a representative of the government based in the community, the NSO was charged with establishing community councils, holding public meetings, and generally instilling a sense of initiative into Inuit, who, bureaucrats felt, had been benumbed by recent changes in the north. A short article entitled "Human Problems in the Canadian Arctic," prepared for the Department of Northern Affairs and National Resources, 1958-59, describes the problem this way:

> The government, in providing care for the aged, the blind and the indigent and in furnishing family allowances and education for the children has taken over responsibilities which used to be those of relatives. There is nothing to replace these lost responsibilities. Moreover, as the new social order supplants the primitive life of the Eskimos, direction is given by the various white men on the scene. In consequence, the Eskimo inevitably tends to lose initiative both individually and collectively. (Canada, Department of Northern Affairs and National Resources 1959)

By encouraging participation at the local level, the NSOs hoped that they could reteach Inuit how to exercise initiative by offering them issues that were more likely to capture their interest than were those covered by the NWT Council.

The use of NSOs began in 1954, and by 1958 there were eighteen NSOs in ten Inuit communities throughout the central and eastern Arctic and northern Quebec, including Cambridge Bay, Frobisher Bay, Baker Lake, Rankin Inlet, Tuktoyaktuk, Kuujjuaq, and Cape Dorset. The Department of Northern Affairs and National Resources (DNANR) reported that NSOs served several useful functions. Primary among these was enabling Inuit to make a useful contribution to national life and to become better citizens. Typical tasks included organizing group efforts, participating in local decisions, and enunciating "responsible and articulate public opinion" on behalf of Inuit (Phillips 1958a). In its 1958-59 annual report of activities, the Office of the Administrator of the Arctic described the NSO as a bridge between Inuit and their new lives:

> Moving among the Eskimo people he is expected to get to know them, gain their confidence, respect, friendship and co-operation and help them to help themselves ... His chief concern is to foster leadership among the Eskimo people so that they may be given local authority and responsibility. (Office of the Administrator of the Arctic 1959, 2)

The goal, in short, was to cause democracy to flourish at the local level, a process that involved distinct developmental stages.

Initial avenues for local discussion were community meetings or residents' association meetings, which were most often attended by local government personnel and their wives, along with representatives of the HBC, and the Anglican and/or Roman Catholic missions. Sometimes, these meetings would formalize themselves as community councils. The position of Inuit on these councils varied from community to community. In some communities, the community council was almost entirely composed of Inuit. In other communities, with larger Qallunaat populations, only a small number of Inuit representatives would be invited. The role of Inuit representatives was to communicate meeting decisions to other Inuit rather than to make the council members aware of issues of concern to the Inuit population. At Frobisher Bay, two Inuit representatives on the council were elected at separate Inuit-only meetings, and a third represented Apex, the settlement over the hill from Iqaluit and the site of the original Inuit community. Often, the NSO encouraged the creation of Eskimo councils as well. If established, these councils would send representatives to the community council but would also meet separately to discuss issues of particular interest to Inuit. In

1959, the NWT Commissioner suggested the establishment of joint councils, but apparently this was not a popular idea among Inuit, who were often obliged to sit and listen to debates in English, while in the Eskimo councils they could speak freely. By 1959, there were Eskimo community councils in Baker Lake, Cape Dorset, Sugluk, and Cambridge Bay. At the first Eskimo community meeting in Frobisher Bay, items discussed included dog problems, the desire of Inuit to move into tents in the summer, and, according to the NSO, the advantages of hygiene and household cleanliness. During the same period, the community council discussed items such as the need for a bakery, bath house, coffee shop, recreation facilities, and improved garbage collection. Later on, a curfew for residents, community freezers, and the rules governing the acquisition of liquor became frequent topics of discussion. In Baker Lake, by contrast, the community councils were essentially all-Inuit affairs, with members consisting of all male adults over sixteen. Most of the members were from the settlement, although at each meeting there were usually one or two individuals who were temporarily in from the land. According to the NSO, typical discussions addressed the new camps to be established, the identification of the head man at each camp, and the progress made in setting up savings accounts. At times, the meetings also presented opportunities for DIAND to communicate with residents. Minutes for one meeting of the Frobisher Bay community council in 1967 indicate that DIAND wished to know whether Inuit would be interested in operating "an old-style Eskimo village" as a tourist attraction.

The establishment of community councils and Eskimo councils was usually followed by the establishment of an array of committees, including, among others, a housing committee, a hunting and trapping association, and a recreation committee. In the late 1950s and early 1960s, most of these councils and committees would have seemed remarkably similar. Without jurisdiction to enact by-laws or policies, without funds to begin local improvement or community support projects, each of these committees would have provided an opportunity for citizens to get together, to visit, and to discuss various community events. Despite the wishes of the territorial administration, the sense that the community council was owed a greater level of devotion than were other committees was not apparent from the minutes of meetings, in large part because the goals and powers of the council were not discernibly different from those of various other committees. This changed in the mid-1960s.

First, in 1964, the creation of the community development fund provided a pot of money to which community councils – and only community councils – could request access for community projects. In some communities, any spending by the community council would also have to be approved by the local Eskimo council. This would have begun a process of differentiation between the community council and other community committees. Second, the Carrothers Commission recommended the development of a southern form of local government, with formal elections to settlement councils or, when the settlement had developed sufficiently, hamlet councils. It was hoped that, by providing Inuit with formal political opportunities to deal with local affairs that might interest them and with which they might be familiar, a generation of political leaders might be trained. The Inuk secretary writing minutes for the 1969 Keewatin Regional Eskimo Advisory Conference summarized the relevant issues as follows:

> Some time we have to start voting for [community councils] in our communities. This community is going to look after everything about our community. Anyone who has been in the settlement for three months can join the council. The people who are in the council have to speak up for all the people, not just three or six. If the Government of Yellowknife give money to the council they have to be real wise to spend it. The council is going to look after everything in the settlement such as airstrip, water, garbage, et cetera. Also the people have to make their own rules that is if the people want to. The rules are for their own settlement such as traffic rules, school rules, et cetera. If the people want to make their own rules they have to be real careful to see what kind of rules they are making because the rules we are making are going to become real rules to our settlement as we make them. (Keewatin Regional Eskimo Advisory Conference 1969)

If we remember the statement in the 1962 government pamphlet *Voting*, that politicians were the bosses in Ottawa, then the heavy attention to rules in the preceding quote makes sense. It also calls to mind the emphasis on changing rules that was prevalent during the conversion to Christianity. Those involved in politics were not seen as those working toward the improvement of community life, nor were they seen as regular members of the community but as those of elevated station enacting rules that governed daily life and individual behaviour.

Changes in the mid-1960s served to better fund and formalize political opportunities at the local level as well as to distinguish the community council from other organizations. At the same time, though, the decision-making authority of other bodies also increased. The 1968 minutes for the Cambridge Bay Housing Association outline the procedures by which access to housing would be determined. Those who regularly paid rent would get the first choice of new homes. When families moved, the housing association would determine who would get the empty house. Those who had not paid rent for three months would receive a notice and, if payment was not received, would be moved to a smaller house.

The same period also saw the development of regional bodies. Initiated so that delegates from existing Eskimo councils could meet, exchange ideas, and discuss issues of common concern, the regional Eskimo councils also provided an additional opportunity to gain experience with the practice of local government. Although the regional Eskimo councils had no official status, the Northern Administrative Branch expected not only that they would serve the goals of individual socialization but that they would provide a handy opportunity to articulate the broad trends of Inuit opinion. Community Eskimo councils each selected their own delegates. The first meeting of the Keewatin regional council, which took place in 1966, had representatives from Rankin Inlet, Baker Lake, Coral Harbour, Whale Cove, Arviat, and Churchill. Two years later, the Baffin regional Eskimo council held its first meeting.

Unlike those of territorial council meetings, the proceedings of the regional Eskimo councils were interpreted to enable the full participation of unilingual Inuktitut speakers. Inuit delegates identified items to discuss, and NSO reports indicate that the delegates were well prepared, that they often arrived with formal notes, and that they kept written records of the views of others. The field officers also indicated that most of the comments were expressed at a policy level and that very little time was spent discussing issues exclusive to one community or one individual. Typical topics of discussion included education, engineering and municipal services, game, and welfare. When delegates returned to their communities, they began various campaigns to petition their community councils and the NWT commissioner on issues such as the improvement of local water delivery, the need to increase funding for Inuktitut education and traditional skills, and the need for a hospital in the north. In response, one territorial official indicated that "the government cannot operate by petition, particularly if our policy on placing increased responsibility in the hands of local governing bodies is to be successful. We must listen to the people as they speak through their own chosen representatives" (Horton 1968, 1). The regional Eskimo councils may have been intended to serve as a one-stop shop for those seeking to understand Inuit public opinion, but the NWT Council members did not believe they were actually expected to act on any of their discussions. Nevertheless, these councils provided the first opportunity for Inuit from various communities in the Arctic to meet and discuss issues that affected them as a people. It was, in other words, the first expression of an Inuit political voice.

The regional councils were not the only method of seeking Inuit opinion. The NWT Council had always maintained an impressive travel record, and the House of Commons Standing Committee on Northern Affairs and National Resources also toured the north on occasion. In 1966, the House of Commons committee spent its first day in Frobisher Bay at a public meeting in the Apex Community Association hall. Here, Inuit had an opportunity to express their views on federal policy in the north, and, according to the records of the meeting, they apparently found it wanting. Typical comments included complaints that the system of adult education was inferior to that for young people and that, without funding, the co-ops would not develop properly.

The minutes of community and Eskimo council meetings are, of course, an invaluable source of information about Inuit public opinion in the 1960s and 1970s, and they put to rest notions that Inuit had homogeneous visions of their own political integration. The Inuit population was divided, in particular, on the issue of exposure to the southern education system. For some, the education system was a way to guarantee the future success of younger generations, while for others it was a method of socializing young Inuit so that they would forget who they really are. At one meeting of the Keewatin Regional Eskimo Council, an Inuk resident of Whale Cove suggested that, if young people really wanted to learn how to make an igloo, then certainly the National Film Board could "take a few shots of making an igloo" and show it in schools. Clearly, this person felt that the lack of curriculum attention to traditional skills was no reason to avoid the school system entirely.

Not surprisingly, this flurry of democratic activity also led to the growth of petitions and requests for community plebiscites, including three in 1968 on access to alcohol: one in Cambridge Bay and two in the predominantly

Qallunaat, western communities of Fort Providence and Fort Simpson, respectively. In each case a petition from the community preceded the plebiscite. That same year, a community council meeting in Igloolik prompted a petition about education. The sixty-seven people who signed their names wanted it known that they were not opposed to formal education for their children but that they wanted a school closer to home. The late 1960s, then, saw an explosion of opportunities for public participation and witnessed levels of public engagement with decision making that were unheralded in the territories. Does this mean that the NSOs were successful?

The various councils did, of course, serve as a training ground for political involvement. Abe Okpik, who later became the first Inuk appointed to the NWT Council, was, more than a decade earlier, the secretary for the Eskimo council in Aklavik. At the 1959 meeting of the Eskimo Affairs Committee, Okpik noted, however, that the Eskimo community councils made little impact as its members only wrote unanswered letters to the government officials. Okpik's criticism, of course, was that the council was an ineffective agent of change –something that it was never intended to be – not that it was an ineffective agent of political education and socialization. Judged through the lens of political socialization, the community councils clearly introduced a generation of Inuit to the territorial decision-making process. As Okpik's comments indicate, however, Inuit participation brought with it an expectation of influence. The various bodies were not really intended as agents of change or, in the case of the regional Eskimo councils, as more than one-stop shops for a survey of Inuit opinion. It is possible, then, that Inuit experiences on community councils and committees raised expectations about their level of influence and the capacity for change in the north, expectations that would have surprised government officials.

Federal and territorial officials had, of course, a multifaceted approach to the political development of individuals. One plan was to bring promising young Inuit south to expose them to southern ways and in so doing to provide them with a political education that they could not get in the north. Those who were identified as leaders in the Keewatin region, for example, had the opportunity to participate in a "southern exposure course." Territorial officials routinely debated what to do with Inuit who were already living in the south and at various times considered using Inuit in southern sanatoria as the vanguard of southern migration.[4] Civic engagement was not fostered solely through meetings among adults. The Office of the Administrator of the Arctic was particularly proud of the work of the Northern Administrative

Branch in the formation of Girl Guide and Boy Scout troops. In 1965, there were 103 Scouts, 35 Wolf Cubs, 40 Girl Guides, and 12 Brownies in Frobisher Bay alone.

Impact of Inuit Integration

If we are looking for lessons that can be drawn from the attempt to integrate Inuit into the Canadian political system, several present themselves:

- that representation is universal, except when you can be excluded for practical reasons;
- that representation is based on geography, except when it is based on ethnic characteristics;
- that one group, because of its ethnicity, can rightly find an avenue of political expression in ethnically defined political groups and that such groups will be recognized by territorial and federal authorities;
- that politicians are bosses and make rules for us to live by;
- that the federal and territorial governments will not necessarily respond to the attempts of Inuit to influence policy; and
- that regional bodies provide an opportunity for Inuit to meet together to discuss common issues of concern.

In the late 1960s and early 1970s, two events transformed these lessons into political action. First, the federal government was forced to recognize its obligations to Aboriginal peoples, including their rights to land claims. Second, the election of Pierre Elliott Trudeau marked a shift in federal rhetoric toward individual rights. The first change reinforced links between Inuit and the federal government. If the federal government was responsible for negotiating a land claim with an ethnic group as a whole, and if the territorial government had no power to negotiate such an agreement, then the most important political actor in the lives of Inuit became, almost instantly, the federal government. This is not to say that the federal government had not always been the most important political actor in the NWT. Certainly its dominance over territorial affairs until 1967, and its near total funding of territorial affairs long after that, meant that the federal government was never far from the centre of power. That it was the federal government that was in charge of negotiating with Inuit, however, emphasized the important role for a particular ethnic group. If the recognition of Aboriginal rights brought Inuit and the federal government closer together, the emphasis on individual over collective rights served to distance them. Since their integration into the Canadian political system, Inuit have been treated differently, whether by the unchanged application of rules thus inhibiting their full inclusion or by the creation of special rules just for them. Inuit were encouraged to create their own councils, at the community and regional levels, and were invited to committee meetings, where they, as a people, were the subject of conversation. Since their integration as voters they have been treated differently by virtue of their indigeneity. In a series of federal statements about Aboriginal policy it became clear, however, that the federal government saw their collective identity as a sufficient basis for a land claim but as an insufficient basis for differential political treatment. So, on the one hand, the federal government had acquired an obligation to negotiate with Aboriginal groups – with ethnically defined collective groups – about land claims, and, on the other, it employed rhetoric that prioritized individual rights over collective rights and suggested that ethnic boundaries were no basis for special treatment.

The late 1960s and early 1970s saw a flourishing of ethnically and regionally defined groups. In the eastern Arctic, this included the Inuit Tapirisat of Canada (ITC), three regional councils, three regional Inuit associations, and the Inuit Land Claims Commission (ILCC). In the western Arctic, these were joined by Aboriginal organizations such as the Indian Brotherhood of the Northwest Territories, the Inuvialuit organization COPE (Committee for Original Peoples' Entitlement), the Native Women's Association of the NWT, and the Métis Association of the NWT. At the same time, political development at the local level continued apace, and original committees were joined by groups dedicated to juveniles, welfare, welfare appeal, alcohol and drugs, and land claims. Community leaders held conferences at which members from different settlements and hamlets could discuss issues of common concern.

Regional councils, including the Baffin Regional Council and the Western Arctic Regional Municipality, began calling on the territorial administration to devolve power to the regional level so that the diverse needs of residents could be met. At the same time, there appears to have been considerable suspicion between national or territorial organizations for indigenous peoples, such as the Indian Brotherhood and the ITC, and the regional councils, who were perceived to be under the thumb of southerners or administrators. At one point, ITC head Eric Tagoona lamented the membership of the Baffin Regional Council, noting that its members were "not the most intelligent and aggressive Inuit." Aggression, it is worth noting, was not seen by the ITC as a negative trait. The result, then, was an explosion of bodies, each trying to grab power, responsibility, and funding from the other. In the midst of this storm, territorial officials threw their hands up.

How did territorial and federal officials react to the flowering of democracy that they witnessed? First with confusion and later with concern. In some cases, officials appeared baffled by the level of Inuit interest in political participation. In 1958, territorial official R.A.J. Phillips presented a conference paper to the Ottawa chapter of the Canadian Political Science Association in which he outlined a hierarchy of Inuit development (Phillips 1958b). Phillips distinguished, for example, among what he saw as the most primitive Inuit (located in the inland Keewatin region), the more developed coastal Inuit (located in the Baffin region), those close to wage employment, those engaged in permanent wage employment, and, most developed, those who had left the Arctic. His remarks suggest a certain confusion about political developments in the North. According to his hierarchy, the least developed Inuit, those in Baker Lake, established the first Eskimo Community Council. That they could have achieved such a high level of political development while so "primitive" was clearly a puzzle to Phillips.

Officials at DIAND were clearly disturbed about the heightened activities of various community councils, Eskimo councils, local committees, and regional councils. In a 1967 letter to Commissioner Hodgson, one federal official warned of the "danger of haphazard proliferation of local agencies of control which could drain off authorities which should properly belong to local Councils" (Canada, DIAND 1967). Inuit were going to be confused by all this activity, it was going to detract from the authority of the council, and it was going to result in them wasting their own time:

> The different roles and functions of the individual groups become hard for local people to distinguish. Where this occurs, local social action can be diverted into duplicatory and fruitless activity, and may eventually be dissipated. Unless steps are taken to avert this danger, the development of local self-government in unorganized communities could be seriously retarded.

If officials were concerned about the wide range of political organizations in the 1960s, political developments in the 1970s only made things worse.

Territorial and federal officials appeared concerned by the patterns of Inuit political participation in the 1970s. At times, this clearly stemmed from a perception that the newer organizations were supplanting the role of government officials. In letters to the ITC, territorial officials reminded the organization that the establishment of regional and community associations was the responsibility of the federal government, not the ITC. Most federal reaction, however, involved a bureaucratic enunciation of jurisdiction. The tenor of territorial reaction was decidedly different.

In a 1971 letter to Minister of Indian Affairs and Northern Development Jean Chrétien, Commissioner Hodgson complained about the considerable confusion felt by residents who were not sure whether they were supposed to pay attention to the territorial government, the federal government, the regional council, the community council, or an ethnic organization, most of which were funded by the federal government. If initially there might have been confusion among local bodies because they were all equal in their lack of funding support and power, now there appeared to be confusion because everyone was funded, albeit from the same pot, and no one was certain about jurisdiction. As Hodgson (1969b) said to Chrétien: "The Council feels that the long-term interests of the native people will not be served if they are encouraged to express themselves primarily through para-political associations rather than the normal political institutions that are available to them and are puzzled by the Federal Government's apparent support of this course."

Hodgson's comments are noteworthy in part because they indicate the start of a period of ad hominem attacks on Aboriginal leaders and intemperate comments about Aboriginal organizations. These comments were not restricted to Inuit leaders and organizations. Indian Brotherhood president James Washie, for example, is described as "manipulated by his wife and [B.W.] a CUSO worker from Toronto." Clearly, Commissioner Hodgson believed that part of the problem stemmed from the individuals involved: "On the other hand, if someone replaced Mr. Washie or Mrs Cournoyea, then everything would be alright, however, I would not want to wait for that to happen." Or, later in the same letter, "The Indian Brotherhood paper has become a purveyor of hate and advocates only the Indian and/or Eskimo for the North – no pipeline, no development – and the old way of life." Part of the concern, it appears, stems from the rhetoric used by these organizations: "The leadership of the Indian Brotherhood and similar organizations advocate that the interests of the native people are different from those of the majority within the Northwest Territories."[5] This is an odd comment from the head of a bureau that spent much of its time arguing that Inuit were different from other Canadians and, therefore, needed to be treated carefully, lest they be bowled over by those who did not have their interests in mind.

Several things are apparent from bureaucratic reactions to Inuit political organization in the 1970s. First, it is clear that federal and territorial officials felt that Inuit and other Aboriginal peoples were being manipulated or led astray by their leadership and by their organizations. As a result, Inuit were seen as victims of leaders and organizations that were less beneficent than those associated with the territorial administration. Second, one gets the impression that territorial and federal officials were so used to selecting the "appropriate" representatives of Inuit opinion, and so blind to the fact that they were selecting those already predisposed to southern ways, that they were unable to fathom an alternate view. At one point, an official expressed surprise that the best leaders are more interested in being out on the land than in sitting on councils. Since traditional leaders were selected in part on the basis of their hunting prowess, it is not surprising that Inuit leaders would be hunters rather than wage labourers in settlements.

Third, early documents suggest that government officials were not responding appropriately to the manner in which Inuit opinion was expressed. At the 1959 meeting of the Eskimo Affairs Committee, for example, one of the two Inuit delegates, Ayaruark, spoke only once. In his speech he thanked the government for the invitation to speak and for all the hard work that it had accomplished in the north. Ayaruark then proceeded to carefully and gently point out the need to modify the education system and to reunite families. He mentioned Inuit frustration at the loss of traditional practices, identified the cultural gap between Inuit workers and non-Inuit employers, mentioned anxiety over the non-voluntary relocation of Inuit, and raised concerns about the limited sense of common identity among the Inuit in Rankin Inlet. Throughout his remarks, however, Ayaruark spoke in what has been described as a typically Inuit non-confrontational style, and the tenor of his remarks therefore appeared to non-Inuit to be gentle and appreciative. Reactions to the meeting mentioned only the positive things Ayaruark said about the federal government's activities in the north. His damning indictment of the federal government's record in the eastern Arctic was missed entirely. Given that their opinion, when presented in a gentle manner, did not appear to register in the way they intended, it is unsurprising that Inuit would come to believe that different tactics were necessary. Federal and territorial officials were so used to the gentle Inuit approach to politics that any change would have seemed intemperate and sudden. This becomes clear when we look at the campaign for a land claim in the eastern Arctic.

5
Institutional Design in the Eastern Arctic

The creation of a new territory in 1999 provided an exciting opportunity to design a new network of political institutions within Canada. Any notion that this was a tabula rasa polity, however, would be far from the truth. The creation of Nunavut was as marked by its extrication from the Northwest Territories as it was by the establishment of its legislature and bureaucracy, devolution having as much to do with institutional division as with institutional creation. However distant the eastern Arctic might have appeared from the centre of power in Yellowknife, it was part of a territorial political culture sustained by institutions that had been created over the course of a century of political development. Viewed in this light, the creation of a new set of institutions for Nunavut is but the latest institutional design experiment in the Canadian Arctic. Beginning with federal administrators in the early twentieth century and ending with the work of the Nunavut Implementation Commission, this chapter tracks the changing views of successive generations of reformers regarding territorial institutions and accounts for some of the distinguishing institutional features of territorial political life.

Throughout the political development of the NWT we can identify six distinct visions of its institutional design. Federal dominance characterized the first vision, in which the territory was treated as a Canadian colony, its institutional development plotted according to an acknowledged template within the British Empire. Debates concerning division of the territory in the early 1960s were entirely in keeping with previous territorial development in Canada. Although division was delayed by disagreements, the second vision did not emerge until the publication of the Carrothers Commission report in 1966, which marked the beginning of a period of northern territorial administration. Territorial officials subscribed to a third vision of institutional development, which differed from that espoused by federal administrators.

However imprecise the administrative divisions between federal and territorial officials, their views of political and economic development deviated sharply. Conflict between these views became further complicated in the 1970s and 1980s as Inuit land claims negotiators articulated a fourth vision of political development, which was distinct from the two traditional options. These three actors – federal, territorial, and Inuit – were not themselves homogeneous. A fifth vision was offered by the federally appointed Drury Commission, which was charged with identifying a sensible path to institutional development in the north. The commission's members had different appetites for reform, as did Inuit leaders, with those active in community or regional councils having different ideas about political development than those active in the land claim movement. Following the signing of the NLCA, the Nunavut Implementation Commission offered a sixth vision of institutional design. I look at each of these visions and identify not only the ideal models for institutional development but also the changing rules for participation expected by various actors.

These distinct visions offer discrete ideas about political development and the institutions necessary to deliver political autonomy. General topics for debate include the division of the territory, the inevitability of provincial status, ownership of non-renewable resources and control over financial affairs, subsidiarity and the role of municipalities, the existence of public or ethnic political bodies, universal elections, responsible government, power-sharing, and the presence of political parties. While wildly different visions of the political future emerged among various groups, actors in the 1970s and 1980s, in particular, disagreed on the process by which political visions should be identified. Debates over what method by which to identify consensus, the expected level of exposure to the public, who should have authority, indeed the very rules governing institutional design, all suggest that there were fundamental disagreements among territorial bureaucrats, federal officials, Inuit land claims negotiators, members of the Drury Commission, and those active in regional councils regarding who had the right to determine the institutional structure of political life in the north.

The Changing Boundaries of the NWT

The political development of the NWT began before the first elections to the NWT Council in 1951 and before division in 1999. In the nineteenth century, the NWT began at the western edge of Ontario's borders and extended west and north. The political process that, between 1870 and 1905, saw the carving away of land to create Manitoba, the Yukon territory, Alberta, and Saskatchewan provides us with an opportunity to identify any consistent patterns in institutional development and, perhaps more useful for our purposes, any sense of exceptions with regard to the NWT. The motives of federal administrators and the extent to which particular design elements were perceived as inevitable help us to determine whether the pre-division territorial culture of the NWT was the product of accident or design.

In many respects, political development in the NWT was seen as part of a larger process of development occurring within the British Empire and was intended to deviate little from established patterns. Federal and territorial administrators kept close tabs on other jurisdictions both within the "white dominions" of Canada, Australia, and New Zealand, and elsewhere within the empire, the United States, and farther afield. The comparative cases that government officials identified are noteworthy for their heterogeneity. In 1957, the Arctic Division of the Northern Administration and Lands Branch gathered information about the expansion of the decision-making power and jurisdiction of native councils in Papua New Guinea. NWT Commissioner Robert Robertson compared the evolution of political development in the NWT to the process undergone by the colony at Massachusetts Bay. The forms of municipal organization in Greenland and the political organization of Aboriginal peoples in Alaska were frequent topics of interest (Rowley 1969, 10). Writing on preparations for the arrival of the territorial administration in Yellowknife in 1967, the clerk of the Territorial Council noted with concern some of the ways in which the NWT might deviate from patterns of political development elsewhere in the colonies, citing in particular Australia's Northern Territory. In the same period, the commissioner sent requests to the Northern Administrative Branch, asking for background information about the process by which areas in Western Canada became provinces. When describing political development in the NWT, territorial officials considered the process akin to the development of responsible government in Upper Canada or the modification of relations between the King and Parliament in the United Kingdom (Hillson 1968). The impression, then, is of an administration with a keen sense that the process of political development in the NWT was indistinct from the process that occurred earlier in the United Kingdom and elsewhere in Canada and that was continuing apace in other colonial outposts. Nowhere was that attention more finely tuned than to the process of political development in previous incarnations of the Northwest Territories.

In the eyes of territorial officials, political development in the NWT began with the purchase of Rupert's Land in 1870. Previously governed under the Hudson's Bay Company, the semi-autonomous District of Assiniboia already had an appointed twenty-member council and a governor, but political development proceeded at a slow pace. Opportunities to participate were extended only slowly, and colonial officials generally ignored the emerging sense of common identity among settlers of the Red River colony. The resulting conflict is viewed as the likely product of a clash between the hesitant rate of political development counselled by Ottawa and the impatient demands of a colony that was far more developed than had been anticipated. With the creation of Manitoba as a province, federal officials believed it safe to return to their previous cautious approach. In the rump NWT, federal officials observed no discernible call for decision-making bodies or self-government. This, in large part, was due to the absence of white settlers. Aboriginal peoples were not seen as potential citizens but, if anything, as wards of the state. There is no discussion of Aboriginal participation in decision making, whether through membership in councils or through elections. The claims we see in later documents about the unsuitability of Aboriginal peoples for decision making are likewise absent. Within the context of political development the indigeneous population is ignored; participation in decision making was seen as a topic worthy of discussion only once an area had a sufficient number of white settlers. Without these settlers, it was assumed that there would be no interest and certainly no benefit in the existence of a governing council.

After the creation of Manitoba, the rump NWT proceeded to move toward the attainment of responsible government. The original appointed council was soon supplemented by elected members drawn from constituencies in the southern portions of the territory. Before the end of the nineteenth century, the council was composed entirely of elected members and it offered representative government, although once again great swaths of the territory – including the Arctic – were excluded from constituencies. Territorial officials viewed this process as the method of best practice, and there are continuous references to it as a model of institutional development for the NWT.

We know, of course, that not only provinces but also new territories were carved out of the NWT. The first modification to NWT boundaries after the creation of Manitoba came in 1876, with the establishment of the Keewatin as a separate territory. With the lieutenant governor of Manitoba as the ex-officio lieutenant governor of the Keewatin, a council of six – all non-Inuit – was appointed to deal with an epidemic of smallpox. Once the epidemic had run its course the council disbanded and was not reconvened before the separate territory was reunited with the NWT in 1905. Although this experiment provides little in the way of lessons of political development, it reinforces the practice of first establishing an appointed council.

The last development lesson of note was the establishment of the Yukon as a separate district in 1895 and as a separate territory in 1898. The appointed commissioner of the Yukon, who was also in charge of the North West Mounted Police, had considerable discretion to act unilaterally, in large part because of the general chaos perceived to reign in the Yukon during the gold rush. This is also the first time that the chief executive officer in the territories was referred to as a commissioner, and not as a lieutenant governor.[1] When it formed as a territory, the Yukon had an appointed council of five officials. One year later, two elected members were added, and, in 1902, the number of elected members equalled the number of appointed members. By 1908, the council was composed of ten members, all elected, who chose their own speaker and who met without the commissioner, thus marking a clear division between executive and legislative responsibility. Political development in the Yukon is noteworthy for two reasons. First, the sheer pace of change is remarkable: representative government in the Yukon arrived within a decade of its establishment as a territory. This, no doubt, was at least partly influenced by the remarkable increase in the population in the region. Indeed, the Yukon's eventual population decline led to the elimination of various federal positions, including the Office of the Commissioner. The governor general in council was given the power to abolish the elected council and replace it with an appointed body, an option that was not exercised. Second, the pattern of development in the Yukon represents a significant deviation from established colonial process. Here, the executive was not contained within the legislature but sat, for a considerable time, outside it. At the time, federal officials were obviously concerned that this represented a shift toward American patterns of institutional design and away from a British model of responsible government.

Taking these examples in the aggregate, we can identify a relatively clear pattern of institutional development: first, establish an appointed council and a governor, slowly begin to add elected members to the council, establish a sense of equilibrium between appointed members and elected members, reduce the proportion of appointed members, and ensure the withdrawal of the appointed governor. The result is a fully elected legislature that houses a responsible executive. At times, the attainment of responsible government was paired with the acquisition of provincehood and the establishment of party politics. In terms of previous patterns of development, then, Nunavut is the only territory created since 1870 that, at the moment of its creation, housed an elected council that operated according to the principles of responsible government. The required time between each developmental stage is elastic. In the Yukon, the march toward a fully elected council proceeded quickly, but the process of attaining fully responsible government took seventy years. In the pre-1905 NWT, moving from an appointed council to responsible government took far less time. Regardless of the somewhat flexible pace of change, the pattern of institutional development was quite clear in territorial Canada. This changed with the redrawing of the NWT's boundaries in 1905.

After the creation of Alberta and Saskatchewan in 1905, there was only a negligible population of white settlers in the rump NWT. Although the authority to create a council existed, none was appointed until 1921, and until 1946 the council was composed entirely of federal officials living in Ottawa. The language of those writing at the time suggests that democracy was only for white adults. References to the Aboriginal populations living in the north are made only in passing, as though they were the trees surrounding white settlers. Population figures used to identify potential costings for policies, and to assess potential institutional development, report figures "exclusive of Indians." Although an improvement on earlier documents, which make no reference at all to Aboriginal peoples, these documents demonstrate an abiding belief that political development and Aboriginal affairs were two separate and unrelated spheres of policy.[2] Details of the changing personnel and departments responsible for the administration of northern political development and Inuit affairs may be found in Table 5.1 (see pp. 110-11).

The NWT Council welcomed its first elected members in 1951, when three members elected in the western Mackenzie region joined its five appointed members. With this election, the territory reached the same stage of political development that it had reached seventy years earlier. Electoral terms were set at three years, and, in the subsequent election in 1954, a fourth member was added, creating balance between the two types of members that lasted a decade. In 1962, when discussing the division of the territories into western and eastern halves, Commissioner Robertson noted that the sparseness of the population in the eastern Arctic would justify the creation of a council composed entirely of appointed members from the eastern territory of Nunassiaq, while the western territory would retain its elected members and move more quickly toward responsible government. Federal Minister of Northern Affairs and National Resources Walter Dinsdale suggested, in response, that the habit of creating constituencies only in areas with larger populations, such as in the southern Baffin or southern Keewatin regions, might prove useful in the new territory. As before, division was expected to restart the process of political development. According to Commissioner Robertson (1962, 28), "[the] unbaptised territory ... has before it the entire process that began with the purchase of Rupertsland in 1870 ... the western region of the Territories ... is now capable of more rapid development toward responsible government."

Federal public servants working on territorial files were certain that territorial institutional development would be characterized by the same markers of progress as were found in other jurisdictions and that it would lead to responsible government, the emergence of a system of party politics – preferably a two-party system – and the acquisition of provincial status. Writing in 1962 on the evolution of the political system in the NWT, Commissioner Robertson suggested that, since 1951, there had been a sense that the NWT Council was the "embryo of a legislative assembly for a future province" and that every effort was being made to ensure that the "legislative, financial and administrative arrangements ... would lend themselves, over the years, to a smooth evolution into provincial status" (Robertson 1962, 16). In its own review of operations four years later, the council recommended that it should "evolve into full provincial status in four stages over 10 or 12 years" (NWT Council 1966, 1). Federal politicians did not appear likely to view provincial status as an immediate goal, much less an inevitable one. Writing to Commissioner Hodgson on the event of his appointment, Minister of Northern Affairs and National Resources Arthur Laing (1967) noted that self-government and moving the territorial bureaucracy to the north were far more pressing goals than was the transfer of provincial-type responsibilities: "Provincial nor even fully responsible government are not immediate goals." Any disagreement between territorial and federal officials, however, was over the pace and order of change, not the eventual goal. The goal was clear: a jurisdiction that did not differ from others in Canada, an elected assembly housing a responsible government, provincial status, and party politics. We know, however, that this does not describe the contemporary political situation in the NWT.

An Emerging Territorial Vision

Almost sixty years after the last change in boundaries, there was sufficient economic activity in the western portion of the NWT, and sufficiently high hopes for resource development, that some federal administrators believed it appropriate to once again divide the territory. The less developed eastern portion of the NWT would then become host to a new centre of activity, likely based in Frobisher Bay. This, however, did not occur. For some, the opposition to division took the form of institutional pragmatism. Far better for a united territory to lobby for federal attention than for two smaller ones to do so. For others, division would ensure that the developed western portion of the territory could carry on without having to cope with whatever development issues might surface in the largely unknown eastern portion. That division did not occur ensured that the pace of change was dictated, at least in part, by the needs of the less economically and politically developed eastern portion of the territories. This, in addition to the administrative structure employed by the federal government in its management of territorial affairs, served to heighten federal control in the north.

When the Supreme Court ruled in 1939 that Inuit were a federal responsibility, the administration of the NWT was being run through the Department of Mines and Resources, and the federal government saw no reason to change this arrangement once it became responsible for Inuit inhabitants in the eastern Arctic. In 1950, the Department of Mines and Resources changed its name to Resources and Development and, in 1953, to Northern Affairs and National Resources, but it was not until 1966 that the administration of social policy for Inuit was coupled with the administration of social policy for status Indians under the Department of Indian Affairs and Northern Development.[3] Until the mid-1960s, then, the top bureaucrat for the NWT was a man concerned with renewable and non-renewable resources. Wrestling control of that file from the federal government became a challenge for subsequent territorial authorities and Inuit organizations. Within the Department of Northern Affairs and National Resources the Ottawa-based Northern Administrative Branch contained federal civil servants working on territorial files, serving as public servants of a nascent territorial bureaucracy. Until 1964, the commissioner of the Northwest Territories occupied his role on a part-time basis, serving at the same time as a deputy minister for whichever department was then responsible for the north. Deputy ministers are, of course, profoundly political appointments and sit at the pleasure of the current head of government; thus, it is not unusual for deputy ministers to have strong partisan ties to the government of the day. Before the transfer of the territorial administration in 1967, those working on territorial politics were federal bureaucrats living in Ottawa, and they saw their jobs as "a purely departmental responsibility within the area of federal jurisdiction" (Robertson 1962, 15). There would have been no understanding at this time that the interests of the territory and the country might not be coterminous and no separate sense of territorial identity for those working on the territorial file. Territorial administration was indistinguishable from the administration of the economy, foreign trade, and human resources: the interests of the party in office were paramount. Even once the pattern of double appointment ceased, commissioners continued to act as the end of the bureaucratic chain for federal employees working on territorial files. The appointed commissioner was a political appointee, with partisan ties to the government in power. Given the power exercised by the commissioner in the NWT, it is not surprising that competitive party politics were not encouraged by federal officials: the commissioner and each of the members of the NWT Council received their appointments from the Liberal Party.

At the bureaucratic level, then, those working on territorial matters were all federal operators, working within a federal department, under federal masters, and ultimately under the partisan appointees of the government. Outside the bureaucracy, the government minister in charge of northern affairs also exerted considerable influence in territorial matters. Members of the territorial council appeared to be far less concerned with the behaviour of bureaucrats than they were with the behaviour of elected ministers. In 1963, Commissioner Ben Sivertz wrote to Arthur Laing, minister of northern affairs and national resources, and requested that he stop answering questions about the territories in the House and begin referring those questions to the NWT Council. Failure to do so, Sivertz noted, "will cause people to think that the federal member is fighting their battles on the Territorial front" (Sivertz 1963). Years later, the chair of the NWT Legislative Assembly's committee on constitutional development expressed pleasant surprise that Liberal Minister of Indian Affairs and Northern Development Warren Allmand referred to the Legislative Assembly as the principal political body in the NWT. Clearly, members of the council, and later the legislature, were concerned about the amount of authority exercised by the federal government.

The failure to achieve responsible government in the 1960s postponed the development of a territorial identity. Rather than focus its efforts on the acquisition of responsible government and provincial status, the NWT Council devoted its energies to integrating a predominantly indigenous population that had little prior exposure to the formal political system. Uncertain about how to proceed, the federal government appointed a commission to examine the issues of territorial division, provincial status, and institutional development. After several trips to communities in the NWT, the three-person Carrothers Commission published its report in 1966 and made several key recommendations, chief among them a call to move the entire territorial administration, including the commissioner, to Yellowknife. This was coupled with the recommendation to retain a united territory and to delay acquisition of provincial status while fostering institutional development by transferring some province-type responsibilities and generating a system of democratic accountability at the local level. Had Carrothers recommended division, Yellowknife or Fort Smith would have become the capital of the western portion and Frobisher Bay, which would have been ruled by Ottawa, would have been the administrative centre of the eastern portion. For those in the east, the decision to delay division likely accelerated the northern arrival of territorial administrators but likely dampened federal attention to the eastern Arctic.

In a territory that retained responsibility for the eastern Arctic, the costs of managing policy and the sheer scale of operations ensured that the only actor capable of delivering or funding policy was the federal government. This, of course, delayed the transfer of responsibility and authority from the federal government to the territorial administration. While a nascent territorial government in a divided west might have been able to expand its role in the financial management of its own affairs, the undivided NWT was too large and too expensive to be managed by anyone but the federal government. The postwar explosion of governmental responsibilities meant that any new province would encounter policy obligations not faced by provinces created earlier. The expanded scope of government served to dampen federal enthusiasm for creating another province. It did not, however, lessen territorial interest in acquiring province-type responsibilities, and the goal of provincial status remained.

The emergence of a distinct territorial identity accelerated in 1967, when the government rented two airplanes and transferred fifty-one staff, along with their families, files, and pets, to Yellowknife.[4] The Carrothers Commission's recommendation that the administration of northern affairs should occur in the north had been viewed favourably, and the commissioner and the territorial council were sent north to fulfill this goal. From this point, we start to see the emergence of a sense of territorial identity among bureaucrats and increasing disagreements over control of resources and provincial status. We also see a continued resistance to federal influence among NWT Council members and the NWT commissioner. This frustration is directed at officials in federal departments and in the government, although council members did not shy away from criticism. While discussing their view of Carrothers, NWT Council members complained about ministerial interference in the selection of appointed members. This point is worth stressing: the members of the council, most of whom had been appointed due to the influence of ministers, were concerned about further appointments made under the influence of ministers. Any emerging sense of territorial interest or territorial identity came not from the bureaucrats but from council members, and they directed their concerns not toward federal bureaucrats but toward the elected members of the House of Commons. The appearance of appointed members complaining about the undue influence of elected ministers is not without irony.

At times, federal officials sharply curtailed territorial attempts to assert independence. In 1968, DIAND Deputy Minister John A. MacDonald wrote to Commissioner Stuart Hodgson and reminded him that territorial officials must notify the federal government when they wish to attend federal-provincial meetings and that they must remember that they participate not as separate actors but as advisers to the federal delegation. Any comments, MacDonald noted, were to be directed to the minister in charge; the role of territorial delegations was not to represent territorial views on par with provincial delegations. Writing in response to an editorial in the Fort Smith paper, Minister of Northern Affairs and National Resources Arthur Laing expressed bewilderment that members of the NWT Council apparently saw themselves as members of the "unofficial opposition" in Ottawa. How could a body of Liberal appointees see themselves as the opposition? As for the editorial's complaint that the commissioner had been appointed and not elected, Laing pointed out that the commissioner was appointed by a democratically elected government, a government that, incidentally, was responsible for about three-quarters of the funds spent by the territorial government. The sheer scale of its financial involvement in the NWT ensured the federal government's continued participation in territorial affairs.

Federal, Territorial, and Inuit Views of Institutional Development

At the start of the 1970s, federal policy suggested that provincial status would only be possible once the political system in the NWT had reached a sufficient stage of development. This included the capacity to assume increased financial responsibility with regard to the administration of territorial social programs, in addition to a widening and deepening of democracy throughout territorial institutions. This approach coincided with three developments relevant to Inuit. First, Aboriginal reaction to the federal 1969 white paper, which, in the eyes of some, counselled assimilation for Aboriginal peoples, served as a lightning rod for political participation. Second, in 1973, the Supreme Court *Calder* decision confirmed unextinguished Aboriginal title to land, leading the government to identify a process for Aboriginal groups who had not signed treaties to negotiate comprehensive land claims. Third, the cohort of politically active Inuit, initially the generation raised on the land and welcomed slowly into territorial administration, was joined by a bilingual generation educated in residential schools and more suspicious of federal and territorial methods of integrating Inuit.

The early 1970s saw a flurry of organizational activity among Aboriginal groups in the NWT. Initially an umbrella organization for all indigenous peoples in the NWT, the Committee for Original Peoples' Entitlement (COPE), was joined in 1971 by the newly created Inuit Tapirisat of Canada (ITC), a pan-Canadian organization for all Inuit. To these were added the Inuit Land Claims Commission (1977-79), the Nunavut Land Claims Project (1979-82), the Nunavut Constitutional Forum (1982-93), and the Tungavik Federation (1982-99). In 1976, the ITC published its proposal for a land claim, which included calls for the division of the territory (ITC 1976). Division was seen as integral to the claim: "two inseparable parts of a logical whole" (Dacks 1993). If we recall earlier debates about representation and the way in which Inuit were integrated simultaneously into public political institutions and various ethnic committees, it is perhaps not surprising that Inuit negotiators called for both types of institutions when negotiating the claim. These two separate elements to the Inuit proposal survived each transformation of organizational structure among the negotiators. They appear, for example, in the streamlined claim proposal put forward in 1977 by the Inuit Land Claims Commission as well as in the 1983 main document of the Nunavut Constitutional Forum (see also Western Constitutional Forum and Nunavut Constitutional Forum 1987), and they were consistently supported by the Tungavik Federation. The negotiators wanted more than had been promised in 1975 to Inuit in northern Quebec and, following the Inuvialuit claim in 1978, became convinced that division was the only way to ensure sufficient control over resources, which, they believed, provided the key to autonomy. These demands were concrete and financial and had little relation to the desired operational culture of political institutions, although the desire for a political system that operated in Inuktitut and according to Inuit needs and wishes was mentioned at various times (ITC 1977, 1979). For the federal side, matters affecting the political development of Inuit were of wider constitutional significance and, therefore, had no place in a process designed purely for the administration of comprehensive land claims. Both Liberal and Conservative administrations appeared to believe that a document designed for one group as defined by its ethnicity should not address the political rights of all individuals within a geographic area as this could undermine the universality of rights enjoyed by Canadians. Inuit negotiators argued that the two were inseparable; federal officials argued that the processes available were designed to deal with one thing at a time. No doubt some part of Ottawa's concern was linked to events in Quebec. A federal government seen to be engaged in the process of institutional creation for a separate jurisdiction would have found it harder to counter the demands of Quebec separatists. The government was not opposed to general political development in the north. In 1972, before the claims proposal, Minister of Indian Affairs and Northern Development Jean Chrétien (1972) identified the evolution of northern government as a goal, and the 1975 amendment of the Northwest Territories Act furthered development by ensuring that all NWT Council members were elected rather than appointed.

If Inuit proposals saw division as a way to achieve political development, and if federal officials hesitated to include references to political development in a land claim, territorial officials opposed division and viewed the semantics of the land claims process as irrelevant. Political development, they reasoned, could be dealt with in other ways. For very different reasons, the specific institutional proposals that Inuit offered – for the bureaucratic structure of a public government, that it operate in Inuktitut – fell on deaf federal and territorial ears. Territorial officials were less concerned with the purity of process and terrified, instead, by what any reference to political development might include. The territorial commissioner viewed Inuit calls for division as folly and appeared to believe that federal concern about "process" masked a degree of sympathy toward division:

> From where it stands at the present moment, the idea is ludicrous ... It's bloody ridiculous ... How in hell can you support something along that line in the Territories ... the whole idea of breaking up

the Territories is a suggestion, a theory, a hypothesis – call it what you like – that bears the stamp on it "Made in Ottawa." Period. (Hodgson 1979b)

Commissioner Hodgson and the NWT Council appeared to believe that division would sound the death knell for provincial status. Denied provincehood in the 1960s because the territories were not divided, territorial politicians now viewed unity as integral to its attainment. In an effort to swing things their way, the members of the legislature called on the federal government to establish a special inquiry on division and provincial status.

In fact, Hodgson had overestimated federal support for division. A 1977 cabinet statement on northern political development saw two constitutional obstacles to division: the creation of an ethnically defined political jurisdiction and the transfer of control of non-renewable resources to a polity less developed than the existing NWT. The federal government responded to the territorial request by appointing a special representative, Bud Drury. In a sense, this was the federal government's attempt to separate two issues that Inuit negotiators kept presenting as united. Inuit leaders immediately saw what the government was doing and reacted with considerable hostility to the Drury Commission.

Then working for the Inuit Land Claims Commission, John Amagoalik (1978) wrote to Drury and complained: "It annoys us that we were not consulted as to how an inquiry should be set up and what its terms of reference should be." The establishment of the Office of the Special Representative (OSR) he continued, removed the political component of development from the claim: "This compromises the negotiation process and attempts to lower the status of the [Inuit Land Claims] Commission to that of a Rotary club." Amagoalik not only warned that Drury's distance from the claim process would hinder its credibility in the eyes of Inuit but noted that an investigation into political development was unlikely to excite Inuit interest: "Most Inuit in settlements are still relatively unsophisticated political[ly], and much education needs to be carried out in this area." The appropriate venue for Inuit discussion was the office of constitutional development set up by the ITC, which was working with the Inuit Land Claims Commission on constitutional arrangements. The letter ends with an imperative: "Change your terms of reference to integrate your work into the framework of negotiations." Amagoalik's missive was forceful, but it was hardly a unique expression of northern concern. In a 29 January letter to Drury, Peter Kattu (1979), chair of the Sanikiluaq hamlet council, mined a similar theme:

> We are against an outsider deciding for us on how our future government should operate, because you don't know how the Inuit live, you have never lived as an Inuk and you've never been born here. We will not give you recommendations to change the government because we have our own people doing this for us through Inuit Claims negotiations.

This is not to say that Inuit abandoned their reputed practical approach to things. While its negotiators were condemning the operation, the ITC sent the OSR a letter asking for $97,600, with which it hoped to conduct a consultation exercise on none other than Inuit approaches to political development (ITC 1978).

Despite the opposition of claims negotiators, the Drury Commission waded into the debate about division, provincial status, and the decentralization of federal authority. The NWT Council and the NWT commissioner wasted little time informing the new body of the necessity of provincial status. Any delay could only imply federal intentions to continue a decidedly colonial relationship with the north. Other actors were less certain. Inuit negotiators, for example, did not believe that the creation of a province would further their own interests but that it would provide an additional layer of institutions designed by non-Inuit for non-Inuit. Federal views on the inevitability of provincial status varied. Minister of Northern Affairs and National Resources Arthur Laing was perceived to be sympathetic (despite his official pronouncements), but a decade later the federal government still did not believe the territory to be administratively capable of handling provincial-type responsibilities. It also feared that provincial status would complicate federal relations with Aboriginal peoples in the Arctic, relations that had become more complex since Laing's tenure as minister. Among staff of the Drury Commission, it appeared that, since the arrival of Chrétien as minister of Indian Affairs and Northern Development, the federal government had prioritized its relations with Native organizations over public government in the north (Barnabé 1979c). Very little of this dialogue appeared tied to the qualities of Aboriginal peoples in the territory. Thus it did not appear to be the case that the federal government opposed a move toward provincial status because this would mean putting status Indians, Métis, and Inuit in charge but that it felt those currently in charge of administering territorial affairs, including the commissioner and his territorial council, lacked the resources and training necessary to perform the job.

The resource issue was an evocative one. Inuit negotiators saw resources as a way of controlling their future. Funds acquired through the land claim were seen only as part of a larger package; resources made available to a new territory could guarantee eastern Arctic residents sufficient decision-making autonomy to make meaningful decisions about economic, social, and cultural development in the north. Documents from the Tungavik Federation of Nunavut suggest that only with sufficient resources could Inuit create policy that would provide quality formal education as well as the possibility of a life on the land, options that were not necessarily seen as anathema. Their pairing of the land claim with a program for political development points to a comprehensive assessment of the capital at their disposal, both land-based and social. Federal unwillingness to negotiate a new territory signalled to Inuit Ottawa's desire to deny them access to resources that would enable their own development. Territorial officials were equally frustrated by the tight rein that federal administrators kept on resources, not that they wanted Ottawa to pass resources to a new, divided, Inuit-led territory. Instead, the commissioner and NWT Council wanted control over non-renewable resources, the expected revenue from which was perceived to be sufficient for the expensive policy needs of eastern Arctic residents (Malone 1989). Commissioner Hodgson's 1979 admission that elected members of the council had no interest "in managing the service functions of finance, personnel and public works" only fuelled federal fears about territorial preparedness for the devolution of financial control (Hodgson 1979a).[5] Both Inuit and territorial officials equated control over resources with autonomy over the direction of political development. Drury recognized the Catch-22 that federal policy had created. In an October 1978 speech to the territorial council, he acknowledged:

> In a sense in the north, there is a vicious circle: because [the federal] government is paying, [the federal] government is making the decisions ... it is senseless for [the federal] government to talk of the devolution of decision-making as long as it continues to intervene in the name of protection of the individual against his own mistakes. It is equally irrational for reformers of the political system to advocate the assumption of power without responsibility, includ-

ing the burden and the costs of managing power and suffering the consequences of mistakes.

At times the Drury Commission acted independently of the federal government, exploring institutional solutions far more innovative than those discussed by either territorial or federal officials (Porteous 1978); at other times, however, it functioned as a bridge between the two governments, explaining the position of one to the other. It was in this spirit that Drury explained to the NWT Council that it wouldn't acquire responsible government until it was able to pay for the cost of running things, that it wouldn't be able to pay for the cost of running things until it acquired control over non-renewable resources, and that it wouldn't get control of non-renewable resources until it was deemed capable of administering funds in the proper way. The council's response was simple: let us increase the number of members so that control might be possible and then give us the resources to do what we need.

Most of these issues – the inclusion of political development in the land claim, territorial division, provincial status, and resources – point to three separate views of political development in the north. Although territorial or federal officials disagreed with Inuit approaches, they often did so in different ways. It was not unusual for one or the other government to support Inuit approaches, if not the logical extension of the argument. The issue that united both federal and territorial governments, however, was the anticipated avenue of political development. Federal and territorial officials saw political development in the north through the creation and buttressing of local public institutions rather than through the creation of pan-territorial ethnically specific bodies. Their desire to develop existing institutions and to discourage participation in other forms of political expression is very similar to the position of the Royal Commission on Electoral Reform and Party Financing, which, in 1992, sought to channel the political participation of Canadians through political parties rather than through grassroots organizations or citizen movements. Both bureaucrats and the royal commission displayed a clear preference for mainstream avenues of political expression.

Within the two governments there were varying degrees of support for local versus regional councils, but support for subsidiarity to public institutions was clear. When complaints about process got them nowhere, federal officials pointed out that the development of local institutions was a matter for the federal government, not claims negotiators. In a letter to ITC head Eric Tagoona, Minister of Indian Affairs and Northern Development Hugh

Faulkner acknowledged that, although the Inuit Tapirisat viewed "political aspects" as part of the claim, Ottawa viewed the development of community and regional institutions as its responsibility (Faulkner 1979). In *Goals of the Government of the NWT*, NWT Commissioner Hodgson (1974) saw local government as a way to encourage political awareness among territorial residents. Later, he made it clear that part of the appeal was the public rather than ethnic nature of the various hamlet, village, and settlement councils. As he put it, "ethnic states are bad" (Hodgson 1977). The legislature added that the preference was for three levels of government, not four, and so, while "there is no place for a regional level of government" (Northwest Territories, Legislative Assembly 1979, 9), strengthening local democracy was fine. The reference to regional government was likely a response to Drury.

The Drury Commission clearly believed that political development for the territories lay in the expansion of local democratic institutions. Much of the commission's work involved a democratic audit of various local institutions, which included how they were perceived, what tasks they fulfilled, and who participated in them, in addition to a mapping exercise of the relationships among community councils, regional councils, regional Inuit associations, the NWT Council, and the ITC. The local councils in particular were surveyed and were asked to identify the main challenges facing their respective settlements as well as to describe the relationship among various institutions. Information from this exercise clarified the extent of regional variation across the territory.

The OSR floated regional government as one possible method of decentralizing federal authority in the territories. In their democratic audit of local councils, Drury's staff noticed that local activities were characterized both by a general problem with capacity and by the over-burdening of a few individuals: "What happens very often is that the same people get re-elected to these types of councils; hamlets, settlements, etc., and get very tired of going to meetings" (Barnabé 1979a). The result was a considerable narrowing of political influence: "The [name withheld] family, Anni, Tommie, presently on council and Charlie, presently Settlement secretary, reflects the predominance of one family leading in [name withheld]" (Porteous 1979). This likely explains what Drury perceived to be minimal levels of autonomy for local councils. In a 13 March memo, he viewed the institutional authority of Greenlandic municipal councils favourably, noting that they were responsible for more than the usual mix of "water, sewer, garbage and dogs." Part of the problem was the plethora of full-time jobs in the community, all of which provided better pay than did council positions. Even those interested in political affairs made more money as bureaucrats than as politicians. Personal economic decisions also affected the development of political institutions.

Drury Commission recommendations are normally summarized as having "advocated against division" (Canada, Special Representative on Constitutional Development, 1980; Dacks 1980) but in its investigation of local government the commission proved to be far more adventurous in their vision of institutional development than territorial or federal officials, or even Inuit negotiators. Documents in the Drury files suggest that while the OSR was aware that the BNA Act limited possible constitutional options it did not dictate institutional homogeneity across the north. Drury spent a considerable amount of time exploring the problem of "fit" between the varied norms and structures of territorial society and southern Canadian political institutions. The Carrothers Commission was seen as something of missed opportunity, given the tabula rasa nature of the political space that then existed. Documents relating to the development of political parties suggest that Drury envisioned a system of territorial parties that cut across ethnic lines, employing a consociational expression of political voice. He supported the conclusions of the Berger inquiry (the federally appointed inquiry into the Mackenzie Valley Pipeline), which called for the establishment of political institutions that were better suited to Aboriginal peoples in the north.

In 1978, staff at the OSR summarized the possibilities for institutional development as status quo, some form of consociational democracy, or a confederation of regions. Under this third option, local democracy would flourish at the regional level rather than at the hamlet or settlement level. This would solve the capacity issue by drawing on a wider pool of individuals. Regions would thus be large enough to manage resources that would guarantee them a degree of decision-making autonomy but small enough to create policy based on local needs. It was a plan to which Inuit negotiators were rather hostile.

The plethora of local bodies created by the federal government in the 1950s and 1960s was continuing to grow in the 1970s. Each community had a local council with several local committees. Regional Inuit associations provided opportunities for Inuit to meet separately. The development of public, regional bodies rivalled the authority of regional Inuit associations, which, at that time, were the only bodies expressing the wishes of Inuit at more than a local level. Organs of local decision making were seen as mouthpieces for the territorial government. Advocates of regional councils felt that regional Inuit associations were concerned with political development at the expense of local issues. When community councils in the Baffin formed the first regional council in 1977, the ITC feared that the government had encouraged the participation of more docile Inuit at the expense of those advocating division and the land claim. Even the NWT press release announcing the establishment of the Baffin Regional Council noted ITC hostility to its creation (Northwest Territories, Department of Information 1977). The ITC believed that the Baffin Regional Inuit Association (BRIA) was already organizing people and, therefore, that a regional council was not needed, particularly if the territorial government was beginning to provide the money needed to solve community problems. This issue highlights three cleavages of opinion regarding institutional development in the NWT. The first concerns the distinction between ethnic bodies and public bodies. Territorial and federal officials displayed a clear preference for public bodies of governance, while Inuit negotiators felt that ethnic bodies would be most responsive to northern residents, the bulk of whom were Inuit. Second, this disagreement points to divisions between those Inuit concerned with local problems and those concerned with political development. Advocates of political development prioritized the involvement of ethnic bodies, which they felt would secure resources through land claims, while advocates of local issues believed the focus on land claims detracted from the day-to-day problems faced by individuals and communities. Relations between the Baffin Regional Council and BRIA were often strained, but the dividing line was organizational rather than ethnic. Third, this disagreement points to the tangled fight over resources. For Inuit negotiators, regional councils were an additional layer of government designed to draw Inuit into the territorial fold and to distract them from the fundamental problem of a lack of economic and political resources. Rather than creating regional councils, Inuit activists believed territorial officials should hand over the resources needed to solve community problems. Territorial officials, who supported local but not regional development, believed that they were short of resources because the federal government refused to release them. The federal government, for its part, had no intention of releasing resources until the territory had proved itself capable of managing its financial affairs.

Political development in the 1980s achieved many of the aims identified by colonial administrators. In 1979, following the second elections for a legislature composed entirely of democratically selected members, legislators elected from among their own number eight people to sit as an executive. As the 1980s began, then, the NWT enjoyed responsible government. In 1986, the NWT commissioner withdrew from active administration and turned the management of the public service over to the executive. These two achievements marked what, in previous centuries, would have been seen as the end stage of political development, the addition of political parties the only remaining procedure. The same period saw more modern innovations, the transfer of authority from the federal government to the territory, and an increase in autonomy for regions and communities. While these might not have had a direct impact on the negotiation of the land claim, they did define the pre-division institutions that served as a model for the creation of a political system in Nunavut.

Institutional Development after the Land Claim

The process by which claims negotiators eventually reached a consensus has been well documented (Armstrong 1999; Dacks 1993; Flumian 1999; Henderson 2001; Ironside 2000; Jull 2001a, 2001b, 2001c; Kusugak 2000; Légaré 1996, 1997, 1998, 1999, 2002; Loukacheva 2004; Merritt 1993a, 1993b, 1993c; Merritt, Ames, Fenge and Jull 1989; Merritt and Fenge 1990; Timpson 2006a; White 2000; Widdowson and Howard 1999b, 2002) and will not be repeated here. The NLCA provided for the creation of Inuit-specific organizations and joint Inuit-government co-management bodies, while the Nunavut Political Accord outlined the creation of public government in Nunavut. The co-management boards were mentioned specifically, but the rules governing the creation of the public government were limited. References to the inevitability of provincial status were absent, as was mention of local or regional councils, although the accord calls explicitly for decentralized government. In an effort to ensure that the transfer of responsibilities began on time, the Nunavut Act called for the creation of the Nunavut Implementation Commission, which was given a very wide mandate and was expected:

> to advise the Government of Canada, the Government of the Northwest Territories and [Nunavut Tunngavik Incorporated] on the establishment of Nunavut and, in particular, to advise on:
>
> a the timetable for the assumption by the Government of Nunavut of responsibility for the delivery of services;

b the process for the first election of the members of the Assembly, including the number of members and the establishment of electoral districts;
c the design and funding of training programs;
d the process for determining the location of the seat of government of Nunavut;
e the principles and criteria for the equitable division of assets and liabilities between Nunavut and the Northwest Territories;
f the new public works necessitated by the establishment of Nunavut and the scheduling of the construction of the works;
g the administrative design of the first Government of Nunavut;
h the arrangements for delivery of programs and services where the responsibility for delivery by Nunavut is to be phased in; and,
i any other related matter referred to it by the Minister, with the consent of the government leader of the Northwest Territories and of Tunngavik. (s. 58)

The nine members of the NIC were nominated by the three parties to the claim and were Inuit or long-term northern residents. It was led by John Amagoalik, former head of the Inuit Land Claims Commission and a key negotiator throughout the claims process. Nine of the ten members of the NIC were Inuit who had had no prior experience in the design of government. The commission was supported by a ten-member staff, five of whom were stationed in Iqaluit, two in Ottawa, one in Yellowknife, and one in each of the three regions. Six of the ten staff members were Inuit. The NIC met for the first time in January 1994 and identified a workplan that would allow its recommendations to be reviewed and implemented before 1999.

The NIC held public consultations throughout the new territory. When Nunavummiut were asked to identify their ideal polity, most reported that they wanted a democracy and the continued practice of consensus government. The public consultations did not reveal an appetite for radical institutional reform in Nunavut. Rather, voters wanted a territory of their own, with a more proximate capital and with Inuit in positions of power. If the creation of a new territory provided the opportunity to engender a radical departure from "politics as usual," there is no evidence that members of the public felt this to be necessary.

The NIC issued two comprehensive reports, *Footprints in New Snow* in March 1995 and *Footprints II* in October 1996, as well as a number of smaller reports on such specific topics as the choice of a capital, the design of the electoral system, the selection of the premier, and the telecommunications requirements of the legislature and bureaucracy.[6] The first report of the NIC contains a series of recommendations, some unsurprising, some revolutionary. It recommended that employees of the Government of the Northwest Territories (GNWT) residing in Nunavut be "rolled over" into the same or similar positions in the Government of Nunavut (GN). It argued that the federal government should pay for the construction of infrastructure, including office buildings and staff housing, to meet the needs associated with the NIC's GN design model. It also suggested some departures from previous practices. It recommended that the GN be established with full legal responsibility on 1 April 1999 rather than have its responsibilities phased in over a number of years (which had been the widely held expectation). It recommended doing away with the administrative regions, regional health boards, and regional education boards that had been created by the GNWT and argued, instead, for a decentralized organizational design consisting of ten departments (plus a legislative assembly) with approximately 550 "headquarters" positions to be located in the capital. Many of the recommendations were eventually implemented or modified only slightly.

The location of the capital itself was discussed by the NIC, which presented three options. While the analysis clearly pointed to the largest community, Iqaluit, as the most logical and cost-effective choice, the NIC shied away from recommending one community over its competitors and, instead, suggested that the eventual decision be made by the federal cabinet rather than by plebiscite. The decision was, however, eventually put to a public plebiscite in 1995, and 60 percent selected Iqaluit over Rankin Inlet as the new capital.

In terms of political vision, the NIC opted for a rather conventional political system. Although direct election of the premier was discussed, the commission turned away from this as well as from modifying the electoral system to include some measure of proportional representation or more consociational arrangements. Nor did the NIC recommend the implementation of party politics. In its research note on the first election, the commission stated: "It is not possible to predict with any confidence whether or not party politics will emerge in Nunavut in the early days of its Legislative Assembly" (Nunavut Implementation Committee 1996c). The NIC's break from "politics as usual" involved eleven two-member constituencies, with each constituency electing one member from a list of male candidates and one member from a list of female candidates. This innovation had not been raised in public consultations and was put to a public plebiscite. The turnout in the referendum was less than 40 percent, and, of those who voted, almost 60 percent did not back the innovation. In other words, only 16 percent of Nunavut residents cast a ballot in support of gender parity, by far the lowest measure of support for any of the plebiscites held between 1982 and 1995. This suggests that pubic reactions to the proposal varied from indifference to hostility.

Decentralization, mentioned in the Nunavut Act as a call for "decentralized government," became, for the NIC, a call for decentralized bureaucracy. This represents a significant shift in how communities were viewed. Although federal and territorial officials initially saw the development of community-level decision making as a key element in political development, this view is absent from the accord and from NIC recommendations. This suggests that the ITC vision of regional development emerged as dominant, with the status of regional Inuit associations being secured in the post-claim political landscape. This shift transforms local communities from venues of decentralized political activity into seats of bureaucratic employment, decentralization a system of resource distribution rather than a program of political development. Nowhere is this more clear than in the NIC's (1994, 10) document on the principles guiding devolution: "The reality of regional diversities and identities in Nunavut should be translated into a design for the [Government of Nunavut] that results in the government offices ... being allocated fairly among the regions." Predictably, reactions to the set of institutions mentioned in the claim and designed by the NIC are varied. *Nunatsiaq News*, the weekly newspaper with more political coverage than its rival *News North*, has been a consistent critic of the bureaucracy and legislature, particularly with regard to staffing levels and decentralization. Indeed, for some, the success of decentralization has become the benchmark against which devolution of power to Nunavut can be judged.

Institutions are both products and agents of political culture. They often emerge from rival visions regarding the best way to organize a state and, once established, become powerful forces in the entrenchment of the successful vision. From 1905 to 1999, institutional creation in the NWT helps us to identify the primary influences on territorial culture. For much of this period, the federal vision of territorial development dictated political events, its dominance ebbing only slowly. As the costs of administering the territory increased, federal interest in pursuing the well-worn process of political and institutional development waned. As a result, the NWT commissioner and the NWT Council remained appointed positions far longer in the twentieth-century NWT than in its previous incarnations. The emergence of a separate territorial bureaucracy within the federal administration and the arrival of responsible government also occurred at an unhurried pace. Federal influence on NWT political culture was thus much stronger than it had been in, for example, the Yukon. Upon their relocation to Yellowknife in 1967, the NWT commissioner, the NWT Council, and the NWT bureaucracy began to develop a territorial identity. Although the federal officials who controlled the purse strings may have advocated a conservative approach, territorial officials desperately wanted control over resources and provincial status, at different times seeing one as a way of securing access to the other. Views on how best to attain provincial status changed over time. In the 1960s, division was seen as a way to ditch an unknown and possibly expensive eastern population. Resources could have been shared among a smaller number and could have served to control demand if not supply. By the 1980s, territorial officials viewed division as an obstacle to provincial status, in part because it heralded negative changes to supply-side resource access. That the chief dispute about political development concerned control over resources rather than, for example, whether executives should be housed inside or outside the legislature, made it easier, in a way, for Inuit negotiators to frame their resource-based claims for a territory.

Running parallel to disputes over resource control were visions of public institutions and ethnic organizations. The debate over the creation of regional government and the reticence to deal with the Drury Commission demonstrated Inuit resistance to public bodies that offered them few rewards. The existence of such bodies was viewed as an obstacle both to the transfer of resources to Inuit and to the development of a political space that would ensure their economic independence. The NLCA and the Nunavut Political Accord spelled the demise of federal and territorial visions of regional and local political development. Instead, the NIC pursued goals that were identified by Inuit negotiators, fostering the role of both regional and pan-territorial ethnic bodies and focusing attention on local economic issues rather than regional political development. Any cultural benefits to be derived from the NLCA related neither to the institutional culture nor to the political culture of a new territory but to a cultural renaissance among Inuit.

TABLE 5.1

Administration of political development in the NWT, 1936-99

Federal department	Federal minister	NWT commissioner	NWT premiers
1936-50 Department of Mines and Resources	1936-45 Thomas Alexander Crerar (L) 1945-48 James Allison Glen (L) 1948-49 James Angus MacKinnon (L) 1949-50 Colin William George Gibson (L)	1936-46 Charles Camsell 1947-50 Hugh Llewellyn Keenleyside	
1950-53 Department of Resources and Development	1950-53 Robert Henry Waters (L)	1950-53 Hugh Andrew Young	
1953-66 Department of Northern Affairs and National Resources	1953-57 Jean Lesage (L) 1957 Douglas Scott Harkness (C) 1957-60 Francis Alvin George Hamilton (C) 1960-63 Walter Gilbert Dinsdale (C) 1963-68 Arthur Laing (L)	1953-63 Robert G. Robertson 1963-67 Ben Sivertz	
1966- Department of Indian Affairs and Northern Development	1968-74 Jean Chrétien (L) 1974-76 J. Judd Buchanan (L) 1976-77 Warren Allmand (L) 1977-79 J. Hugh Faulkner (L) 1979-80 Jake Epp (C)	1967-79 Stuart Hodgson 1979-89 John Parker*	

1980-84	John Munro (L)		1980-84	George Braden
1984	Doug Frith (L)		1984-85	Richard Nerysoo
1984-86	David Crombie (C)		1985-87	Nick Sibbeston
1986-89	Bill McKnight (C)		1987-91	Dennis Patterson
1989-90	Pierre Cadieux (C)			
1990-93	Thomas Edward Siddon (C)		1991-95	Nellie Cournoyea
1993	Pauline Browes (C)		1995-98	Don Morin
1993-97	Ron Irwin (L)			
1997-99	Jane Stewart (L)		1998-2000	Jim Antoine

NOTE: Between 1950 and 1966, First Nations affairs were dealt with by the Department of Citizenship and Immigration, but Inuit affairs were dealt with by the Department of Northern Affairs and National Resources.

* Stopped functioning as head of executive in 1980 with election of first premier. L = Liberal; C = Conservative.

6
Consensus Politics

One of the most distinctive features of political culture in Nunavut is the operation of party-free consensus politics, an institutional feature borrowed directly from the pre-division Northwest Territories. Candidates for the nineteen seats in the Nunavut legislature run as independents. Once elected, legislative members select from among themselves a speaker, a premier, and the members of the cabinet. Although the premier is unable to impose his or her wishes on cabinet selection, he or she is able to assign portfolios to cabinet ministers. Lauded as less prone to needlessly aggressive partisan debate, consensus politics has been portrayed as a compromise between British parliamentarism and an Aboriginal preference for consensual decision making (O'Brien 2003; White 1991). Political parties have been portrayed as alien to Aboriginal models of governance and, as such, have been seen as an unwelcome potential addition to political life in the north. The following chapter explores the impact of consensus politics on political culture in Nunavut, focusing in particular on relations between the public and the legislature.

Consensus Politics in Nunavut

There are a number of unsubstantiated myths or claims surrounding the political development of consensus politics. One claim, repeated by both academics and practitioners, is that the current institutional settlement reflects Aboriginal wishes and decision making and that it was designed with these in mind. It is more accurate, however, to note that the current system of consensus politics stems from two related features of political life in the pre-division NWT. First, the failure of division in 1962-63 ensured that the development of political institutions proceeded more slowly in the unified NWT than it might have done in the western portion of a divided territory. Second, the reduced pace of change kept political life in the territories so completely under the thumb of the administration in Ottawa that the introduction of political parties would have been a useless invention at least until the 1980s, at which point the tenor of political culture in the north had changed entirely. That consensus politics *currently* reflects the wishes of a northern Aboriginal population is not in question, but it was not designed to be a permanent feature of northern political life, it had nothing to do with efforts to acknowledge Aboriginal preferences, and its current existence owes as much to the tenor and pace of political change in the NWT as it does to the original intentions of administrators.

The near total appointment of all territorial officials in the 1960s can easily explain the absence of party politics in the NWT Council. Members were not only appointed, but were appointed by Liberals. In a sense, the NWT was a cultural fragment of political culture in Ottawa. If we believe what Bell (1970), Hartz (1964), Horowitz (1966), Lipset (1968, 1986, 1990), and McRae (1978) have to say about political culture in Canada – namely, that it stems from cultural fragments inherited from French, British, and American settlers – then the same could be said with regard to the relationship between Yellowknife and Ottawa. That for over twenty years, at a critical stage in its development, the NWT was run, with varying degrees of intensity, by appointees of the Liberal Party of Canada must have had a profound impact on the tenor of political debate.

In the 1970s, with the increase of elected members in the legislature, and later, with an entirely elected legislature, the absence of party politics can also be explained by the influence of an executive that was still controlled by appointees. Party politics did not develop in the Yukon, for example, until the executive was housed within the elected legislature. The operation of party politics at the legislative level, while absent at the executive level, would have reinforced the division between the two entities and likely made the NWT seem far closer to an American model of government than to a modified Westminster model.

Who would have introduced parties as a form of political organization, and how would either federal or territorial officials have prevented their emergence? In the Yukon, and in contemporary politics in the NWT, it is the political parties who determine whether or not they will field candidates. In the early 1980s, there was one stillborn effort to run party candidates in territorial contests. Ultimately, however, it is up to voters whether they choose to back those candidates or vote for independents. Federal and territorial officials did not explicitly delay the introduction of party politics; rather, given the institutional settlement in the NWT, there would have been no logical point at which political parties could begin contesting seats on the council or the legislature. This was the case because (1) at first there were so few seats over which to quibble; (2) the scale of operation necessary to field and fund candidates would have been impossible for political parties to handle; and (3) the Liberal Party so clearly had a lock on political authority and participation in the north that any competition would have been laughably uneven. Even still, well into the 1980s territorial officials viewed the development of political parties as an inevitable and ordinary stage in political development, and federal officials, although conservative about the desired pace of change, tended to agree.

Following the successful negotiation of the Nunavut Land Claims Agreement and the Nunavut Political Accord, the NIC turned its attention to the institutional design of the new territory. While it was not within the remit of the NIC mandate to compel political parties to field candidates in the first territorial election, the recommended size of the legislature, the choice of electoral system, the decision not to directly elect the premier (Nunavut Implementation Committee 1996b, 1996c, 1998), and the fact that all other institutional features so closely resembled NWT political life suggested that non-partisan politics was a virtual certainty in the territory.

Most academics who have studied political development in the NWT or Nunavut have viewed the absence of political parties in the north in a favourable light (Dacks 1986; White 1991), and assessments by northerners are, for the most part, also positive (O'Brien 2003). Political parties have not yet attempted to field candidates for territorial electoral contests in Nunavut, but the NDP has tried, on isolated occasions, to field single candidates or, in some cases, a complement of candidates in NWT elections. This has not been successful. Clearly, there is continued support for the consensus system, and it is possible to identify five reasons why it is preferred over partisan systems. First, political parties are seen as alien to the north. Graham White (1991), in his seminal article on politics in the Northwest Territories, noted that parties would bring artificial divisions within the population. Such a strategy would discourage individuals from acting in concert on issues that could unite them. White mentions Dene and Inuit specifically, although a similar argument could surely be made with regard to partisan politics in southern Canada. Second, political parties are perceived as engines of political acrimony, something that is seen to be at odds with Aboriginal decision making and is regarded as unwelcome in northern politics. The extent to which this is actually true is up for debate, but clearly northerners are happy with the lower levels of aggression witnessed in their own legislatures. Almost 60 percent of respondents to the 2004 NuHS believe that parties do more to divide the country than to unite it, and just under 80 percent are satisfied with the way democracy works in Nunavut. For political scientists, the benefit of this is obvious, as survey results from southern Canada clearly show that cynicism is driven, in part, by negative views of political parties and the rather unseemly tenor of partisan political debate.

Third, the financial relationship between the territories and the federal government argues against the establishment of political parties. Partisan legislatures in the territories could produce governments of a different political stripe than the one in Ottawa, something that could have a negative effect on the size of federal transfer payments. Given the dependence of the territories on the federal government, an institutional feature that eliminates the possibility of partisan conflict between the two levels is seen as a prudent choice. Fourth, the size of the legislature and the population it represents are also seen to be better served by consensus politics than by political parties. One common refrain is that there are insufficient numbers of quality candidates to ensure that all the people elected from one party would be "cabinet material." Good candidates for cabinet positions could be excluded on the basis of their partisanship. Fifth, the absence of political parties has resulted in no discernible set-back to the territories. The absence of Liberal premiers has not resulted in the NWT, and now Nunavut, being denied access to resources to which they might have laid claim. The absence of political parties has not served to exclude territorial leaders from federal-provincial meetings. Indeed, the recent degree of cooperation among the territorial leaders of the NWT, Nunavut, and Yukon has shown that a common partisan stripe is not a necessary precondition for cooperation.

Coinciding with this positive evaluation of consensus politics are negative predictions about the absence of parties. Writing about the NWT, Widdowson and Howard (1999a, 37) criticize consensus politics, arguing that they are the result of an ill-advised "attempt to combine aboriginal culture with parliamentary democracy." This view is grounded in a belief that the establishment of consensus government was a conscious effort to appeal to Aboriginal norms and values, something that is not borne out by evidence. Although the various Aboriginal groups living in the Arctic may now prefer consensus politics as a method of decision making, this does not explain the presence of consensus government in the north. Whatever its origins, Widdowson and Howard identify several problems with it, in particular the absence of coherent views among cabinet members, the lack of public scrutiny, and the lack of incentive for regular MLAs to question suspect ministerial behaviour by ministers (38). In the absence of vibrant opposition in the legislature, Widdowson and Howard predict insufficient media coverage of government scandals (39). Their conclusions are dire:

> Because of the focus on maintaining tribal values rather than satisfying current aboriginal needs, the territorial system is regressing to an archaic form of political organization, preventing the social evolution required for full participation in the world of the 21st century. (40)

More general concerns are raised in other venues. Writing in a public forum addressing the cynicism caused by political parties, Hugh Berrington (2003) warned that, without parties, voters would be hard pressed to know what candidates believed, that elections would essentially become popularity contests devoid of policy discussion, that representation would be guided solely by personal opinions, and that it would be difficult for voters to evaluate the voting records of their members. Furthermore, governments would become unstable, torn apart by internal conflict, indecision, and the lack of a central and unifying vision. Clearly, these are empirical statements that contain a normative element. We assume that governments should be stable and that it should be easy for voters to evaluate the voting records of their members. If we turn our attention to consensus politics in Nunavut, we find that some of these statements are true. Election campaigns in Nunavut, and in the NWT for that matter, have not been prone to overarching policy debates that occupied the attentions of candidates or voters. One is left wondering, therefore, whether the absence of parties really does produce a polity that is distinct from the ones we recognize in southern Canada. Do we really lose anything by the absence of political parties? And, if we do, is this loss offset by the gains that might be made? We know that parties serve certain functions. What happens when they are not there to function as organizations capable of articulating particular interests? The following analysis focuses on the integration of citizens and the articulation of interests both within the legislature and during election campaigns. If political parties in Canada are seen to exercise a greater role within the legislature and a less prominent role during election campaigns, it is perhaps surprising that when examining the impact of their absence we find a far greater distance between consensus and partisan systems with respect to the integration of citizens and the articulation of interests during campaigns, and an almost negligible difference when we compare the behaviour of actors within the legislature. The chapter addresses each of these in turn.

The Role of Political Parties

Literature on the role of political parties in advanced industrial states identifies a number of possible activities that political parties might be expected to perform (Boyce and Bischak 2002; Dalton 2002; Laski 1938). A first theme deals with election campaigns, in which typical activities include the recruitment and identification of candidates to stand as party representatives in electoral competition. Apart from the mechanics of the campaign itself, parties may use campaign periods to enunciate issues of interest to citizens and to integrate them into the political process. Whether through leadership contests, candidate selection, or voting, parties can use campaigns to lure potential partisans into their fold and, by taking a particular stand on certain issues, can also give partisans cues about how they should feel about a specific topic. By articulating a basic platform, parties also identify issues of interest to the wider electorate. As a result, parties not only provide substantive information about how to evaluate particular issues but also help to identify which issues are important by framing the political debate. While this is most obvious during an election campaign, parties can also provide these types of information shortcuts to citizens throughout the life of a government and, in so doing, reduce the costs for citizens of staying informed. After an election, parties set about the task of ensuring the selection of a government and, eventually, of governing. Because membership in the government is usually unambiguous, opposition members and voters alike know whom to hold accountable should they be displeased with legislation and whom to reward for the introduction of popular measures. Within the legislature, parties can serve as interest brokers among different groups and individuals and, in so doing, help to transform the local or personal desires of voters into an overarching program that balances the needs of all, or at least most, within the polity. Campaigning, passing legislation, integrating citizens, and articulating interests are tasks that place parties at the centre of the political system. Or, put another way:

There is hardly a serious student of democracy who does not seem to believe that political parties provide by far the most important linkage between citizens and the political process and that party platforms provide the best possible means for aggregating diverse interests and passions into a coherent, system-wide mix of public policies and that competition between these parties provides the most reliable mechanism for ensuring the accountability of rules and that cooperation within and between these parties provides the only feasible way of forming viable governments. (Schmitter 2001, 67)

And yet we can reasonably assume that not all of these tasks are created equally and that different types of parties will place greater emphasis on some than on others. Certainly the numerous typologies of parties, based on function or organization (Neumann 1956; Kitschelt 1989; Katz and Mair 1995; Duverger 1954; Gunther and Diamond 2001; Anderson 1998), point to the various ways that parties can discharge their assumed roles. If we are to understand what we might lose or what we might gain in the absence of political parties, it is worthwhile determining how the roles of Canadian political parties differ from the roles of those in other advanced industrial states.

Our typical understanding of Canadian political parties as brokers of diverse regional interests suggests that they are less concerned with ideology and more concerned with forming governments (Carty 2002; Carty, Cross, and Young 2000; Carty and Stewart 1996; Sayers 1999; Young 1998). Party discipline is seen to be strong, but party organization has typically been described as weak, with permanent and sufficiently resourced party head offices only a relatively recent development. For much of the past century, party organizations emerged at election time but faded shortly thereafter. Until 1993, Canada was assumed to have two cadre brokerage parties (the Liberal Party and the Conservative Party) and one mass party, the NDP, which was seen to have a higher level of permanent organization and a greater devotion to ideology than either of the other two. The emergence of the Reform Party and, later, the Bloc Québécois ensured that mass parties, and ones with clearer ideological positions, now outnumbered the cadre brokerage parties. The first-past-the-post electoral system has ensured a long line of single-party majority governments, with minority governments being both rare and short-lived. These features not only describe the current influence of parties on political life in Canada but they have also assumed a normative position.

Single-party majority governments are not only a feature of political life but are seen to be a positive feature. Strong party discipline, likewise, is viewed by some as a necessary and positive component of legislative politics.

In a comparative sense, party influence over voting within the House is often portrayed as a more relevant concern in Canada than it is in the United States or in the United Kingdom. In the case of the United States, this stems from a greater willingness on the part of representatives to vote according to local constituency concerns, while in the United Kingdom the sheer size of the legislature mitigates the impact of any potential backbench rebellion. Certainly in the United States the Democratic Party and the Republican Party have been more likely to woo recalcitrant legislators with carrots rather than to employ the various sticks of partisan punishment. Within the legislature, then, Canadian parties could be seen as exercising greater power than their counterparts elsewhere. In terms of campaigns, however, Canadian parties might be seen as a less relevant presence. Brokerage politics has ensured a relatively fluid position for parties on any of the left-right or issue spectra that might dominate campaigns, and a low proportion of partisans means that, with each campaign, parties must begin anew to woo voters rather than to rely on a steady supply of support. South of the border, by contrast, the practice of individuals registering as partisans, participation in presidential primaries, identical partisan contests at numerous levels, only two partisan choices, and more frequent elections are seen to have increased the salience of partisanship during campaigns. For this reason, the assumed importance of Canadian political parties appears to be heightened when we explore legislative behaviour, but within the context of campaigns, Canadian parties seem to have a weaker role and a more tenuous connection to citizens than might be the case in American electoral contests.

If these beliefs structure our perceptions of what parties contribute to political life, then we might expect their absence to have a noticeable impact on legislative developments but a less well-defined impact on electoral contests. As the following analysis illustrates, however, the absence of parties in Nunavut is least evident in the daily operation of the legislature and more obvious in the articulation of interests and in the integration of citizens, something that is particularly visible during election campaigns.

Election Campaigns in a Consensus System

In a consensus system, all individuals run as independents for elected office. Candidates might wish to create flyers or pamphlets that outline their views on the issues facing the constituency or the territory. They might wish to participate in all-candidate debates within the constituency, should others choose to arrange them. There is no obligation on the part of any political actor, whether the incumbent MLA, the candidates themselves, or the elections office, to organize public meetings, though local organizations and the media have often arranged informal events. In large constituencies, for example those containing more than one community, campaigning is expensive and time-consuming. Before division in 1999, constituencies in the eastern Arctic contained communities hundreds of kilometres apart but unconnected by roads, and even after 1999 constituencies in the north Baffin and Kitikmeot remained geographically dispersed. The air connections between some neighbouring communities are infrequent and indirect. Candidates wishing to visit each community in their constituency are required to cover the cost of airfare themselves or travel by snowmobile, using precious resources of money or time. Admittedly, communities are not large, and so the cost of travel may be offset slightly.

In consensus systems, candidates themselves bear the sole financial burden of their election campaign, and any fundraising must be accomplished without the aid of a party structure or party name. The exact financial costs will vary, but each candidate must provide a $200 deposit and may incur pre-election and election expenses of no more than $30,000. Contributions from individuals and corporations, whether as cash or in kind, may not exceed $2,500. The maximum tax receipt, both for donors and the candidates themselves, is $1,500. There are three exceptions to the $30,000 maximum. Candidates may incur reasonable expenses above the limit for transportation, childcare expenses, or expenses related to a disability. Candidates must identify their own networks of support, based on personal rather than on partisan ties. This is not to say that party organizations in place for federal elections are not pressed into service in territorial campaigns, but it is not unusual in some of the larger communities to have partisans of a similar stripe competing against each other, all drawing on the same pool of federal sympathizers. Even though the costs to those engaging in gladiatorial activities are higher in consensus systems than they are in partisan systems, this has not had an impact on the number of candidates. The 1999 election saw seventy-one candidates, while the 2004 election involved eighty-two candidates and only one acclaimed seat.[1] If we examine the number of registered voters compared with the number of candidates, we find that consensus systems produce a higher proportion of gladiatorial participants than do partisan systems (Henderson 2004c).[2] While this addresses the number of candidates rather than their talents, these figures belie the claim that consensus politics is necessary in the north because the talent pool is too shallow to warrant a steady supply of candidates for two or three or four parties.

Perhaps the most striking impact of consensus campaigns is on the individual voter. Given the shortcuts that parties make available to voters, whether with regard to the types of issues at the heart of a campaign or how voters should approach them, the absence of such cues in consensus campaigns is significant. In many respects, there is not one election campaign in Nunavut but nineteen, each fought on different issues and concerns. This decreases the extent to which there can be a coherent policy discussion within the territory during an election. Most voters, however, do not have information about how candidates feel on any of the issues facing the community or the territory. This has two results: first, campaigns tend to be fought on local or community issues, with a considerable amount of attention devoted to the infrastructure needs of communities; second, organizations other than the candidates or voters themselves are able to set the agenda for the campaign. Evidence of the former can be seen in the results of a candidate survey conducted for the CBC during the 2004 Nunavut election.

During the 2004 election campaign, the CBC contacted each of the candidates, initially in English and later, if necessary, in Inuktitut, and asked for basic information, including prior political and employment experience, reasons for standing as a candidate, and the issues on which the candidate was running. The motivations of candidates, summarized in Table 6.1, are particularly interesting. When asked why they were running in the campaign, 42 percent of candidates mentioned representation for the local level, 20 percent mentioned personal reasons, and 15 percent mentioned issue-driven politics or territory-wide issues.

Evidence of a vibrant policy debate within the territory is not necessarily precluded by these local motivations. More explicitly, candidates were asked about the issues they felt were important to Nunavut. Here, there appeared to be consistent attention to issues of housing, education, and training, but for the most part these were expressed as issues facing the community rather than the territory as a whole. Issues of local infrastructure were seen to be particularly pressing. When asked about the main issues on which he was running, one typical candidate noted that he wanted a new community hall and a swimming pool, a youth drop-in centre, an elders hall where they can discuss health and care, a camping ground, a medium security jail, a new church, more housing, a traditional healing centre, a women's shelter and an FM radio station. (Henderson 2004b)

TABLE 6.1

Candidate reasons for running in the 2004 Nunavut election

Issue	n	%
Local concerns	30	43.5
Community needs a voice in the legislature	8	
Give back to the community	8	
Constituency needs a voice in the legislature	7	
Know community/constituency needs best	4	
Current MLA is not good	2	
Economic development in community	1	
Personal reasons	14	20.3
Friends/people in community convinced to run	8	
Feel should stay as MLA for continuity	3	
I have appropriate qualifications	2	
No one else was going to run	1	
Issue-driven politics	10	14.5
Social issues	2	
Language and education	2	
Family issues	1	
Housing and employment	1	
Hunger	1	
Erosion of Inuit culture	1	
Health care	1	
Economy in bad shape	1	
Territory-wide	10	14.5
A lot of work to be done	5	
Want to serve the public	2	
Want to contribute to Nunavut	1	
Want to make a better future	1	
Want more unity between partners in development	1	
Ethnic concerns	5	7.3
Want to represent/know best Inuit concerns	3	
Constituency needs an Inuk in the legislature	2	

NOTE: Not all candidates provided a reason for running.
SOURCE: CBC Candidate Survey February 2004, $n = 82$.

Just six months after the election, the 2004 NuHS asked individuals about the most important issue facing Nunavut. Individuals were overwhelmingly interested in measures of economic vitality, things like affordable housing, employment, the cost of living, and job training. Only a handful mentioned local infrastructure such as docks or community halls. If we compare the issues mentioned by candidates in the election campaign to the responses provided by respondents in the 2004 NuHS, we find some interesting results.

Table 6.2 highlights the schism between the interests of voters and the issues identified by candidates. For the most part, the results are *relatively* similar. Voters and candidates place higher emphasis on the acquisition of economic vitality than they do on cultural vitality, which we might expect, given the explicit attention to resources throughout the land claim process. Neither voters nor candidates are likely to identify broader issues of social policy as the most pressing concern. What is most striking, however, is that candidates pay far greater attention to local economic vitality than do voters, who seem to place the economic vitality of the territory above all else. There are a number of conclusions we might wish to draw from such data. Clearly, candidates are seeking to identify themselves as the best representative for a local area, and, thus, their attention to the concerns of local citizens and the needs of the constituency should not surprise us. Candidates in electoral systems employing single-member districts often try to portray themselves as the best representative of and for a given locality. In partisan systems, however, candidates are obliged to at least pay lip service to the wider policy issues identified by their respective parties and, in so doing, ensure that the local electoral campaign shares something with the wider campaign throughout the polity. This, clearly, is not the case in Nunavut, where there is not necessarily a wider policy debate to tap into and where there is no incentive for candidates to identify one. This has obvious ramifications for citizen engagement and the articulation of interests.

At first blush, it would appear that candidates do a poor job of articulating issues for voters if the citizenry has different priorities than does its political class. Equally worth noting, the integration of citizens can be seen as a two-stage process. By encouraging participation at the local level, political parties can help to bring partisans into the political fold and, in so doing, to integrate them into a wider polity, one that transcends the local environment. While candidates for the territorial election may help to ensure the participation of campaign workers, this does a far more complete job of integrating citizens to a local political event than it does of integrating them into

TABLE 6.2

Issues identified by voters and candidates

	Voters		Candidates	
Issue	#	(%)	#	(%)
Territorial economic vitality	380	(47.0)	14	(20.3)
Financial situation in territory	123	(13.7)	1	(1.4)
Jobs	104	(11.6)	4	(5.8)
Education	74	(8.2)	7	(10.1)
Costs	51	(5.7)	1	(1.4)
Economic development	28	(3.1)	1	(1.4)
Local economic vitality	189	(23.4)	34	(49.3)
Housing	181	(20.1)	12	(17.4)
Local infrastructure	3	(0.3)	13	(18.8)
Other local issues	5	(0.6)	9	(13.0)
Cultural vitality	103	(11.4)	7	(10.1)
Status and quality of Inuktitut	31	(3.4)	0	
Inuit Qaujimajatuqangit	22	(2.4)	2	(2.9)
Hunting/fishing/quotas	15	(1.7)	1	(1.4)
Article 23	14	(1.6)	1	(1.4)
Role of/treatment of Inuit elders	8	(1.0)	3	(4.3)
Cultural change	8	(1.0)	0	
Inuit leadership	5	(0.6)	0	
Socio-political issues	137	(16.9)	14	(20.3)
Health	40	(4.4)	7	(10.1)
Mental health/suicide	34	(3.8)	1	(1.4)
Political development in the territory	19	(2.1)	0	
Alcohol and drugs	12	(1.3)	0	
Equal opportunities for all	9	(1.0)	0	
Youth issues	8	(1.0)	5	(7.2)
Crime/justice system/abuse	8	(1.0)	1	(1.4)
Family/marriage/same-sex marriage	4	(0.4)	0	
Recreation and sports	3	(0.3)	0	

NOTES: There are 186 unclassified responses. Results are counts, with percentages in parentheses. NuHS participants were responding to the question "What is the biggest challenge facing Nunavut?" Election candidates, by contrast, were asked to identify the most important issues in the election. The first response mentioned has been coded.
SOURCE: 2004 NuHS (*n* = 900).

the wider imagined community of the polity. And yet, even though our traditional understanding of parties is that they help individuals to transcend their personal and local interests, to aggregate these interests and so help to create a relatively coherent mandate, Table 6.2 suggests that individuals perform that task without the aid of political parties. Candidates, not their electors, are far more concerned with local issues, while voters appear more concerned with the needs of the aggregate.

Finally, it is worth noting that not all candidates had a declared platform on which to run. Thus, while some articulated predominantly local concerns, others indicated that they or their campaign team had not yet identified the issues central to the campaign. If candidates themselves do not establish an overarching policy debate, this provides an opportunity for other organizations to identify central issues and, in so doing, to articulate interests to the voters. Much of this task is assumed by the media, an onerous job in a territory with two weekly newspapers, one public radio network, community radio, and only a handful of local or private radio stations.

We know that campaign coverage in southern elections has become dominated by public opinion polls. In the territories, such an endeavour would prove useless as each constituency would require its own poll in order to say anything meaningful about voter intentions. This has not eliminated public opinion polls completely. During the 2004 Nunavut election, one Iqaluit establishment offered a variation on the long-standing American practice of flouting polling regulations by offering "candidate burgers." Individuals would place an order for the Hunter Tootoo burger or the Ed Picco burger, and running tallies for each of the three Iqaluit constituencies were updated daily and put on display. Not surprisingly, the results bore no particular resemblance to the eventual results on election day. Deprived of their staple of public opinion data, the media in Nunavut have taken on a clear role in the identification of key campaign issues. In 2004, the CBC published a list of twenty questions that individuals should ask their candidates and, in so doing, articulated issues to voters just as parties might have done. Each set of questions, on topics such as employment, decentralization, and housing, was prefaced by a short backgrounder that sought to establish for voters the key issues at stake. In some cases, though, the backgrounder seemed to identify not only the key questions one might ask but also the "correct" answers. Voters were urged, for example, to ask candidates how they feel about the devolution of control of resources from Ottawa when, earlier in the document, we read: "Nunavut can't benefit from development until it controls its resources through devolution." The document not only served as a way to articulate interests to voters and thus to integrate them into the polity but also as a method of identifying favoured responses. Attempts to frame other issues were similarly blatant: "Communities need better water and sewage treatment and garbage disposal systems." This material appears surprisingly similar to the party campaign material made available to candidates in partisan systems, except here the same material was made available to all candidates within the polity.

We might expect voters in consensus systems to avoid the polls on election day, given the absence of all the natural cues for making voting decisions. Despite these challenges, turnout during territorial elections points to healthy levels of participation. For each of the 1999 and 2004 elections, levels of turnout were very high, far higher than they are in most southern jurisdictions, and in excess of 100 percent in certain constituencies. Turnout levels above 100 percent are made possible by the enumeration process and the ability of individuals to cast ballots on election day even if their names had not appeared on the voters list. By taking the total number of people who cast ballots and dividing it by what might be considered an artificially low number of people on the electoral register, we are able to produce turnout levels in excess of 100 percent. Even if we use the more conservative American method of dividing by the total number of eligible adults, we find that over two-thirds of adult Nunavummiut are participating in elections, a proportion that compares favourably to that in southern jurisdictions. By comparison, turnout in the most recent NWT election was 68 percent, which included a turnout as high as 150 percent in one constituency.

Consensus politics thus has an obvious impact on the nature of election campaigns. Without political parties to provide institutional or financial support to candidates, the costs of political involvement in consensus systems are far higher for individuals than they are in partisan systems. The costs of political involvement for voters are similarly high as they lack the cues that parties provide regarding issue positions and political information. And yet, within Nunavut, both candidates and voters appear willing to bear those costs. The impact of consensus politics on citizen integration and interest articulation becomes clearer when we look at the operation of the legislative assembly.

Legislative Behaviour in a Consensus System

Consensus politics has a more mechanical influence on the operation of the legislature. In a consensus system, all MLAs, once elected, vote for a speaker and a premier, and then select members of the executive. In such a system the premier does not select his cabinet colleagues, retaining only the right to assign particular portfolios to individuals. A well-liked colleague with whom the premier agrees might be given an important portfolio, while one with whom the leader shares little might be given a minor role or, as happened to Jack Anawak in 2003, be labelled a minister without portfolio. Members of the territorial cabinets do not necessarily share ideological views, goals, or policy preferences. As a result, there is no predetermined coherence, ideological or otherwise, to the mandate of any government, something that observers of brokerage systems might find familiar. And yet cabinet members are still bound by notions of cabinet solidarity. They might have a difficult time arriving at policies, but once cabinet decisions are reached, members are expected to support them regardless of their own preferences or those of their constituents.

Those not elected to cabinet are referred to as "regular members." These MLAs may well lack a shared ideology, goals, or preferences. Without an ideological mooring, the way in which regular members choose to exercise their role as "official opposition" and hold the government to account can vary according to circumstance. In some cases, regular members might act in concert; in others, they might not. Regular members are not whipped to vote as an opposition block, largely because there is no opposition leader to compel obedience, and only on rare occasions have they voted against the government. Decisions in the legislature are based on majority support, and, as Dacks (1986) notes, this means that politics in the north is characterized less by a sense of consensus than it is by an absence of parties. Unanimity on government decisions is neither required nor sought, and, as in partisan systems, 50 percent plus one is all that is needed to pass legislation.

Assessing the role of political parties within a legislature can focus on two discrete tasks: the selection of government and the passing of legislation. With respect to the selection of government, there is clearly a difference between consensus systems and partisan systems. As stated earlier, all members of the legislature have a hand in electing the speaker, premier, and members of the cabinet. While this system may offer a regular member the opportunity to influence the choice of premier, and therefore provide the MLA with greater influence than might otherwise be the case, it denies voters the opportunity to determine who will form a government. Voters have no way to know whether their candidate is going to be elected. Even when a voter's candidate has been elected, there is no way of knowing whether or not the

MLA will become premier or will sit in cabinet. Some voters might hope that their representative would seek a cabinet position, as this might ensure greater financial rewards and infrastructure projects for the community. For others, the demands on cabinet ministers might effectively keep their representative away from the community, thus adversely affecting his or her ability to be an efficient conduit between the community and the legislature.

This lack of influence functions in an active and reactive sense. Voters cannot determine who is in cabinet, nor can they decide who is to be removed. The ability to throw out a government if displeased with its performance is thus not a possibility for voters. At best, individual cabinet ministers can be defeated at the polls, and thus the face of the cabinet can be changed one representative at a time. This lack of opportunity to influence who is in the government could have a psychological impact on citizens, serving to distance them from political affairs and to deny them a political voice that they are able to exercise in federal contests.[3] In the wake of the 2004 election, an editorial in the Iqaluit-based weekly bilingual paper echoed this point (*Nunatsiaq News* 2004a), while an editorial following the previous election claimed that support for a directly elected premier clearly stemmed from "a frustrated public fed up with their inability to influence government policy at election time" (*Nunatsiaq News* 1999).

If we think of the job that the Legislative Assembly could be doing with respect to the integration of citizens, we find some cause for concern. One of the touted benefits of consensus politics is the absence of a needless division between cabinet ministers and regular members. Although the latter have their own committee, they meet regularly with cabinet ministers in sessions that are not open to the public. As White (1991, 521) noted of the NWT, this has a negative impact on the integration of citizens: "NWT ministers are far more accountable to the Assembly than their counterparts elsewhere in Canada, but overall accountability of the government to the people is weak." In other words, there may be lower levels of secrecy between cabinet ministers and regular members, but the public is largely excluded from these deliberations. The publicly accessible plenary debates are, in many respects, merely a summary of decisions taken earlier during in camera meetings. There is evidence, though, that Nunavummiut take advantage of the opportunity to follow political debate. One-quarter of respondents to the 2004 NuHS indicated that they watch televised legislative coverage either nightly or three to four times a week, with a similar proportion indicating that they never watched it. There also appears to be a significant relationship between language and exposure to political information. Unilingual English speakers are far less likely to watch the proceedings than are unilingual Inuktitut or Inuinnaqtun speakers or those able to watch without the need for simultaneous interpretation.

Within the Legislative Assembly two features of consensus politics work at cross-purposes. The first is the tendency for political expertise to be located on one side of the house. All but one of the cabinet ministers who were re-elected in 2004 found themselves again in cabinet, a pattern mirrored in the 2003 NWT election. Within Nunavut, cabinet ministers had higher rates of electoral success than did regular members. Only two of the seven incumbent regular members were returned to Iqaluit. One should note, however, that regular members had a higher success rate in the NWT election, where nine of eleven were returned. These patterns are, of course, quite similar to what we find in legislatures in which one party has been in government for a long time: the government benches remain well stocked with experienced political operators, while the opposition benches contain few with experience of government. This imbalance, then, is not unique to consensus systems. At the same time, a consensus system inhibits incumbency among government leaders. Unlike in partisan systems, where heads of government need only be re-elected by their constituencies, heads of consensus governments must first win re-election in their constituencies and then must secure a second term from fellow MLAs. In a partisan system, the considerable resources of the party can be pressed into action should the incumbent candidate need assistance at the constituency level. This is not the case in consensus systems, where, again, the full costs of the campaign are borne by the candidate and where legislative rivals may emerge to unseat an incumbent premier.[4]

In terms of the selection of cabinet members, the preference for representation of different groups is as evident in consensus systems as it is in partisan governments. Just as there is an effort to find linguistic, gender, ethnic, and regional balance within the federal cabinet (Bakvis 1991; Smith 1985), so, too, do MLAs take certain factors into consideration when electing cabinet ministers. For the most part, these are geographic and informal. The NWT cabinet, for example, has long been composed of representatives from Yellowknife, the southern constituencies, and the northern constituencies, a move recently entrenched by having separate cabinet selection ballots for Yellowknife, the south, and the north.[5] MLAs from Yellowknife, then, compete against each other for Yellowknife positions in cabinet. In Nunavut there is a similar balance among those from Iqaluit, those from the north Baffin, and those from the Kivalliq, and each cabinet has had at least one woman and one representative of the Kitikmeot. In Nunavut, however, the system of regional accommodation is informal.

Despite the fact that cabinet ministers do not share an ideological mooring and regular members have little to bind them, we find remarkably partisan-type behaviour within the Nunavut Legislative Assembly. In part, this is because the legislature still operates according to the principle of cabinet solidarity, with the result that headstrong ministers are effectively whipped into line by their premier. Those refusing to comply with cabinet solidarity face two consequences: they can either be assigned a lesser (or non-existent portfolio) by the premier or be removed from cabinet by their fellow MLAs. This has happened in both Nunavut and the NWT, so the threat is real. In 1987, one NWT minister was voted out of cabinet after he sent a threatening letter to another member, indicating that funding for projects in the latter's constituency might disappear unless the regular member backed the government in a key vote. More recently, Jack Anawak (former Nunatsiaq MP, former interim commissioner of Nunavut, and rival for the premiership) was demoted by the premier to minister without portfolio and was voted out of cabinet by his fellow MLAs for speaking out against a government plan to decentralize jobs in the territorial bureaucracy from Rankin Inlet to Baker Lake.[6] This is not to say that cabinet stability is the hallmark of consensus systems. Cabinet ministers have resigned from time to time in both the NWT and Nunavut for the same types of reasons that bring down cabinet ministers elsewhere in Canada: allegations of fraud and corruption, inappropriate behaviour, and assorted brushes with the law. That breaches of cabinet solidarity have not been a persistent issue in Nunavut raises a number of questions about the motivations of MLAs to speak out or to hide their discontent, about the uniformity of their preferences, or about the limited remit of their decisions. One might wonder whether individual MLAs fail to speak out because the issues they are debating invite no real opposition, because there is universal agreement on these issues, or because the penalties for speaking out are so severe.

On the other side of the house, we have reason to doubt the cohesion of regular members. The much-touted minority status of the executive is, at first blush, of little relevance, given how rarely the regular members have voted together against the government (CBC 2005a, 2005b, 2005c). As White (1991,

513) noted of the NWT, the "ordinary members are simply too disorganized and apprehensive to be effective against the cabinet." Indeed, White noted that the biggest divisions between cabinet and regular members were less salient than the geographical and cultural cleavages that divide them. In the former NWT, far greater divisions existed between representatives of the east and representatives of the west, or between MLAs from Yellowknife and everyone else. In some cases, the divisions were ethnic, grouping Inuit, Dene, and Métis on the one hand and non-Native representatives on the other. When White (1993) asked MLAs about the divisions among them, 60 percent cited cultural divisions as being the most significant.[7]

If we look to Nunavut, we can identify four possible types of divisions. The first of these is geographic and has multiple formulations. One geographic cleavage involves representatives from larger communities on one side and representatives of smaller communities on the other. In Nunavut, smaller communities would include those too small to receive decentralized jobs. Candidates from the smaller communities identified the uneven benefits of decentralization as a frequent campaign issue; smaller hamlets that had not received decentralized jobs have seen little of the positive economic impact anticipated for larger communities. Another geographic cleavage involves representatives from the capital on one side and representatives from all other communities on the other. Debates about capital expenditures often focus on the wealth of infrastructure contained within Iqaluit and the limited availability of capital projects in other communities. A third geographic cleavage is regional. While we have yet to see a cleavage that pits those from the three regions (the Qikiqtaaluk/Baffin, the Kivalliq, and the Kitikmeot) against each other, there is reason to be cautious of a growing sense of western alienation, fuelled both by geographic distance and concerns over the status of Inuinnaqtun. Indeed, for residents of the Kitkimeot, government seemed perhaps closer to the people before 1999, when the capital, Yellowknife, was located in the same time zone and was fewer than two hours away by plane. As of 1999, the new capital, Iqaluit, is two time zones away and can be reached only after two days of travel.

A second type of possible division is ethnic. White's original formulation for the NWT suggests that the interests of Inuit and Dene MLAs might be different from those of non-Native MLAs. In Nunavut, the assumed corollary would be between Inuit MLAs on the one hand and Qallunaat, or non-Inuit, MLAs on the other. We should be cautious of such a formulation. The extent to which this cleavage continues to be salient depends on the continued presence of Qallunaat members in the Legislative Assembly. While the first legislature contained four non-Inuit members, the second contains only two, one of whom is in cabinet. There is also evidence to suggest that Inuit MLAs remain unconcerned by the differences of opinion that might exist across ethnic lines. Inuit MLAs have always entrusted their non-Inuit peers with a number of positions of responsibility, including cabinet positions, committee chairships, and, in the first Legislative Assembly, Speaker of the House.

In what might be considered a variant of ethnic divisions, a third division between MLAs involves those who emphasize Inuit Qaujimajatuqangit (IQ), or Inuit traditional knowledge, and those who do not. This is not quite a division between regular members and cabinet ministers, or between Inuit members and Qallunaat members, although those advocating a greater focus on IQ have been Inuit and have come predominantly from the "regular" side of the house. The presence of older, often unilingual, MLAs from the Baffin region has ensured a focus on and belief in the importance of IQ to the extent that, within the first Legislative Assembly, IQ eventually became a coherent plank from which to attack the executive. When, on the day he was voted out of cabinet, Jack Anawak defended his critique of decentralization, it was not surprising that he did so through the prism of IQ. There are obvious exceptions to this homogeneity. Hunter Tootoo, the sole Iqaluit MLA not in cabinet, has consistently criticized the executive not from the perspective of IQ but from one of transparency and accountability, maintaining that there has been far too little of both.

A final division among MLAs concerns religion. The spread of Christianity throughout the north, facilitated by Roman Catholic and Anglican missionaries, has left the territory dotted by a patchwork of denominational clusters (Remie and Oosten 2002). Some communities are overwhelmingly Roman Catholic, while others contain a clear majority of Anglicans. Only a very few communities contain roughly equal proportions of either denomination. There has been increasing attention to the role of religion in political debate in Nunavut, and news reports from southern Canada regarding the 2004 election campaign suggested that it was the central issue dividing candidates (although such claims have not been borne out). In the first Legislative Assembly, the debate over the Nunavut Human Rights Act couched opposition to protection from discrimination on the grounds of sexual orientation in both religious and ethnic terms. Same-sex marriage, which was not mentioned in the act, was portrayed as anathema to Inuit traditional culture and as irreligious. The religious division operates in different ways. While initially division would have been between Christians and those practising more traditional forms of Inuit spirituality, and later might have characterized itself by rivalry between Christian denominations, it might now distinguish between evangelical and non-evangelical Christians (or between evangelical Christians and everyone else).

Many of these cleavages are crosscutting. Notable by their absence, however, are divisions pertaining to ideology. If we define ideology in left-right terms, there was little evidence of significant ideological divisions among MLAs in the first Legislative Assembly, and there is little evidence of them in the current one. There are a number of possible reasons for this. First, if left-right divisions enunciate rival visions of the state, in the north there is broad-based support for an activist state, something that would make an ideological debate rather lopsided. Second, the structure of campaigning in the north encourages attention to local issues. Third, while MLAs might be well aware of the possible ideological grounds from which to examine any given policy issue, they might believe this to be divisive and, therefore, something best avoided.

If these are rival cleavages to the divisions between regular MLAs and cabinet members, they do not help to explain the low salience of divisions between the two sides of the house. One possible explanation lies in the much-touted Inuit norm of non-confrontation. Another is the incentive structure for regular members. In a partisan system, opposition members are expected to vote according to party lines, lines that are often contrary to the interests of the executive. In a consensus system, the reward system works in the opposite direction. There is little incentive for members to vote against the government. In part, this is because regular members have an opportunity to air their views to cabinet ministers in camera and to ensure that they are incorporated in government legislation. This is, of course, an optimistic justification for low levels of political discord in the legislature. It is equally likely that the reward structure within the Legislative Assembly ensures that MLAs are well aware of the benefits of compliance. As in southern systems, rewards include committee chairs, future cabinet membership, or infrastructure projects for a given member's community, all of which depend on MLAs not running afoul of the powerbrokers within the legislature. In such a situation, regular members have a vested personal interest in not critiquing the government.

Related to this is the issue of federal partisanship. Parties might not operate at the territorial level in Nunavut or the NWT, but it would be unwise to assume that federal partisan structures are irrelevant. In part, this is an artifact of institutional design. While the NWT Council remained the governing body in the Northwest Territories, politics were clearly under the control of the NWT commissioner, who, for many years, was also a federal deputy minister. Ties to federal parties were thus a consistent and unquestioned part of the supposedly non-partisan politics of the NWT. For the most part, it has been the Liberal Party that has colonized territorial politics, and its hold on political life should not be ignored. In spite of the arrival of responsible government in the NWT, there is continued evidence of Liberal dominance. First, the Liberal Party has far more members, far more voters, and far more financial resources in the north than all the other parties combined. Within Nunavut, for the past three elections the Liberal Party has earned more contributions than have all the other parties, gathering upward of $50,000 for each election campaign and usually spending about half this amount. Only in 2004 was Liberal campaign spending in Nunavut rivalled by the spending of other parties; in the previous two elections, the party outspent its rivals by a margin of two to one. These patterns are similar, it should be noted, to the fundraising and spending habits of the Liberal Party in the Western Arctic constituency as well (although it lost that consitutency in 2006). Second, political elites within Nunavut and the NWT have often been members of the Liberal Party, at times holding positions of authority at the territorial and federal levels of the party structure. Every NWT premier since Dennis Patterson has been openly Liberal, a high proportion of cabinet ministers have been Liberals, and a number of senior mandarins are closely identified with the Liberal Party. In the first Nunavut administration, Finance Minister Kelvin Ng sat on the Liberal Party's national executive, cabinet minister and candidate for the premiership Jack Anawak was a former Liberal MP, and cabinet minister Manitok Thompson, upon leaving the legislature, openly contemplated running for the Liberal Party. The method of organization used in territorial politics might not depend on political parties, but we should not ignore the fact that partisanship itself could be a relevant feature in determining cabinet positions, campaign support, and voter recognition, and could affect the perceived degree of consensus within the legislature.[8]

Whatever the reasons, regular members have not been in the habit of voting down government legislation in either the NWT or Nunavut, and non-unanimous votes are relatively uncommon. A lack of support among regular members for certain pieces of government legislation has, however, ensured that such initiatives fall off the order paper, the most noteworthy example of this being the Education Act. Recently, however, this general pattern of compliance has changed. In the second term, regular members have twice voted down government budget items (CBC 2005a, 2005b, 2005c). In March 2004, regular members voted to cut half a million dollars from the budget for the Department of Community and Government Services because they felt the reason for it was no longer relevant. In order to avoid defeat, government ministers abstained from the vote. Later in the same month, regular members passed a motion to withdraw $150,000 from the Department of the Environment's budget because they wanted the money to go to a hunters' support program. Again aware that they were going to lose, ministers abstained from the vote. Both motions, incidentally, were put forward by Tagak Curley, the man who ran for the premiership and lost. If candidates who fail to attain the premiership sit not in cabinet, as was the case with Jack Anawak, but on the other side of the house, then regular members may gain a leader around whom to rally.

Extra-Parliamentary Actors

If the regular members of the Legislative Assembly are largely supportive of the government, and are unable to bring it down even when they stand in cohesive opposition to it, one might ask how effectively consensus governments are critiqued when in office. Part of the answer lies in the multiple sources of opposition to the government. Within the Legislative Assembly, regular members have a formal mechanism for co-ordinating their opposition. The Regular Members Caucus provides an opportunity for members to ensure that the government is accountable. Furthermore, as in southern Canada, the media serve to critique the government. Although tempered by the frequency with which it appears, *Nunatsiaq News* might be considered a second opposition within the territory, publicly criticizing government policy on education, decentralization, and wildlife management. A third source of opposition is Nunavut Tunngavik Incorporated. The successor to the Tungavik Federation of Nunavut, NTI has a four-person executive (elected by all Inuit beneficiaries over the age of sixteen) and a larger board that contains representatives of the three regions in Nunavut. The body charged with ensuring that the NLCA is implemented properly, NTI is not set up as a natural opposition to the government in Nunavut and, more often than not, has the federal government in its sights (although it has also been critical of territorial handling of the Nunavummi Nangminiqaqtunik Ikajuuti [NNI] policy).[9] At times, though, NTI has acted as an unofficial opposition. This was clearest in the years between the signing of the land claim and the first Nunavut elections. In 1997, NTI established a shadow cabinet in which eight of its executive members assumed responsibilities for monitoring eight of the portfolios in the NWT cabinet. According to NTI, this had less to do with holding the NWT cabinet to account than it did with ensuring that there were individuals within Nunavut who had some knowledge of cabinet responsibilities. In such a situation, one might wonder whether regular MLAs are analogous to backbench representatives of the governing party in a partisan system rather than to an official opposition.

What, then, might we conclude about consensus systems? First, the costs of participation are higher for both voters and candidates than they are in partisan systems, but these appear to be borne relatively willingly by both groups. The proportion of people putting themselves forward for election is higher in the north than in the south, and levels of turnout remain above provincial averages. Not all news is positive. In the 2004 NuHS, over 60 percent of Nunavummiut indicated they felt that "people like me have no say" in politics, compared with only 40 percent of southern Canadian respondents to the 2004 CES. Similarly, almost three-quarters of Nunavummiut believed that "politics is so complicated that people like me can't understand it," while just over half of southern Canadians felt this way. Evidence derived from political behaviour is encouraging, but attitudes suggest there is some cause for concern.

Second, in terms of the articulation of interests, we see evidence of a schism between the interests of voters, on the one hand, and candidates, on the other, with candidates appearing to be more interested in local concerns than voters. This contradicts what we might expect in a consensus system and challenges also perceptions that we need parties in order to raise the interests of voters above the local level. This also has an obvious impact on the integration of citizens within an imagined community of voters. Candidates, as agents of political socialization, appear to serve less effectively in this role than they might. Clearly, candidates and the legislature in which representatives sit are not the only agents of political socialization or integration within Nunavut. Rival agents include the media, which play a significant role in the articulation of interests, and Nunavut Tunngavik, which serves to integrate Inuit into an ethnically defined polity. In short, organizations such as the media and land claim bodies might be considered additional means to integrate citizens into the polity, just as they might be considered rival sources of opposition to the government. We should, of course, be wary of equating consensus politics with an automatic concern for local interests. Attention to community and constituency matters often stems from the urgent need for local infrastructure. Concern for local issues might have less to do with consensus politics and more to do with the stage of economic development in the north.

Finally, within the Legislative Assembly, cabinet ministers remain whipped by notions of cabinet solidarity and are often supported by regular members, but even when the latter rebel and vote down the government, political stability is not imperilled. The absence of a coherent government mandate, the greater degree of political experience on the government benches, and cabinet solidarity all mean that consensus politics retains many of the elements familiar to observers of brokerage systems. Cleavages among MLAs have not tended to emerge around legislative functions but reflect the cultural and economic divisions within the north. We might begin to see less of this if losing candidates for the premiership sit outside cabinet and thus provide a rallying point for regular members. The prior absence of regular member rebellion implies, though, that the institutions and individuals within them have created a reward structure that mirrors the activities of political parties. This suggests that the desire for power, rather than its overt use by poliical parties, ensures government stability.

7
Political Participation in Nunavut

Canadians are constantly being bombarded with news that their participation in traditional avenues of politics is decreasing, something that is most evident in the declining turnout rates for federal elections. The same is true in Nunavut, where 54 percent cast a ballot in the 2006 election, although even this level is an improvement on the 44 percent who voted in the federal election two years earlier. And yet there are signs of healthy civic engagement in the eastern Arctic. Since 1999, turnout for territorial elections has been higher than the national average for substate elections. The process through which the NLCA was acquired expanded avenues of civic engagement in the form of plebiscites on the principle and boundaries of division, the location of a new territorial capital, and the gender parity proposal, although turnout rates varied between 29 percent and 79 percent. In addition, Inuit residents in Nunavut have other opportunities to vote. In 1992 Inuit went to the polls to ratify the NLCA with an 81 percent turnout rate. More regular opportunities for participation include elections to the executives of NTI, regional Inuit associations, and hamlet councils and elections within hunter and trapper organizations. These forms of electoral participation take place within a political system in which the costs of staying informed are higher than they are for other Canadian voters. In addition, demographic indicators suggest that levels of political participation should be lower in Nunavut than in the rest of Canada, particularly given the lower levels of income and educational attainment in the territory. Higher rates of participation in territorial elections seem puzzling in light of these facts. In this chapter, I address this puzzle and argue that rates of participation are far lower than is usually estimated and that this is a product of the way voters are enumerated and turnout is calculated. At the same time, the plethora of electoral positions for which one might stand has created a very active political elite, which occupies a larger proportion of the electorate than it does in southern Canada. Participation in territorial elections is thus not greater in Nunavut than it is in other jurisdictions, but rates of participation are far more uneven.

Avenues of Political Participation

Political participation is an essential part of political culture. The avenues available to those seeking to become involved vary among states, as does the willingness of citizens to participate. There are many ways to participate in politics. Individuals can cast a ballot in elections, join political parties, or run as candidates. This avenue of electoral politics has been summarized by Lester Milbrath (1965), who identifies a unidimensional hierarchy of political activity. Those who do not vote are classified as apathetics, those whose primary activity is voting or who are more informed than others are classified as spectators, and those most active, including those belonging to parties or running in elections, are classified as gladiators. According to Milbrath, in any given society there are many spectators and apathetics but very few gladiators. The hierarchy is cumulative, in the sense that apathetic citizens are typically expected to become spectators before they turn to gladiatorial activities. Critics of Milbrath's theory argue that it prioritizes electoral behaviour and, therefore, ignores the possibility that individuals could belong to community organizations or grassroots movements. Such bodies might seek to influence politicians or they might operate without reference to publicly elected officials (Verba, Nie, and Kim 1978). The complaint is that Milbrath does an insufficient job of mapping the plethora of political activities in which individuals might participate. At the same time, his restricted definition of participation serves to exclude from consideration as politically active citizens those individuals most likely to participate in grassroots or community organizations. It is also possible that definitions of gladiatorial activities could vary over an individual's lifetime. Teenagers helping to organize anti-globalization marches or community activists lobbying their local council to provide sidewalks for residents are each engaging in political activities, but neither of these would be considered gladiatorial according to Milbrath's hierarchy.

Research on the *types* of participation possible co-exist with a normative literature about the *amount* of participation that is appropriate for individuals or communities. Generally speaking, communities composed of individuals who are active in social organizations are better able to withstand economic recessions or periods of tumultuous change than are communities in which individuals are isolated. Of course the type of activity matters. Individuals belonging to gangs could be described as engaged members of society, in the sense that they are active in social groups, though this equates gangs with social groups whose purpose is the betterment of society. Participation that prioritizes positive social interaction reinforces the bonds among individuals, creating networks of trust. The result is social capital that can be accumulated and used in the same way as other forms of capital (Bourdieu 1983; Coleman 1988; Putnam 1993).

Canadian research suggests that participation in electoral politics is decreasing. Membership in political parties, never involving much more than 5 percent of the population, is lower now than it was in the 1970s, as is participation in elections. Levels of social capital are assumed to be lower in urban communities than they are in rural areas (Turcotte 2005), among older Canadians, and among the religiously observant. In general, accounts of political participation in Canada suggest that things have changed since the postwar period, when levels of trust, satisfaction, confidence, and deference were higher (Nevitte 1996). Patterns of political participation are changing, as Canadians show themselves to be ever more supportive of unconventional or informal models of participation, such as petitions or boycotts. Indeed, Canadians seem more sympathetic to these modes than do voters in other advanced-industrial countries (Dalton 2002; Nevitte 1996). These patterns are not uniform. In the 1970s and 1980s, Simeon and Elkins (1974, 1980) indicated that provincial borders help to create significant cultural boundaries and to produce differing patterns of efficacy, trust, and involvement. Recent research continues to suggest that there may be provincial subcultures operating within Canada (Adams 2003; Henderson 2004d). Such research typically avoids a discussion of northern Canada, in part because of the paucity of available data. By demography and political institutions, Nunavut and the NWT are distinct entities within Canada (Cameron and White 1995; Clancy 1994; Dickerson 1992; Gibbins 1990; Irlbacher Fox 2004; Ironside 2000; Irwin 1989a; Matthiasson 1992; Mayes 1982; Stabler 1989; White 1991; Whittington 1985). Sizable Aboriginal populations and diseconomies of scale as a result of small populations located within vast geographic spaces point to the existence of a separate regional political culture in the north (Henderson 2004c), something that also serves to separate the provincial north from the urban centres of southern Canada (Coates and Morrison

1992). Demography and the development of institutions in the north have together created a distinct environment for political participation.

Political Participation in Nunavut

In some respects, political life in Nunavut follows the same rhythm as it does in other parts of Canada. There are three levels of government: federal, substate, and local. Parties contest seats in federal elections, and candidates running as independents campaign for seats in local elections, whether for hamlet, settlement, or town councils. The territorial Legislative Assembly operates according to the principles of representative democracy and responsible government. We know, however, that the process of political development in the north has created institutional anomalies. The absence of political parties, although common in municipal councils across Canada, is rare in substate legislatures. After the ratification of the Nunavut Political Accord, the NIC did not see it as part of its remit to recommend the creation of party politics for elections in Nunavut. As the previous chapter explains, the absence of political parties affects access to resources for campaigning, something that, in the north, is further compounded by demography. In her contribution to the research conducted for the Royal Commission on Party Financing and Electoral Reform, Valerie Alia (1990) notes that large distances make political campaigning difficult not only because of the great amount of time required to travel to communities but also because of the cost of that travel. Political campaigns are expensive even in concentrated ridings in southern Canada, but flights among the northern communities in the Baffin and Kitikmeot regions cost thousands rather than hundreds of dollars. Most significant, though, the absence of parties has an obvious impact on voters, for the partisan cues made available to them are absent.

Research on party identification suggests that parties are the main recruiting agent in political life and that they provide individuals with shortcuts and cues to aid them in their electoral participation. Voters need not read the fine print of every piece of legislation but may find it helpful to know how their preferred party feels about various policies. The absence of parties not only makes it harder for individuals to identify the goals of candidates, particularly in the context that Alia describes, but also raises the costs of participation for anyone trying to identify the main issues in any given debate. If parties are a key political recruiting agent, then their absence suggests that citizens might not be drawn to political participation in the way that they might in partisan systems. The absence of an organized opposition and executive within the Legislative Assembly makes it harder for individuals to identify with various aspects of political debate. In this, the structure of political debate in Nunavut appears similar to that described in early civic studies of the United States, where citizens were deemed to possess low levels of knowledge and engagement (Key 1949). In the absence of political parties we would expect individuals to have trouble placing political issues on a meaningful spectrum, identifying the issues upon which candidates campaign, and, therefore, feeling connected to political life.

Demography further compounds the effects of institutions. Studies of political participation demonstrate that younger people tend to participate much less than older people. A young median age for Nunavut could thus result in lower rates of political engagement. Demography has also led to the creation of constituencies that house more than one community. Even after division, seven of the nineteen constituencies contain two communities, while one contains three. On occasion, all candidates come from one community within the constituency, something that is further exacerbated when the constituency houses communities of unequal size. Access to candidates before the election, in addition to access to MLAs after the election, thus varies within these multicommunity constituencies. If consensus elevates the costs of participation, then adjustments for demography ensure that these costs are not spread equally among different communities. This is further compounded by another feature of political life: the absence of media outlets that, in southern Canada, would be essential organs of political debate. The two main sources of print news, *Nunatsiaq News* and *News North*, are both weekly operations, available each Friday and Monday, respectively. Radio and television provide more frequent opportunities to follow political and community affairs, especially the weekly Inuktitut call-in show on CBC North. This reinforces the high costs of political participation in Nunavut. Those seeking to cast an informed ballot must work harder in Nunavut than in partisan systems.

This is the legacy of how residents in the eastern Arctic were integrated into the Canadian political system. And yet, traditional Inuit society offered important lessons for contemporary understandings of political participation. We know that, until the 1950s, individuals living in the eastern Arctic lacked government institutions in which they could participate and that the right to vote in elections was only extended in 1962 for federal contests and in 1966 for territorial elections in the eastern Arctic. At the same time, the small social units that made up Inuit traditional life could be described as high social capital environments. Individuals helped others, providing food, assisting with shelter, clothing, transportation, and hunting implements. We should be wary of equating such behaviour with altruism. Although nurturing behaviour was prized, it was undoubtedly linked to self-reliance (Briggs 1982). Unlike in southern Canada, where social capital is seen to stem, in part, from membership in social clubs, Inuit social capital was not the by-product of social entertainment but stemmed directly from a focus on the link between cooperation and quality of life. Whatever the origins of social capital, northern transitions in the 1950s and 1960s served to erode traditional social networks. The period that produced the greatest increase in opportunities for electoral participation brought relocation to the High Arctic, residential schools, and a dramatic decrease in the amount of time that children spent with their parents. The transition to communities, although placing people in greater geographic proximity to relatives, brought an increase in troubling behaviour. Many of the elder interviews conducted by the NRI suggest that the move to communities facilitated anti-social behaviour (IE 090; IE 214).

> Today we as parents are not controlling our children as they did in the past. This mainly is due to the fact that our children have to attend school and our youngsters have to be taught the white man's way of doing things, which is the only way they can make money to survive as we know it. So if we were to control our children by having them to concentrate on hunting, we would be responsible should they not be able to make a living on their own. (IE 129)

When people moved off the land their days were no longer occupied with particular tasks. The resulting disruption or boredom led some to engage in violent or mischievous behaviour. Although such actions would typically have been addressed by moralizing from an elder, the bonds among individuals were so loosened in community life that admonishment from adults carried far less weight than it had previously. Once traditional social capital weakened, the methods for reinforcing positive behaviour no longer guaranteed the same compliance. If the 1950s and 1960s brought new opportunities to participate, it also weakened the healthy social bonds among individuals.

The distinction between electoral politics and social capital can be seen as a distinction between formal and informal modes of participation. Electoral politics is a formal political contest in which potential lawmakers are selected. Social capital, by contrast, refers to the informal social networks within which individuals operate. The decreased strength of informal networks, brought about by the transformation of life in the 1960s, coincided with an increase in formal opportunities for participation in social life. These included a wealth of elected and unelected bodies devoted to discussing political affairs. The opportunity to participate in community affairs through local councils and committees continues today in the form of local council and district education authorities. Although these two provide the opportunity to engage in formal elections, other local organizations include hunter and trapper organizations. Women's organizations, such as the Nunavut Status of Woman Council and Pauktuutit, the Inuit women's organization, offer more specific opportunities for participation, as do the multiplying IQ councils and groups. Civil society in Nunavut provides its citizens with organizations similar to those found in the south. Sometimes these organizations are the same as the ones found in southern Canada, such as the Royal Canadian Legion, the Elks, or the Girl Guides.[1] Regional, territorial, or national organizations for Inuit provide a significant avenue for political participation (Ittinuar 1981). Although in the 1960s Inuit-specific bodies would have been limited to local Inuit councils and the regional Eskimo councils, these gave way in the 1970s to the Baffin Regional Inuit Association, the Inuit Tapirisat of Canada, the Inuit Land Claims Commission, and the Nunavut Constitutional Forum. As has been mentioned, the Tungavik Federation of Nunavut, established in 1982 to negotiate the land claim, was reconstituted in 1993 as Nunavut Tunngavik Incorporated, which promotes the rights and manages the responsibilities that Inuit beneficiaries received under the NLCA. The four-member executive of NTI is elected by all Inuit beneficiaries over the age of sixteen. Terms for the executive are four years and are staggered so that two positions become available every two years. In the event that, for any reason, members do not complete their terms, elections are more frequent. Three regional Inuit associations – Qikiqtani, Kitikmeot, and Kivalliq – also provide positions for which Inuit land claim beneficiaries may vote or campaign. The Qikiqtani Inuit Association, for example, is the successor to the Baffin Regional Inuit Association and offers sixteen positions for which voters may stand, including president, vice-president, secretary-treasurer, and thirteen general board positions.[2] QIA ensures that the principles of the land claim agreement are upheld in the Baffin region, and selected members of QIA sit alongside members from the other regional Inuit associations on the board of NTI.

NTI and the regional Inuit associations have several roles. NTI represents all Inuit under the land claim and administers all the Inuit-owned land. Along with the regional Inuit associations, it works to facilitate Inuit economic self-sufficiency and cultural well-being. To this end, it offers land-based programs as well as language and cultural programs, and it advocates on behalf of Inuit both within the territory and within Canada. The resources that it accords and the role it has adopted have turned NTI into a second political authority in Nunavut. The existence of two political systems, one public and one for Inuit beneficiaries of the land claim, speaks to the dual nature of political life in Nunavut, something that has its roots in the way Inuit were integrated into the Canadian political system. It was the NLCA that ensured the creation of a public government for all residents of Nunavut. Thus political change, driven by Inuit, resulted in a new territory for all within the eastern Arctic, whether Inuit or non-Inuit. It also means that there are uneven opportunities for Nunavummiut to participate: Inuit may participate in electoral politics through the land claim organizations as well as through the public government. This is in addition to opportunities, particularly for bilingual employees with political experience, to become involved with a number of appointed administrative positions.

The features of political life in Nunavut suggest the following:

- the consensus system raises the costs for campaigners and voters;
- demographic indicators suggest lower levels of participation in Nunavut than in the rest of Canada; and
- the presence of land claim organizations provides rival opportunities for individuals to participate in the political life of the territory.

Each of these would serve to dampen territorial participation, and yet we know that turnout rates are higher than we might expect. There are two possible explanations for this. First, participation in territorial politics is greater than is the case in the south because the territory – rather than the local community or country as a whole – is the primary political community for territorial residents. If territorial politics is prioritized over federal, local, or land claim politics, it might not matter that the costs of participation are high. Second, southern cost-benefit models of political involvement might prove incapable of accounting for patterns of political participation in the north. Here we would expect to find that new Nunavut-specific predictors are better able to explain voter turnout than those typically used in southern Canada.

Assessing Levels of Formal Participation

Before we attempt to explain the different levels of political participation in Nunavut, it is essential to identify the proportion of individuals who go to the polls in any given election. This, of course, is but one form of political participation. Membership in political parties is another, although the absence of parties at the territorial level would likely dampen enrolment figures, making comparisons with other jurisdictions less useful.

The process by which Inuit acquired a land claim and new territory provided five opportunities to vote, details of which appear in Table 7.1. In 1982, residents throughout the NWT voted on the principle of division, and ten years later they voted again on the proposed boundary. That same year, Inuit in the land claim area voted to ratify the land claim in a plebiscite. After the claim, the eastern Arctic electorate voted in 1995 on the location of the capital, and two years later on the gender parity proposal. In four of the plebiscites, turnout was higher than in federal elections but lower than in territorial elections. This is consistent with the 75 percent eastern Arctic turnout for the 1992 referendum on the Charlottetown Accord. Variations in turnout rates can be explained in part by the circumstances surrounding the vote. Turnout in the 1992 boundary plebiscite could have been elevated by fears that a low rate of turnout among Inuit would have allowed the majority of Mackenzie Valley voters to dictate developments in the eastern Arctic. The 1997 gender parity plebiscite, which voters ultimately rejected, prompted

TABLE 7.1

Turnout in land-claim–related plebiscites, 1982-97

		Turnout	Yes	No
1997	Gender parity	39.0	42.7	57.3
1995	Capital	79.0	59.9 (Iqaluit)	40.1 (Rankin)
1992	NLCA ratification	80.9	69.0	31.0
1982	Principle of division	69.0*	82.0	18.0

* Results for eastern Arctic only. NWT results are 53 percent turnout with 56 percent support.

TABLE 7.2

Turnout in federal elections, 1979-2006

	Canada	Nunatsiaq/ Nunavut	Month of election	Gap (Nunavut-Canada)
1979	76.0	65.0	May	-9.0
1980	69.0	66.8	February	-2.2
1984	75.0	69.0	September	-6.0
1988	75.3	74.3	November	-1.0
1993	69.6	67.5	October	-2.1
1997	67.0	59.8	June	-7.2
2000	61.2	54.1	November	-7.1
2004	60.9	43.9	June	-17.0
2006	64.7	54.4	January	-10.3

NOTE: The Nunatsiaq constituency was created in 1976.

the lowest levels of participation. The Inuit leadership involved in the negotiation of the NLCA and the Nunavut Political Accord was relatively united on the issue of the boundary division and the land claim, and was largely silent on the location of the capital. This was not the case for the gender parity proposal, which was more divisive than other issues (Dahl 1997; Gombay 2000; Young 1997). The inconsistent message coming from negotiators, and the general unwillingness of the electorate to embrace a fundamental reform of their institutions (as seen in the public consultations of the NIC), could account for the low turnout in that plebiscite.

For federal elections, turnout in Nunavut is lower than it is in the country as a whole, although it is by no means the least active jurisdiction. Since 1976, when the eastern Arctic acquired its own constituency, turnout rates have lagged behind Canadian rates by an average of seven points, and the gap between voters in Nunavut and those in the rest of the country is increasing. Table 7.2 identifies the gap for each of the federal elections since 1979. In the 1980s, turnout rates lagged behind Canadian rates by three points, and in the 1990s by 4.7 points. Since the turn of the century, however, Nunavut turnout rates have been over eleven points below the Canadian average. Additional information is gleaned from turnout rates in territorial elections.

In the last territorial election for the undivided NWT, the eastern communities reported an average turnout rate of 83 percent. As Table 7.3 demonstrates, these ranged from a low of 25 percent in Nanisivik to a high of 318 percent in Bathurst Inlet. Among current communities, the range is from 64

TABLE 7.3

Turnout in Nunavut communities and constituencies, 1995-2006

	Average turnout	(Standard deviation)	High	Low
1995 territorial (NWT)[a]	83.2	(48.3)	318.2 (Bathurst Inlet)	24.8 (Nanisivik)
1997 federal	59.8	(12.6)	87.5 (Bathurst Inlet)	34.9 (Repulse Bay)
1999 territorial	88.6	(15.8)	111.3 (Cambridge Bay)	23.7 (Nanisivik)
2000 federal	54.1	(10.6)	74.2 (Chesterfield Inlet)	29.4 (Nanisivik)
2004 territorial[b]	97.8	(17.0)	143.0 (Uqqummiut)	77.8 (Nanulik)
2004 federal	42.3	(7.5)	57.7 (Sanikiluaq)	31.0 (Kugaaruk)
2006 federal	53.8	(9.3)	75.3 (Whale Cove)	32.8 (Kugaaruk)

a This is the turnout rate for Nunavut constituencies within the NWT. In this election the western constituencies had a turnout rate of 72.5, producing an overall turnout rate of 76.2.
b Results for the 2004 territorial election are for constituencies, not communities.

percent in Igloolik to 104 percent in Iqaluit. Turnout for the 1999 election, the first for the newly established Legislative Assembly, was 89 percent, higher than turnout in other provincial elections. Within the territory, turnout levels range from 68 percent in the northern constituency of Quttiktuq to 115 percent in Cambridge Bay.[3] Turnout was even higher in the second territorial election, with a 98 percent participation rate. If we compare these to federal elections, we see quickly that turnout in territorial contests is higher. It is also worth noting that there is considerable variation among communities in territorial elections and less variation in federal elections. There are, however, several reasons to treat these numbers cautiously.

First, turnout in territorial elections may be recorded above 100 percent if individuals who were not originally on the electoral list appear on voting day with proof of eligibility. When turnout is calculated, the former denominator is used, which would elevate the reported level of turnout. Second, there is a significant gap between the number of registered voters in Nunavut and the number of eligible voters. This also suggests that the denominator is smaller than it should be, resulting in an overrepresentation of turnout at the territorial level. An example helps to prove this point.

In 2004, Nunavut residents had three opportunities to cast ballots, a fourth if they were Inuit beneficiaries of the NLCA. The second territorial election took place in February 2004, the federal election took place four months later in June, and the municipal elections were the last month of the year. If we calculate the turnout rates for the territorial constituencies in the 2004 territorial and federal elections, we see a significant gap in participation rates.[4] In the federal election, only three constituencies reported a turnout level at or in excess of 50 percent. For the remaining constituencies, less than half of all registered adults cast a ballot. In five constituencies, approximately one-third of adults participated in the federal election. If we compare these rates of participation with those registered in the territorial election, levels of turnout appear healthier. Only one constituency reported a turnout rate below 80 percent. If we examine the number of eligible adults in each of the territorial constituencies, however, the federal electors list contains far more people than the territorial list. Admittedly, this ignores the minor variations in eligibility between the two electoral rolls, but the territorial list underreports the number of eligible adults for each of the constituencies in Nunavut. This varies by constituency. In the Nanulik constituency, the territorial list contains only thirty-one fewer adults than does the federal list. All other constituencies have between 109 and 586 fewer individuals on the territorial list. In the three Iqaluit constituencies 1,986 adults are present on the federal electoral register but are missing from the territorial register. The total gap between territorial and federal voting lists is 5,417, or 37 percent of the total electorate. If we know that turnout is calculated by the following formula:

$$\text{Turnout} = \frac{\text{total votes cast}}{\text{total registered voters}}$$

and we know that the number of total registered voters is one-third smaller than it is in federal elections, then the reported territorial turnout level will appear larger than it would otherwise. We can, of course, adjust these numbers. If we use the number of eligible adults identified on the federal list as the denominator for calculating territorial turnout, we can create an adjusted assessment of participation in the territory. The new results clarify the extent of the overreport problem with territorial turnout figures.

As Table 7.4 indicates, the adjusted figures are lower than the original territorial rates of turnout by, on average, thirty-five points. For the territory as a whole, the new turnout rate is 62.5 percent rather than 98 percent. Because underreporting varies among constituencies, so, too, does the gap between original and adjusted rates. In the Nanulik constituency, which has

TABLE 7.4

Adjusted turnout rates for Nunavut elections, 2004

	Federal turnout	Official territorial turnout	Adjusted territorial turnout
Akulliq	34.09	93.33	75.90
Amittuq	42.38	120.10	59.85
Arviat	50.00	81.10	70.46
Baker Lake	36.47	89.50	78.40
Cambridge Bay	59.98	102.13	63.40
Hudson Bay	66.59	96.09	70.91
Kugluktuk	33.09	134.33	65.69
Nanulik	40.64	77.78	73.75
Nattilik	34.43	107.04	71.14
Pangnirtung	45.33	83.95	61.06
Quttiktuq	33.33	81.34	61.31
South Baffin	40.60	109.17	49.61
Tunnuniq	45.95	90.22	62.00
Uqqummiut	43.35	143.34	70.20
Iqaluit	49.02	105.74	51.24
Total	43.90	98.00	62.90

NOTE: The figures for Iqaluit report the average turnout for all three constituencies within the capital.

the smallest gap between the number of registered voters on territorial and federal lists, the new adjusted figure is only four points lower than the original estimate. In Amittuq, where there is a 586-person gap between the territorial and federal lists, the adjusted turnout rate is half the original reported rate. Kugluktuk, which had one of the highest turnout rates in the territorial election, reports only average participation rates in the new adjusted figures. Turnout in territorial elections is not significantly higher than in federal elections, although participation rates are certainly elevated. The general pattern of greater participation in territorial elections holds, although the extent of the gap is smaller than originally believed. Table 7.4 also clarifies which communities are most active and which record lower rates of participation.

The existence of Inuit birthright organizations such as NTI and the regional Inuit associations provides additional opportunities for Inuit to vote. Turnout rates for recent elections appear in Table 7.5. All Inuit beneficiaries may cast votes for NTI board positions and one of three regional Inuit associations (Qikiqtani, Kitimeot, Kivalliq). Turnout for these organizations is

TABLE 7.5

Turnout for NTI executive positions, 1999-2006

	Turnout
2006 1st VP	23.0
2004 president and 2nd VP	37.0
2001 president, 1st, and 2nd VP	45.0
1999 president + 2nd VP	32.0

generally lower, although it is worth noting that, in this case, the electorate includes sixteen- and seventeen-year-olds. We know from existing research that younger members of the electorate are less likely to vote than are those in their forties and fifties. This suggests that, if voting patterns in Nunavut are consistent with those in other parts of Canada, the inclusion of sixteen- and seventeen-year-olds in the voting population could produce lower levels of turnout. Since the signing of the NLCA in 1993, turnout for birthright elections has ranged from approximately 30 percent to, on occasion, 60 percent. Turnout for the most recent NTI presidential election in 2004 was 37 percent, which is about average for these types of elections. Participation rates in non-presidential elections, for the first vice-president, for example, are lower still, as is turnout for the regional association elections. Turnout for the 2000 and 2002 QIA elections were 40 percent and 33 percent, respectively. These rates obviously have more in common with turnout rates for municipal elections across Canada than they do with rates for federal or territorial/provincial elections.

Identifying Predictors of Turnout

In most Canadian jurisdictions, turnout rates are usually highest for federal elections and lowest for municipal elections, with provincial or territorial rates falling in between (Johnston 1980; Kornberg, Mishler and Clarke 1982; Studlar 2001; Wilson and Williams 1998). In Nunavut, territorial rates are higher than federal rates, with NTI election turnout rates comparable to those at the municipal level. To better understand political participation in Nunavut, we can explore why territorial turnout rates are higher than federal turnout rates. We can also attempt to identify the general factors propelling voters to the polls. It is helpful, of course, to look at the known predictors of turnout. Factors likely to increase turnout include both individual factors, such as age and level of education, and systemic factors, such as a proportional election system and the perception of a meaningful electoral contest (Blais 2000; Blais and Dobryzynska 1998; Crewe, Fox, and Alt 1977; Franklin 1999; Franklin 2002; Gray and Caul 2000). Factors likely to decrease turnout include the frequency of elections and a geographically dispersed electorate. Nunavut possesses several factors that would lead one to predict low levels of voter turnout.

There are several possible reasons for the low rates of federal voter turnout, some more plausible than others. Variations in Canadian turnout rates have been linked to seasons. Elections held during vacation periods or in inclement weather are thought to result in lower levels of turnout. An examination of federal turnout in Nunavut suggests that there is no link between colder average temperatures and the lure of seasonal hunting schedules. The June 2004 federal election saw the largest gap between federal turnout and turnout in Nunavut, with 61 percent of Canadians voting federally and only 44 percent of residents voting in Nunavut. The June 1997 election saw much higher rates of participation in Nunavut than in the 2004 election. If we distinguish among seasons and look for patterns in turnout rates, we find no statistical relationship between the two.[5]

Nunavut has the youngest electorate in Canada. The median age of Nunavummiut is 22.1 years. The median age in the rest of Canada, by contrast, is 37.6 years. In Nunavut, only 8.8 percent of the electorate hold university degrees, while in the rest of Canada 17 percent of the electorate do so. These gaps widen if we focus on the Inuit population. The median age of Inuit is 19.1 years, and only 1.7 percent of Inuit have university degrees. If these two features are predictors of political behaviour, we would expect lower levels of turnout in Nunavut than in the rest of the country.

In terms of systemic effects, we know that none of the federal, territorial, municipal, or birthright elections operate according to proportional electoral systems. All employ a majoritarian first-past-the-post method. Furthermore, the electorate is geographically dispersed. None of the communities in Nunavut is joined to any other by roads. While two communities, Iqaluit and Rankin Inlet, contain more than one territorial constituency within their boundaries, eight constituencies contain communities that are separated by hundreds of kilometres. These two phenomena are often associated with lower electoral turnout.

Another factor is the perception of a meaningful electoral battle. We can assume that an electoral battle is meaningful if it is close or if it is fought between diametrically opposing views. At the territorial level, the absence of polling and local daily media makes it less likely that individuals will know whether or not the electoral race is a tight one. Furthermore, the absence of political parties would make it hard for individuals who pay only cursory attention to political campaigns to know whether the views of candidates are similar or remarkably different. The sheer size of the constituencies inhibits all-candidate debates that might expose these differences. In short, it is not that electoral battles in Nunavut are not hotly contested or that they do not involve radically different visions of political life but that it is hard to tell whether they are.

At the federal level, the pattern of hegemonic support for the Liberal Party precludes a meaningful or close electoral battle. The 2006 election was unusual as the Liberal Party gained only 40 percent of the popular vote. In 2000 and 2004, by contrast, it earned 70 percent and 51 percent of the vote, respectively. In Nunavut, the Liberal Party makes money from elections, raising more than it spends. In 2000, it raised $65,000 and spent $35,000. This contrasts with the Progressive Conservatives (PCs), who in 2000 raised and spent about $6,000. In 1997, the PCs raised $4,000 but spent $11,000. The amounts raised by the two main parties, and the gap between fundraising and spending, are indicative of the dominant position of the Liberal Party in Nunavut.

Typically, federal elections in Nunavut involve fewer small parties and fewer candidates than do elections in the rest of the country, where, on average, six candidates contest seats. This is consistent with research that suggests urban electoral contests field larger and more diverse lists of candidates than do rural contests. In Nunavut, the Green Party has joined the three main parties. Candidates from smaller parties are rare, although in 2004 former MLA Manitok Thompson ran as an independent, and in 2006 the Marijuana Party fielded a candidate. The Reform and Alliance parties were less active in the territory than they were in other parts of the country.[6]

A final predictor of turnout is the frequency of elections. As the number of voting opportunities increases, voters feel a decreasing sense of urgency to cast a ballot in each contest. This helps to explain turnout levels in Switzerland and the United States, where elections occur more frequently than in other polities. If trips to the polls dampen turnout, then we have reason to expect low levels of turnout in Nunavut. Since 1992, the Nunavut electorate has had twelve opportunities to cast a ballot: four plebiscites, three territorial elections, and five federal elections. This works out to approximately one election per year and excludes elections for local councils and mayoral positions. For Inuit, this number is higher still, with an additional plebiscite in 1992, NTI elections every two years, and regular elections for the regional Inuit associations. As a result, voters in Nunavut, and particularly Inuit voters, have been to the polls more frequently than have voters in any other province or territory.

Each of these predictors would help to explain why federal turnout in Nunavut would be lower than average. And yet we know that participation rates in territorial elections are higher than the Canadian average. We need to identify potential predictors that would elevate turnout in territorial contests. Research on turnout in federal systems distinguishes between first-order and second-order elections. First-order elections are for legislatures that are perceived to have the greatest impact on the lives of voters. Second-order elections, by contrast, are for legislatures of lesser importance. Voters often cast ballots in second-order elections on the basis of factors relevant to first-order elections. Originally this research was conducted in a European context (Reif 1985; Reif and Schmidt 1980). Residents in Spain or the United Kingdom cast ballots in European elections on the basis of national political events rather than European Union issues. Here, the state-level elections were first-order elections, and the supranational European elections were second-order elections. This works in a federal context as well (Curtice 2003; Hough and Jeffery 2006). Voters living in Nova Scotia might cast ballots for the provincial Liberals if they approve of the work done by the federal Liberals. Such research also argues that turnout in first-order elections is higher than in second-order elections. If this theory accurately described political participation in Nunavut, we would expect territorial turnout to be lower, and we would expect Nunavummiut to cast their ballots on the basis of federal politics. The absence of political parties in territorial contests provides one stumbling block, although it is possible for the informal networks around party membership to affect political participation at the territorial level. More damning, though, turnout rates in the supposedly second-order territorial elections are higher than they are in national contests. Part of the explanation for this may stem from the perceived primacy of the legislature or from the perception of a meaningful political community. Part of what makes state-level elections more important is the perceived influence of the federal legislature on policy that affects the lives of individuals. If, however, another legislature produces legislation of greater importance to people than that produced by the state, it may well assume first-order importance. The presence of a meaningful community is salient here (Henderson 2003c; McEwen 2003; Pammet and Leduc 2004; Parallés and Keating 2003; Parry and Moyser 1984). If Nunavummiut believe that the territory is their primary political community – more so than their local community or Canada as a whole – then the legislature at the centre of that political community will be more important than will a less proximate assembly.

Because the Nunavut Legislative Assembly stems from a land claim that quite literally defined the existence of a political community, we have reason to believe that residents see its elections as first-order contests. The jurisdiction of the legislature is also relevant, relating as it does to cultural issues such as language strength and IQ (Inuit Qaujimajatuqangit), wildlife conservation, and education. Despite the traditional importance of the federal government in the lives of Inuit, the territorial government, through the manner of its creation and through its jurisdiction, most directly affects the lives of territorial residents. This is more true for Nunavut than for other political jurisdictions in Canada because the boundaries are drawn around a political community and because of the cultural components to territorial jurisdiction. The first-order/second-order dichotomy may hold in Nunavut, but it works in the opposite way from what it does in the rest of Canada. In this, voters in Nunavut may share more with the Quebec electorate than they do with voters in Manitoba or Ontario. In Quebec, voters cast their ballots in federal elections on the basis of factors relevant to political debate internal to the substate nation. Although we lack comparable survey data for Nunavut, it is possible that Nunavummiut perform similar calculations when participating in federal contests. This is not to say that all individuals within Nunavut place greater importance on the work of the territorial government, but that in the aggregate this could help to explain territorial participation rates.

The 2004 NuHS asked individuals about their sense of identity and whether they felt closer to their municipality, their region, their territory, or Canada. Inuit respondents were also given the option of identifying most as Inuit rather than with a geographic entity. The results, displayed in Table 7.6, provide interesting findings about divisions between Inuit and Qallunaat respondents. A majority of Qallunaat residents identify with Canada. Most Inuit, however, identify with their ethnic group and only 12 percent identify with Canada. This might explain lower turnout rates in federal elections. If we are looking for proof that Nunavut residents identify most with the territory, however, the results do not immediately confirm this. It is possible that there is a degree of overlap between the political boundaries of the territory

TABLE 7.6

Primary identity attachments among Nunavut residents

	Nunavut	Nunavut Inuit	Nunavut Non-Inuit
Community/region	21.1	18.8	29.9
Territory	11.7	11.0	20.1
Canada	19.8	11.7	50.5
Inuit	46.0	58.2	na

SOURCE: 2004 NuHS, $n = 900$. Results are column percentages.

and the ethnic boundaries of Inuit identity. Thus, a high proportion identifying as Inuit rather than with Canada might indirectly explain high territorial voter turnout. Given attachment to ethnic identity and to community, the results cannot explain the relatively low rates of turnout for NTI elections and municipal elections. In order to better understand the relationship among predictors of political participation, we must turn to a multivariate analysis.

To determine whether any of these predictors affect political participation in the territory, we can perform two tasks. First, we can examine turnout levels by geographic area and compare these with demographic indicators for communities. We can determine whether larger communities, those with older populations, or those with higher levels of income have higher turnout rates. Second, we can turn to individual-level datasets. Here we can see, for example, whether individuals who are older, who earn a larger income, or who are living in larger communities are more likely to vote. The distinction between datasets is an important one. Individual-level data are relatively rare in the north, while aggregate-level data are easier to obtain. Aggregate-level data can explain general links among indicators, but we run the risk of committing an ecological fallacy if we rely on them to say something meaningful about the behaviour of individuals. What is true for the community as a whole is not necessarily true for all individuals within the community. The following analysis uses two datasets. The first explores turnout in the federal and territorial elections since 1995, while the second explores individual-level voting in four 2004 elections: territorial, federal, municipal, and NTI. In each case, the dependent variable is voter turnout.

We can test the impact of different variables on turnout by creating a database composed of all communities in Nunavut. The database contains information about levels of turnout in past elections and basic demographic

TABLE 7.7

Aggregate predictors of turnout in elections

	Territorial turnout		Federal turnout
	1995	1999	2000
Population	.069	.721**	-.290
Inuit	.173	.827**	-.400
Inuktitut	.366*	.048	.574
Income	.961***	.581*	.034**
Adjusted R^2	.431	.383	.230

NOTE: $n = 25$. Results are standardized coefficients from OLS regression. * = $p < .1$; ** = $p < .05$; *** = $p < .01$.

information such as population, population change, and density; economic predictors such as income, unemployment rates, proportion employed in manufacturing, resource, and service sectors; levels of educational attainment; average age; and variables related to ethnicity and language use. Table 7.7 contains the results of three ordinary least-squares (OLS) regression analyses.[7] The tests examine the independent impact of four variables on voter turnout in the 1995 and 1999 territorial elections. The 2000 federal election is included for comparison. The independent variables are population, ethnicity, language, and income, measured as the size of the community, the proportion of community residents who are Inuit, the proportion who report that they speak Inuktitut, and the average family income. Population size is included for two reasons. Larger communities have greater employment opportunities and provide more diverse political environments, both of which could better embed individuals within their political community and increase the salience of elections. The number of Inuit in a constituency is included as a test of civic fatigue. If Inuit enjoy more frequent opportunities to vote, and trips to the polls are seen as predictors of lower turnout, then we might expect that turnout in communities with a higher proportion of Inuit would be lower. The proportion that speak Inuktitut is employed as a measure of political community. It is possible that turnout is higher among residents in Nunavut than it is in the rest of Canada because the territory provides a more meaningful political community than do other jurisdictions. If this is the case, we would expect the proportion of the population speaking Inuktitut to be a significant positive predictor of turnout. Age is not included as the average age across communities does not vary significantly. Similarly, levels of education have little variation.

The results contain several interesting findings. First, income is obviously relevant to turnout. Communities with higher average incomes have higher participation rates than do poorer communities. This holds across time and across type of election. Second, for all other predictors, locus and time matter. Predictors of turnout in 1995 are different from those relevant in 1999. This is to be expected. In the united territory, the proportion of residents who speak Inuktitut is a significant and positive predictor of participation. In 1999, by contrast, the proportion of Inuit residents is a better predictor, as is population size. It is possible that, since the 1999 election was for a legislature created by the NLCA, ethnicity was a more relevant factor than it had been in the united NWT. Third, the predictors relevant to territorial participation are, with the exception of income, not relevant to participation in a federal context. Fourth, the territorial models perform better than the federal model. The adjusted R^2 provides a measure of model fit. The independent variables account for 43 percent of variation in participation in 1995 and 38 percent in 1999. These results are quite high, given the exclusion of theoretically significant variables such as age and education. The federal model, by contrast, accounts for one-quarter of the varying participation rates among Nunavut communities.

We know, of course, that other factors might affect turnout. The nature of the electoral contest itself can propel voters to the ballot box or encourage them to stay at home. If we examine the eventual margin of victory for the winner, the number of candidates in the election, and the presence of an incumbent, none of these proves to be a relevant predictor of voter behaviour in territorial elections. In federal elections within Nunavut, these factors remain constant so we cannot test for their effects. A better understanding of turnout in different contexts can be gleaned from additional data.

Since division there have been two versions of the NuHS. The 2001 survey relied on face-to-face interviews conducted in either English or Inuktitut. The sample for the survey was large, at just over 5,800. The 2004 survey contains a 900-person sample and was conducted over the telephone. Despite the smaller sample size, the second survey is more useful for it asks a broader range of questions related to political participation. Participants were asked, for example, whether they were interested in politics, whether they were satisfied with the operation of democracy in Canada and Nunavut, and what they thought of political parties and various modes of political participation. Four questions are of particular interest. Individuals were asked whether they had voted in the 2004 territorial election, whether they had voted in the federal election, whether they voted in the most recent municipal election, and whether they had voted in the 2004 NTI presidential election. These four questions provide us with an unprecedented opportunity to test for predictors of participation in four very different settings at a fixed point in time.

In the sample, 72.5 percent of NuHS respondents indicated that they voted in the 2004 federal election, 68.5 percent in the NTI election, 63.5 percent in the federal election, and 62.5 percent in the most recent municipal election. These figures point to a significant overreport problem for three of the elections, while lending credence to the notion that the territorial figures for turnout are higher than the federal figures. We know, for example, that the reported turnout for the 2004 federal election was closer to 44 percent. NTI turnout was 37 percent. We can be confident that the NTI community list is accurate, stemming as it does from the list of beneficiaries. Only self-reported turnout in the territorial election is lower than the official estimate, although it is larger than the adjusted figure of 62.5 percent. Overreporting is a common problem. In the Canadian election studies, the proportion of respondents who indicate that they cast a ballot is always larger than the reported turnout rate. This gap may stem from two likely causes. First, the sample might do a better job of capturing those elements of the population more likely to vote and a poorer job of capturing those least likely to vote; the individuals included in the sample are likely more active than the population as a whole. Second, we know that when responding to surveys individuals have a propensity to identify socially desirable answers. For some people, voting is a socially desirable act, and individuals may have claimed to vote even when in fact they did not. A third possibility, likely accounting for only a small portion of the gap between self-report and official turnout, is imperfect recall. Asked several months later whether they cast a ballot in the February 2004 territorial election, individuals may have recalled inaccurately whether they voted or not. While these numbers may prompt us to doubt the reliability of our data, they present problems that are common to quantitative datasets.

The following analysis relies on four sets of independent variables. The first includes demographic variables such as age, income, ethnicity, mother tongue, and community size, variables that replicate those employed above. It also includes gender and dwelling condition. The remaining sets of variables are grouped under three themes: cultural community, political values, and views of the contemporary political system. Cultural community includes two variables created by factor analysis: traditional activities, which includes harvesting and the production of crafts, and land-based activities, such as spending time on the land or eating country food.[8] This theme also includes an identity variable, which was created out of two questions, one asking Inuit and non-Inuit respondents whether they feel closest to their community, region, territory, or Canada, the other directed specifically at Inuit and asking whether this best describes their identity. In the four analyses below, the identity community variable rotates, so that when testing for federal turnout, attachment to Canada is included; when testing for municipal turnout, attachment to community is included; and so on. These variables provide a more robust measure of political community than do the ethnic and language variables employed in the aggregate-level analysis. A third set of variables deals with political values and consists of three variables created by factor analysis. The political activity variable, for example, was created by combining scores for political interest and summing the variables for political contact methods such as petitioning, contacting politicians, attending rallies, working with others, and so on. The deference variable includes questions related to the role of parties and the perception that politics is too complicated. The cynicism variable includes questions that explore views of MPs, the sense that parties divide voters more than they unite them, and the idea that voters have no say. These variables help us to assess a respondent's attitude toward politics in general. The last set of variables includes those that probe the respondent's view of the contemporary political system. These include a factor on democratic assessment, which probes democratic satisfaction in Canada and Nunavut, as well as a question on political developments in Nunavut. Respondents were asked whether they believed the new territory would allow Nunavummiut to better govern their lives. We would expect that those holding more positive evaluations of contemporary politics and those more sympathetic to politics in general would be more likely to vote in elections.

The results of the regression analysis are presented in Table 7.8. First, demographic variables perform consistently as predictors of turnout, regardless of the particular election. Age is positively associated with turnout in three of the four cases: older respondents were more likely to vote than were younger respondents. Speaking Inuktitut was also positively associated with turnout, other things being equal. Being Inuit, however, was largely irrelevant. In NTI elections, of course, only Inuit can vote, so this variable was excluded from the NTI regression. Ethnic status was relevant only in municipal contests,

TABLE 7.8

Individual predictors of turnout in 2004

	Federal		Territorial		Municipality		NTI	
Constant	.108	(.26)	.415	(.22)*	.503	(.23)**	.103	(.16)
Socio-economic status								
Age	.414	(.19)**	.238	(.16)	.352	(.16)**	.658	(.12)***
Gender	-.041	(.10)	.032	(.08)	.132	(.09)	.127	(.07)*
Inuit	-.260	(.19)	-.117	(.15)	-.388	(.17)**	Na	
Inuktitut	.532	(.22)**	.729	(.18)***	.807	(.19)***	.581	(.09)***
Community size	-.220	(.14)	-.255	(.12)*	-.301	(.12)**	.068	(.10)
Dwelling condition	.205	(.17)	.028	(.14)	-.049	(.14)	-.329	(.11)***
Income	.220	(.18)	.581	(.15)***	.034	(.15)	.175	(.12)
Cultural community								
Traditional activities	.061	(.05)	.028	(.04)	.037	(.05)	.002	(.03)
Land connection	-.030	(.05)	-.051	(.04)	-.127	(.05)***	-.030	(.03)
Identity community	.011	(.11)	.080	(.11)	-.090	(.10)	.068	(.06)
Political values								
Political cynicism	-.049	(.05)	-.087	(.04)*	-.027	(.05)	.100	(.03)***
Political engagement	.142	(.04)***	.069	(.04)*	.105	(.04)[b]	.018	(.04)
Deference	.034	(.05)	.091	(.04)**	.006	(.05)	.014	(.03)
Political evaluations								
Nunavut good	.140	(.17)	-.342	(.14)**	-.096	(.15)	.052	(.10)
Democratic satisfaction	-.087	(.05)	.088	(.04)**	.090	(.05)*	.011	(.05)
Adjusted R²	.27		.47		.47		.91	

SOURCE: NuHS 2004; n = 900. Results are unstandardized coefficients with standard errors in parentheses. * = $p < .1$; ** = $p < .05$; *** = $p < .01$.

where Inuit were less likely to vote. Community size was relevant twice, once for municipal elections and once for territorial elections. In each case, those from smaller communities were more likely to vote than were those from larger communities, whether decentralized communities or the capital. Income was relevant once, again for territorial elections. This suggests that the importance of income in the previous aggregate analysis may have been a proxy for other variables not captured by the existing model. Second, membership in a particular cultural community appears to be irrelevant. Thus, participation in traditional activities and time spent on the land cannot explain participation in territorial, federal, or NTI elections. A cultural variable is only relevant for municipal elections. Here, those spending less time on the land are more likely to cast a ballot in a local election, something that may be considered an intuitive finding. This distinguishes these variables from evaluation indicators, which provide counter-intuitive results. Those who are satisfied with the way democracy is operating in Canada and Nunavut are more likely to cast a ballot in territorial and municipal contests than those who are not. Those who feel the territory will help Nunavummiut better govern their lives are less likely to vote in Nunavut elections. This could reflect a schism in the minds of respondents between Nunavut as secured in the political accord and the political system headquartered in Iqaluit. Fourth, political values contribute to our understandings of political participation in each of the four levels of government. For territorial, federal, and municipal elections, levels of political engagement matter. Those most interested in politics and more active in other forms of participation are more likely to cast a ballot. This finding is entirely consistent with research in other advanced industrial political systems. Political cynicism is relevant, but here the results are counter-intuitive. Cynics are less likely to cast a ballot in a territorial contest but are *more* likely to vote in NTI elections. Deference is relevant only to territorial politics, where it propels people to the polls. Last, the degree of model fit varies across the four dependent variables. Our ability to predict political behaviour in federal elections is weakest as the accumulated independent variables explain only 27 percent of the variation in turnout. Model statistics for territorial and municipal elections are more encouraging still. Participation in NTI elections is best captured by our variables. Over 90 percent of an individual's decision to cast a ballot in an NTI election is explained by the variables listed below. Taken together, the results suggest that voters in Nunavut are pushed toward the polls by the same sorts of factors that encourage individuals to vote elsewhere in Canada. The demographic predictors operate in an expected way, as do the political values. If there is anything unique about patterns of political participation in Nunavut, it has little to do with the predictors of political participation.

But how can this explain higher rates of turnout in territorial elections and lower degrees of turnout in federal or municipal elections? The cultural community variables do not appear to propel voters toward the polls in territorial elections and to keep them away during federal contests. Those speaking Inuktitut are uniformly more likely to vote, whatever the electoral contest. The key may be in the relevance of political values to territorial contests. Political predictors that we know to affect participation in other polities are not relevant either for federal/municipal contests or for NTI elections. The relevance of political variables in a territorial context may lend further credence to the notion that residents in Nunavut perceive the territory to be their primary political community.

Political Gladiators

For Milbrath, turnout was the lowest form of political participation. The highest form involved those "political gladiators" who ran for and held elected office. These individuals were at the apex of political involvement: they were more involved, more informed, and certainly more active and influential than other citizens. We know from previous sections that turnout rates for federal elections are lower in Nunavut. In territorial elections, predictors such as age and income have an expected impact on turnout. Indeed, given the presence of multiple factors that would drive down political activity, it is remarkable that turnout is not lower in the territory. If at first glance patterns of political behaviour in Nunavut suggest declining voter participation and engagement, an examination of turnout suggests that this is not the case. These findings are clearer when studied in light of more gladiatorial political activities.

Examinations of electoral office show that there are more elected positions per capita in Nunavut than in other parts of the country. As mentioned previously, there is a wide array of elected positions for which one might stand in Nunavut. Opportunities to vote are accompanied by opportunities to stand as candidates for election. There are 288 elected positions in the territory, not including bodies that elect members from general assemblies such as the Inuit Circumpolar Conference or single-issue bodies such as hunter and trapper organizations, the district education authorities, or the boards of directors of the community housing associations. This number includes all elected posts at the federal, territorial, and municipal levels as well as the positions available in the birthright organizations. In other words, at any one time, 1.02 percent of the population holds elected office. This is more than the proportion in any other community of comparable size. When the Bank of Montreal left Nunavut in 2004, it relocated the accounts of all territorial residents to Pembroke, Ontario, which, according to the 2001 census, has a population of 23,608. Pembroke has elected positions for 0.04 percent of the community.[9] Even a larger community such as Windsor, with a population of 200,000, has elected positions for .0075 percent of the population. If we assume that these electoral contests are fought by similar numbers of individuals, then the proportion of the population competing for electoral seats is 1.6 percent in Nunavut and .02 percent in a typical Canadian community. Milbrath argued that the hierarchy of political participation operated as a pyramid, that most people would vote, fewer would pay attention to politics consistently, and fewer still would hold elected office. This is certainly true in both southern Canadian provinces and in Nunavut. That pyramid, however, would have a slightly different shape in Nunavut, with a narrower base at the bottom and a slightly larger point at the top. We can also compare the propensity of individuals to stand as candidates at the various levels of office.

Table 7.9 summarizes the patterns of competition for elected office in Nunavut and indicates the number of individuals competing for each elected position. With five candidates vying for one seat in the House of Commons, the federal election has the greatest competition for seats. It also involves far fewer individuals than do most other competitions. The 2002 Nunavut municipal elections, for example, involved 198 candidates. These numbers mask, to a certain extent, variations within Nunavut. In the municipal elections, some communities saw twelve or thirteen candidates vying for five positions on council. In other communities, seats remained unfilled as candidates failed to materialize. In Kimmirut, for example, only one candidate stood for one of the four available seats on council. Variations tend to be regional. The Kivalliq has the greatest competition for seats. For every mayoral seat in the Kivalliq, 2.8 candidates presented themselves. This compares with an average two-candidate contest per seat in the other regions. This pattern holds true for council seats as well. In the Kitikmeot and Baffin regions, three candidates contest every two seats on council. The number is much higher in the Kivalliq, where 2.47 candidates contest each council seat.

TABLE 7.9

Competition for elected office in Nunavut, 1999-2006

Election	Candidates	Elected positions	Candidates/seat[a]
2002 municipal election	198	131	1.5
Councillors[b]	185	101	1.8
Mayors	13	30	2.3
2004 NTI election	8	2	4.0
2001 NTI election	9	2	4.5
2006 federal	5	1	5.0
2004 federal	5	1	5.0
2000 federal election	5	1	5.0
2004 territorial election	82	19	4.3
1999 territorial election	71	19	3.7

a This column indicates the number of individuals standing as candidates for every elected position.
b Municipal elections are staggered so that not all positions are vacant during any one election. This number, and the number for mayors, indicates the number of vacant positions rather than the total number of councillors or mayors in Nunavut.

Further evidence of the opportunity for civic engagement surfaces when we examine Nunavut's political classes. We can examine, for example, the declared professions of candidates and MLAs. Before each election, candidates are asked about their previous political involvement and current employment. Table 7.10 reports the results for 1995, 1999, and 2004. The political class in Nunavut differs slightly from those in other parts of Canada. The near absence of lawyers from among candidates and MLAs is noteworthy, although, as in other legislatures, businesspeople and incumbents loom large. The proportion of unemployed candidates and hunters or carvers sets Nunavut apart from the rest of Canada. If we examine trends over time, however, we can distinguish between subtle and striking results. Among candidates, the proportion of white-collar workers is increasing, as is the proportion of civil servants, although in the latter case the jump appeared in 1999. For the first time the 2004 political class does not include those who list their profession as hunters or carvers. Most significant, the proportion of incumbents has increased steadily since 1995 to the point where they now comprise almost half of the legislature. These results suggest that, even in nine

TABLE 7.10

Current employment of territorial candidates and MLAs, 1995-2004, in percent

	2004 Candidates	2004 Elected	1999 Candidates	1999 Elected	1995 Candidates	1995 Elected
Self-employed/businessperson	12	21	20	26	18	0
Hunter/carver/artist	7	0	20	10	18	25
Civil service (hamlet, territory, NIC)	20	16	14	16	8	0
Politician (MLA, IA exec)	19	47	13	32	13	25
Manager	1	0	10	5	8	25
Manual labour	7	0	8	5	8	0
Unemployed	12	0	7	0	8	25
Other blue collar	1	0	3	0	0	0
Counsellor/social worker	3	5	3	0	5	0
Teacher/adult educator	7	0	1	0	8	0
Student	0	0	1	5	0	0
Other white collar	11	10	0	0	8	0

NOTE: Results exclude candidates who did not provide employment information.

short years, the political class in Nunavut has started to resemble political classes elsewhere in Canada, at least in terms of professions.

We can also examine the political experiences of MLAs. Here too we have reason to believe that representatives in Nunavut have considerable experience in other political venues. Of the first cohort of nineteen representatives, five had held elected office at the territorial level in the legislature of the NWT. A further five had served as mayors of their respective communities, and one had served as a deputy mayor. The remaining eight MLAs included among them an MP and three councillors. Only four MLAs had not served a term in elected office for a public government before 1999. Two, including the premier, had no previous electoral experience, a third ran the local hunter and trapper organization, while the fourth was an elected board member of QIA, the regional Inuit association in the Baffin. This pattern was repeated in 2004. Of the nineteen members, eight were incumbents and a further two had previous experience as NWT MLAs. Of the remainder, all but one had served either as a hamlet councillor or as a mayor, as had many of the incumbent MLAs. Fewer had experience in Inuit political associations, although those who did held leadership positions in them. The current cohort contains a former head of BRIA, a former head of the ITC, and a former president of the Kitikmeot Inuit Association. Devolution may have created the opportunity for new individuals to come forward as political candidates. Those elected, however, represent a seasoned political class. Over time, it appears that the turnover rate among MLAs is decreasing and that vacancies are being filled by local politicians or, more rarely, by those active in Inuit organizations. If the 1999 election created space at other points in the political system – with the departure of local councillors and mayors to the Nunavut legislature – the amount of space available with each successive election appears to be decreasing. Since 1999, then, patterns of political participation among elites have become more similar to those elsewhere in Canada, while the predominantly Inuit electorate holds attachments that distinguish them within the wider Canadian electorate, something that is borne out by an investigation of the north-south attitudinal divide in Chapter 8.

8
Ideological Diversity in Nunavut

Federal and territorial management of the Arctic helps to explain the political institutions that have emerged. The size of the Nunavut Legislative Assembly, its electoral system, and the process of member selection create a highly structured environment in which Nunavummiut might participate in political life. What Nunavummiut think about the political system, the social goals they identify, and the issues that divide them are less naturally dependent on political institutions. An exploration of political attitudes in Nunavut allows us to determine whether northern political attitudes have been more or less influenced by southern political culture.

Political attitudes form an essential component of political culture. Conceptually, they are at the centre of early definitions presented in classic works. The advent of large-scale social surveys has eased the methodological burden of acquiring data on political attitudes, and, since their introduction, they have become a more studied aspect of political culture. Attitudinal research on political culture explores such topics as the evolution of attitudes following political reform, the fit between the norms of institutions and the dominant attitudes of the populace, and the homogeneity of attitudes within the nation-state. Each of these is relevant to political culture in Nunavut. First, while technologically, Inuit may have gone from the stone age to the space age within a generation, the transformation is equally significant when we explore political developments. Judged a federal responsibility in 1939 and given the franchise in 1962, Inuit secured a land claim in 1993. It is worth determining, then, whether this pace has affected the dominant political attitudes in the territory. Second, the institutions initially established in the territorial north were little tailored to a territorial reality. Given the culture of institutions and the culture of contact Inuit society, it is worth determining whether this has any effect on contemporary political culture. If Westminster institutions set the cultural parameters for the integration of an Inuit territorial population, a predominantly Inuit population now serves as the bedrock for a political culture that is host to a sizable, mobile non-Inuit population. Third, we know that the process of institutional accommodation in the 1970s and 1980s created divisions among territorial residents in terms of the identified path of political development and the perceived ideal avenues of political participation. MLAs display among themselves divisions over economic development, IQ, and decentralization. Whether contemporary political cleavages among territorial residents reflect these divisions, however, has never been addressed. In this chapter I address first whether Nunavummiut display different political attitudes from other Canadians; second, the demographic foundations of political cleavages within Nunavut; and third, the ideological clusters within the territory.

A North-South Divide?
Is there a Nunavut political culture? The method by which Inuit were integrated into the political system in Canada, the campaign for a land claim, and the institutional features of the current territory each contribute to the general patterns of behaviour in Nunavut. The territorial political institutions encourage voters and politicians to mirror behaviour in other systems, even in the absence of political parties. The predictors of turnout in Nunavut are similar to those in other political systems. The evidence thus far suggests that, even in the face of institutional anomalies, the overwhelming influence of the Canadian political system has served to make political culture in Nunavut far more similar to that found in other jurisdictions than one might expect to be the case. The political behaviours we have studied – particularly turnout – are heavily dependent on the institutions that structure political life, and the institutions with which the general public interacts are more similar than they are different from those in other territories or provinces. We know, however, that there is no necessary corollary between institutions and attitudes. In a comparative context, research on democratization shows us that the presence of democratic institutions does not necessarily instil immediate support for democratic values. Closer to home, we know that minor institutional anomalies are capable, over time, of producing attitudinal variations among provincial electorates (Simeon and Elkins 1974, 1980; Wilson 1974). Three possibilities present themselves. We certainly have reason to believe that the institutions governing political life are capable of

producing, over time, distinct attitudes within Nunavut. At question, though, is whether the institutions have yet had an impact on political attitudes or whether territorial citizens are still so embedded within a federal political culture that their views are indistinct. Here we might seek to determine whether the development of territorial institutions in the 1970s has affected attitudes, or whether the creation of Nunavut allows us to distinguish between the attitudes of those on either side of the new boundary.

A second interest is the impact of traditional Inuit attitudes toward leadership and social interaction on contemporary attitudes in Nunavut. Can we, for example, distinguish between the attitudes of Inuit and non-Inuit, and, if so, do the attitudes of contemporary Inuit bear any cultural imprint of earlier traditional culture? Third, the boundaries that individuals draw around themselves are signs of a distinct political culture. Attitudinal similarity can mask a fierce belief in the existence of a distinct political space. This can function as proof of a separate political culture in Nunavut even in the presence of otherwise uniform attitudes.

Efforts to compare the attitudes of Nunavummiut and other Canadians are complicated by the paucity of data. To facilitate comparisons, the 2004 NuHS replicated questions employed in previous Canadian election studies. Seven of those identified were then put to respondents in the 2004 CES. These tap fundamental aspects of political culture, including voter cynicism and deference, in addition to evaluations of the operation of democracy. They also include a series of questions probing "traditional" values. The wording of questions allows for some ambiguity between the two contexts. The necessity of a return to "traditional" family values could, for CES respondents, appear as a symptom of social conservatism or religiosity; for NuHS respondents, however, a return to "traditional" values could imply a return to life on the land or traditional spirituality. Finding cultural equivalents is often a tricky task for those translating survey questions in different contexts. Finding Inuktitut words to capture "left" and "right" on an ideological spectrum has proven to be particularly difficult. With these caveats in mind, though, we can determine whether Nunavummiut distinguish themselves according to typical indicators of political culture.

The results displayed in Table 8.1 display a fundamental difference between Nunavummiut and other Canadians.[1] Indeed, the differing levels of support for these questions far exceed those found among provincial residents. Nunavut residents appear to display lower levels of internal efficacy, ("People like me have no say") and higher levels of external efficacy ("MPs

TABLE 8.1

Political attitudes in Nunavut and Canadian provinces, percent agreeing

	Nunavut	Canadian provinces
Deference		
People like me have no say	59.4	42.0
MPs lose touch with the people	69.6	76.8
Evaluation		
Satisfaction with way democracy works	80.4	65.5
Efficacy		
Politics too complicated	73.1	56.4
"Traditional" values		
Environment before jobs	76.5	37.7
Welfare makes people not look after selves	72.3	58.0
Should return to traditional family values	80.7	65.1
Working mothers have poor relations with kids	29.9	41.4

NOTES: Wording in CES and NuHS identical unless otherwise stated:
- People like me don't have any say about what the government does.
- Those elected to Parliament soon lose touch with the people (NuHS: Those elected to Parliament in Ottawa ...).
- On the whole are you satisfied with the way democracy works in Canada?
- Sometimes politics and government seem so complicated that a person like me can't really understand what's going on.
- Protecting the environment is more important than creating jobs.
- The welfare state makes people less willing to look after themselves.
- This country would have many fewer problems if there was more emphasis on traditional family values (NuHS: Canada would have many fewer ...).
- A mother who works outside the home can maintain just as warm and secure a relationship with her children as a mother who does not work outside the home (direction of question reversed in table).

SOURCES: NuHS 2004, n = 900; CES 2004, n = 3,050.

lose touch"). Satisfaction with democracy is higher and deference is higher than in the rest of Canada, as is support for a return to traditional family values. Indeed, many of these attitudes appear more similar to those registered by Canadians in the 1970s, before the decline in trust and deference became a hallmark of Canadian political culture (Nevitte 1996). On moral traditionalism and economic development, the results are mixed. A greater proportion believe the welfare state makes individuals lazy, while a smaller proportion believe that working mothers should return to the home. Attitudes to the welfare state are interesting. One possible interpretation is that they reflect traditional Inuit perspectives on self-sufficiency. Despite high levels of poverty and an underdeveloped private sector, over three-quarters of respondents believe that protecting the environment is more important than job creation, compared with half that proportion in southern Canada. Each of these differences is significant at the .01 level.

We know that political attitudes vary across the country. Residents in particular provinces exhibit higher or lower levels of efficacy and deference, a function, in part, of the way their provincial institutions structure political relationships within the jurisdiction. If we examine the Canadian data and disaggregate respondents by province, can we identify a jurisdiction that most resembles Nunavut? Yes and no. On some questions, we can clearly identify provinces in which attitudes are remarkably similar to those exhibited by Nunavummiut. On others, residents in the eastern Arctic are obvious outliers in the Canadian polity. On measures of cynicism, Nunavut political culture appears most similar to that found in the Atlantic provinces. Indeed, on five of the nine indicators, Nunavummiut appear most similar to other eastern Canadians. Nunavummiut appear most like Newfoundlanders in terms of internal efficacy and most like Prince Edward Islanders in terms of party support. Territorial respondents appear most similar to those in Nova Scotia on measures of external efficacy, democratic satisfaction, and views of working mothers. Political culture in eastern Canada is often viewed as distinct, exhibiting lower levels of efficacy and greater levels of deference (Bell 1970; Simeon and Elkins 1979; Stewart 1994), and here we have reason to believe that, on typical indicators, political culture in Nunavut is consistent with these attitudes. Levels of deference, when measured as a perception of "complicated" politics, share more with the views of prairie residents in Saskatchewan; levels of support for traditional values are most similar to those found in Quebec, a particularly "modern" province if we consider rates of cohabitation and religious attendance; and levels of support for the welfare state are most similar to those found in Alberta. Nunavut, then, appears to combine the environmentalism of British Columbia, the self-sufficiency of Alberta, the traditionalism of Quebec, and the efficacy and cynicism of Atlantic Canada. This should not detract from the fact that the territory is more supportive of environmentalism, more supportive of self-sufficiency, and more traditional than are any of the provinces mentioned here. Nunavummiut are more supportive of environmental protection than are residents in British Columbia, the most "green" province by CES standards. Just under half of all BC residents felt that environmental protection was more important than job creation, while over three-quarters of Nunavummiut believed the same. Three-quarters of Atlantic voters, by contrast, prioritized job creation.

Clearly, there is more to political culture in Nunavut than basic comparisons with provinces can suggest. The NuHS also asked several questions typically included in surveys such as the CES and World Values Survey but excluded from the 2004 national survey. These include perceptions of the political class and political interest. Fewer than one-third (28.9 percent) believe that men make better political leaders than women, and more than half believe that parties do more to divide the population than to unite it. Levels of political interest among territorial residents is high. Over two-thirds (67.5 percent) indicate that they have a moderate or high level of interest in political affairs. A less explicitly political series of questions, however, provides us with the most useful insight into political culture in Nunavut.

Maslow's (1943) previously mentioned hierarchy of needs distinguishes between material needs such as food, shelter, and security, and higher-order needs such as self-actualization and belonging. Inglehart (1977, 1990) employed a variant of this analysis in his investigation of advanced-industrial and developing countries. Arguing that the adult populations of states tend to prioritize the things they lacked in childhood, Inglehart distinguished between the materialist needs of countries interested in security and stability and the postmaterialist needs of those interested in quality of life. If this theory is correct, we would expect materialist concerns to dominate the minds of those living in Nunavut, so dominant was the attention to food and shelter in the lives of many adults. The rapid process of industrialization in the eastern Arctic provides a unique environment in which to test theories of postmaterialism.

Postmaterialism was initially measured by a twelve-point scale. Respondents were presented with three different opportunities to identify the two most important societal goals. Choices included two materialist options and two postmaterialist options. Within Canada, the list of options has often been reduced to one question presenting four options: fighting crime, giving people more say, increasing economic growth, and ensuring free speech. Those identifying the two most important goals as fighting crime and economic growth are classified as materialists; those who select having more say and ensuring free speech are postmaterialists. Individuals who identify one materialist and one postmaterialist goal are classified as mixed.

The proportion of "mixed" and "postmaterialist" Canadians has increased since Inglehart employed the scale in the 1981 World Values Survey. In the 2004 CES, just under 60 percent are classified as mixed and 16 percent are classified as postmaterialists. The Nunavut results are initially puzzling. If we

TABLE 8.2

Postmaterialism in Nunavut, in percent

	Nunavut	Canadian provinces
Materialist	19.4	23.8
Postmaterialist	16.6	15.9
Mixed	63.9	58.7

SOURCES: NuHS 2004, $n = 900$; CES 2004, $n = 3,050$.

assume that the childhood scarcity thesis is correct, that adults want what they lacked in childhood, then the adult Inuit population should be predominantly materialist. This is not the case. Indeed, as the data in Table 8.2 show, Nunavut contains a smaller proportion of materialists than does Canada as a whole.

If we examine support for particular goals, we see that CES respondents prioritize economic growth. In Nunavut, however, the most important goal was freedom of speech. Support for both goals presents a fairly even division between the two populations, although there is a slight preference (51.5 percent) for materialist concerns in the CES and a slight preference for postmaterialist concerns (51.3 percent) in the Nunavut survey. The gap is small, though, so we should avoid claiming the two are poles apart. Most significant is where the theory suggests Nunavut responses should be and where they actually are. Rapid industrialization and the move to settlements – a dramatic change in the social conditions of Nunavummiut of today and those of fifty years ago – in addition to a considerable difference between the economic conditions faced by Nunavummiut and southern Canadians, has failed to produce significant variations in terms of postmaterialism. Where differences appear, they are in a direction different from one theory suggests we should see.

The nature of support for postmaterialism in Nunavut is clearer when we differentiate among the "mixed" category of respondents. We can distinguish, for example, between those prioritizing materialist values first and postmaterialist values second. If the territory contains 19.4 percent materialists and 16.6 percent postmaterialists, the mixed group breaks down so that 29.1 percent of Nunavummiut are predominantly materialist and 34.9 percent are predominantly postmaterialist. We can convert these positions to a four-point scale.[2] If we do this, the average scores of Inuit and non-Inuit are significantly different, with Inuit more postmaterialist on average than non-Inuit by a score of .51 to .43. Non-Inuit preferences are not only more materialist but they also display greater heterogeneity than do Inuit preferences, with higher standard deviations around mean scores.

Part of the explanation might lie in the emphasis traditional society placed on belonging and social embeddedness, and part might lie in problems with theory. Traditional society could be characterized by its simultaneous attention to lower- and higher-order needs. The acquisition of food and shelter, although structuring the rhythm of life and the daily tasks of individuals, was not all-consuming in the way we might expect. The theory that societies embark on a linear form of progress from lower-order to higher-order needs, and thus that the preoccupations of citizens will be transformed from materialist to mixed to postmaterialist, does not describe reality in Nunavut. Here, the transformation appears to be from mixed to specialist needs. If Inuit society once sought to meet both lower- and higher-order needs, it has now created an environment in which one or the other needs (materialist or postmaterialist) might be met. Here society has witnessed two different trajectories – one from mixed to materialist, the other from mixed to postmaterialist – rather than a linear pattern of progress.

This is best seen when we explore postmaterialism scores by age cohort and ethnicity. Figure 8.1 reports mean scores for a postmaterialist scale that runs from 0 (materialist) to 1 (postmaterialist). The scores by age cohort show that younger people are clearly more postmaterialist than are older people. Although differences among age cohorts are significant at the .01 level, the relationship is not straightforward. For Inuit, each ordinal increase in age shows an increase in materialism, until we reach the cohort of respondents between forty-five and fifty-four. At this point, the trend reverses so that the two older cohorts show levels of postmaterialism that are more symptomatic of younger people. Similar patterns are evident among the non-Inuit population, although the bottom of the curve occurs earlier. For both groups, young people and elders are more sympathetic to postmaterialism than are adults in their forties or fifties. Although the gap between Inuit and non-Inuit preferences is generally stable, it widens in middle age, when non-Inuit appear more materialist than their Inuit counterparts. Part of this might be explained by the composition of the non-Inuit population in Nunavut. Non-Inuit of working age tend to have spent a smaller proportion of their lives in the north than have non-Inuit in, for example, their sixties, who have typically

FIGURE 8.1

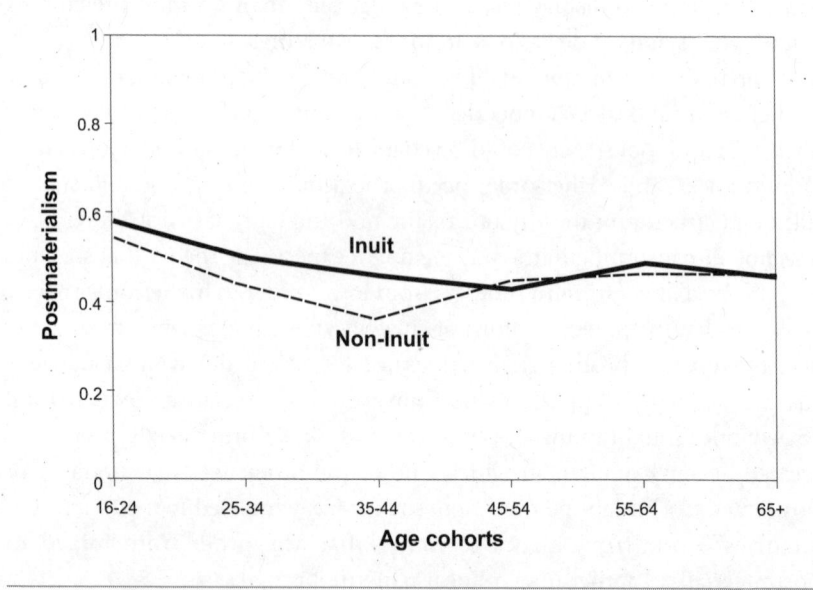

Postmaterialism by ethnicity and age

[Figure: Line graph showing postmaterialism values across age cohorts (16-24, 25-34, 35-44, 45-54, 55-64, 65+) for Inuit and Non-Inuit groups. Inuit line starts near 0.58, declines to about 0.45, slight rise then level around 0.46. Non-Inuit line starts near 0.54, dips to about 0.36 at 35-44, then rises to converge with Inuit line.]

spent their adult life in the territory. The gaps between Inuit and non-Inuit appear largest, then, when we are comparing northerners and southerners rather than ethnic divisions among northerners. This analysis points to the existence of demographic cleavages within the Nunavut electorate.

The Demographic Foundations of Political Cleavages

Not all residents in Nunavut identify the same societal goals. Not all believe that protecting the environment is more important than jobs or that people have no say in political decisions. Whether this is proof of a considerable political cleavage within Nunavut or whether this is the same absence of homogeneity we find in most political cultures is up for debate. One way that we would be able to identify political cleavages would be to determine whether they are aligned with existing demographic divisions. If Inuit tend to exhibit relatively uniform preferences but non-Inuit do not, for example, then we might have evidence of an ethnic cleavage within Nunavut. Demography on its own is, in many respects, irrelevant. Rather, it is the social significance of difference – the fact that men are treated differently from women, that Inuit are treated differently from non-Inuit, that regions created by the government receive differential access to power or resources – that creates politically salient demographic cleavages within society. Political development in the eastern Arctic has produced four potential cleavages among the population. In some ways, these reflect and reinforce perceived divisions among MLAs. We would only see these divisions as the fault lines within a political culture if they were of salience to regular individuals as well as to politicians. The following section tracks the possible demographic foundations of political cleavages in Nunavut.

Geographic

The twenty-five communities of Nunavut are located within three regions: the Baffin/Qikiqtaaluk, the Kivalliq, and the Kitikmeot. These regions reflect very real demographic variations in terms of language use (Inuinnaqtun in the west), levels of traditionalism (north Baffin), and economic prosperity (Keewatin). For the most part, they are not natural regions. Baffin Island is geographically distinct and, to southern eyes, might appear relatively isolated, but frozen seas have always ensured movement across the Kivalliq to the north Baffin between, for example, Repulse Bay and Pond Inlet. The -miut groups of traditional Inuit society, which today are most relevant in the linguistic variations they represent, exist within and across the existing regional boundaries and reinforce the extent to which regional division was artificial. Indeed, the division of Inuit by nation-states is seen by some as an artificial boundary separating the fundamental unity of Inuit populations in Greenland, Chukotka, Alaska, or the Canadian Arctic. The artificial nature of regions is compounded by the fact that existing communities are not located at the site of existing permanent settlement, as was the case for some First Nations communities in southern Canada. In the Arctic, settlements emerged around centres of southern activity, such as trading posts or military bases, and therefore reflect southern concerns rather than northern ones. By far the most explicit example of southern determinism is in the High Arctic, where Resolute and Grise exist because of the federally planned relocation of Inuit from northern Quebec and Pond Inlet.

The creation of regions was a legacy of the pre-division NWT, where program delivery was aided by the presence of regional health authorities and regional educational authorities. The emergence of regional Eskimo councils in the 1960s became the first expression of Inuit political voice beyond the immediate social group, and later the federal government attempted to foster public regional institutions such as regional councils. The formal salience of regions diminished after 1999 with the disbanding of regional boards when the government of Nunavut assumed responsibility for education and health.

The importance of region lives on in three ways. First, and least important, regions form the basis for municipal organization and program delivery. Second, Inuit associations are organized on a regional basis. These associations are of greater significance to Inuit than the nominal administrative regions are to Nunavummiut as a whole. We might expect, then, that region might be more significant to Inuit than to non-Inuit. Third, transportation links among the communities reinforce a regional element to life in Nunavut by creating different poles of influence. For communities in the eastern portion of the territory, Iqaluit serves as an air hub, while for those in the west, Yellowknife and, to a lesser extent, Rankin Inlet provide the same role. Access to southern Canada is served by Ottawa, Edmonton, and Winnipeg, respectively. The market-driven decisions of airlines may appear innocuous in their ability to mould shopping routes or enable family visits during stop-overs, but a sense of regional cohesiveness is aided by the extent to which contact among regional inhabitants is facilitated.

Another manifestation of a geographic cleavage helps to explain the previously discussed divisions among MLAs. The distribution of jobs after 1999, both to the capital in Iqaluit and to the decentralized communities, has created a have and have-not division between communities. While this might not be reflected in ideological divisions regarding moral traditionalism, it could distinguish between higher- and lower-efficacy residents. Despite the conscious effort to create a capital more reflective of Nunavut than Yellowknife was of the NWT, Iqaluit has become increasingly unlike other communities in the territory. The capital contains the bulk of GN employees, and thus, those most active within the political sphere, as well as the vast majority of the territory's non-indigenous population. Its population is also more mobile than is that of any other community. In the 2001 census, respondents indicated where they were living five years ago – whether it was at the same residence, elsewhere in the jurisdiction, or elsewhere in Canada. Most communities in Nunavut have remarkably stable populations. Of the twenty-five communities, seventeen had less than 6 percent of their population living outside Nunavut five years ago. Coral Harbour, for example, has the most stable population, with less than 2 percent living elsewhere in Canada in 1996. A handful of other communities, most notably the regional centres, had extraterritorial mobility rates of 15 percent. In Iqaluit, however, one in three residents was living outside Nunavut five years ago.

If region is salient, it could prove that institutional reform matters. This would contradict research that suggests political culture is resistant to the administrative changes of boundaries. If regions in Nunavut exert a significant impact on attitudes, then this suggests that some political cultures are more susceptible to reform than others, that they are more malleable. And yet, when we ask whether individuals identify with their region of residence, there is little to suggest that region serves as a salient political cleavage. Less than 3 percent of Inuit identify region as their primary identity group, and less than 6 percent of non-Inuit do so. Even if we disaggregate results by region, there is little variation. Less than 3 percent of Baffin residents identify region as their primary identity group, and 4.8 percent of Kivalliq residents feel the same.

ETHNIC

Political culture in Nunavut is overwhelmingly affected by the ethnic composition of its electorate. The Inuit population not only guaranteed through the land claim the very existence of the territory but is also embedded within a cultural tradition that possesses its own approach to social relations and leadership. Two integration processes dominate political culture in Nunavut. From one perspective, it is dominated by the integration of new arrivals and institutions into a predominantly Inuit political culture. Mobility among the non-Inuit population in Nunavut is far higher than it is for the Inuit population. Although Qallunaat represent 15 percent of the population, the short period of time many of them have spent in the north detracts from their potential demographic weight within the polity. From another perspective, the predominantly Inuit population has been integrated into the southern culture of political institutions. At the root of both perspectives is a fundamental ethnic division. Federal administrators sought to undermine the salience of ethnicity by explicitly avoiding the creation of institutions that would reinforce it. This form of northern brokerage politics saw public institutions as organs of political integration and, after the demise of the Eskimo Affairs Committee, expressed a general reluctance for Aboriginal organizations to be anything other than agents of cultural expression. Nor are ethnic divisions within Nunavut binary. The non-Inuit population can be divided between those born in the north and those temporarily resident in the territory, primarily for employment opportunities. The Inuit population can also be divided linguistically among Inuinnaqtun, Inuktitut, and English speakers.

The potential impact of any ethnic division is tied to resources. The bald statistics reported from the census show that Inuit and non-Inuit are living in different social and economic environments. The political salience of these differences has changed since 1999. The simultaneous drive to meet the targets of both Article 23 of the NCLA and decentralization has led to lower levels of job security for non-Inuit than might otherwise be the case. The NNI policy, by which companies competing for government contracts are given extra points if they are owned by or employ northerners, and additional credit if they are owned by or employ Inuit, exposes an ethnic component to public policy. At present, the campaign in Nunavut differs from efforts to alter the composition of bureaucrats in the federal and Quebec civil service in the 1970s. There, the attempt was to create a bilingual bureaucracy, which, given current practices, remains a distant goal in Nunavut, where the civil service operates overwhelmingly in English. For some, hiring decisions grounded purely in ethnic considerations rather than in linguistic skill are problematic. Inuit disappointment at the pedestrian pace at which jobs are being decentralized to communities outside Iqaluit, or the rate at which professional and managerial positions are being taken by Inuit, is matched by the frustration of non-Inuit government employees who feel that their employment contributions are less valued, their tenure in office less secure, and their presence in the territory less welcomed than it was before 1999. Recent charges of racism from non-Inuit GN employees are but one example of this (Younger-Lewis 2004). For the most part, such accounts are limited to newspaper reports and, on both sides, are anecdotal. They suggest, however, an emerging division between Inuit and non-Inuit within the territory. We can see part of this in the identity figures for both groups. Only 11.7 percent of Inuit suggest that their primary attachment is to Canada; almost 60 percent suggest that their ethnic identity is more important than their Canadian identity; and the remainder are split as to whether territory, region, or community is most important to their identity. As for non-Inuit, more than half suggested that their primary attachment was to Canada rather than to a geographic unit contained within the boundaries of the territory.

GENERATIONAL

Every culture displays variations in attitudes and behaviour across generations. This is exacerbated in a culture that has undergone a significant change, whether religious, social, or economic. We know that each of these transformations occurred in Nunavut. An older generation, raised primarily on the land and speaking Inuktitut, has children, grandchildren, or great-grandchildren who, with each successive generation, lead lives less like those of their elders. Equally important, the burdens of cultural change have fallen unevenly on different generations. One cohort witnessed the full evolution of change within its lifetime, while others enjoyed considerably more cultural stability. Sandwiched between unilingual elders who lived traditionally most of their lives and English-speaking young people who have known nothing other than settlement life and full-time education is a bilingual adult population that was placed in residential schools at their most assimilative phase, many of whom are devout Christians, many with rosy employment prospects. Obviously this ignores the variations we find in any age cohort, and so here we are playing up differences across generations, but if the youngest and oldest generation face difficulties in terms of communication – if not in terms of language, then at least in terms of values and goals (Kral and Minore 1999) – this middle generation is caught in something of a cultural half-way house. As the postmaterialism figures show, it is this generation whose political views are more similar to those of southern Canadians. This suggests they have a different cultural trajectory than do those who came before them or those who came after.

The potential impact of a generational cleavage is complicated by the age structure of Nunavut society. The lower age at which women in Nunavut typically give birth, along with the high average birth rate, produces a society with a generational structure that is unique within Canada. While this is a demographic feature rather than a cleavage, it places certain generations in different roles than might otherwise have been the case. In particular, it creates a perceived boundary around elders as a cohort. Noted for their leadership in traditional society, particularly for their role as moralizers or community leaders, their smaller demographic weight within Nunavut has served to heighten their status. The cultural importance of elders is seen in their formal integration into – if not their actual function in – the Nunavut political system. The best examples of this is the outer ring around the debating chamber in the Nunavut legislature and the creation of the elders' IQ katimajiit, an external body containing community representatives who can advise the government on traditional values. The importance of elders is also seen in the emphasis on IQ. It is worth noting that the emphasis on elders is a development particular to Nunavut and is comparatively absent in other circumpolar

Inuit societies. Generational change in Canada thus has both a demographic component and a normative component. Cultural change has created a society in which the lived experiences of younger and older generations are more dissimilar than they are in other Inuit societies. As a result, we would not be surprised to learn that older residents believe one thing and younger residents believe another. Generational cohorts are also the source of a normative cleavage among residents, where we can distinguish between those who think that greater respect and attention should be paid to elders and those who identify other goals for Nunavut society.

Spiritual

The last potential cleavage is spiritual. The 2004 human rights debate in the Nunavut legislature pointed to a significant religious division within Nunavut. It showed, at the same time, that it is not always easy to separate religious divisions from ethnic ones. Spiritual cleavages have, in some sense, characterized social life in the eastern Arctic since the arrival of European missionaries. A cleavage that initially would have distinguished between those adhering to traditional shamanistic spiritualism and Christianity gave way, in some communities, to divisions between Anglicans and Roman Catholics. We have evidence of education being structured along religious lines, and the two churches provided rival authorities in the few communities in which both were active. Usually, communities were deemed the preserve of either Roman Catholic or Anglican missionaries, and so the religious cleavage sits atop regional variations. Whatever the doctrinal difference between the two denominations, their primary importance is in the way that they managed to integrate Inuit spirituality. The easier accommodation of a pre-existing Inuit belief system and spiritual rituals within the Roman Catholic Church has resulted in a contemporary distinction between communities in which Inuit spirituality is more present and those in which it is near absent.

Although the arrival of missionaries fundamentally altered the leadership structure of life in the camps and imposed an external mechanism of social control on Inuit behaviour, religiosity is not in automatic conflict with Inuit traditionalism. Indeed, religious attitudes among Inuit are aligned with social conservatism just as they are in other parts of Canada. All that differs is the traditionalism that is deemed worthy of preservation. Religion divides Nunavummiut by denomination and by religiosity, and it interacts with ethnic and regional cleavages. If religion serves to divide Nunavummiut, it provides further evidence of the malleability of cultures at different points in their development.

Ideological Clusters within Nunavut

We can identify potential divisions among Nunavummiut, but whether they have any impact on political attitudes in the eastern Arctic remains to be seen. We can test for the effect of these cleavages either deductively or inductively. If we choose the deductive method, we can identify the possible sources for division and then determine whether they survive as predictors of political attitudes. If, for example, region serves as a predictor of cynicism or deference even when we control for other demographic variations that exist across those same geographic units, then we can point to a regional cleavage within Nunavut. If we choose the inductive method, we can use the various political attitudes in Nunavut as a foundation and proceed to identify ideological clusters within the population. We can then examine these clusters in light of demographic variables to determine whether one ideological cluster is composed primarily of unilingual Inuit in the north Baffin, one is composed of younger government workers in Iqaluit, and so on.

Table 8.3 reports the results of a deductive approach to political cleavages within Nunavut. The regression analyses test for the independent impact of four sets of variables, three of which reflect the potential demographic cleavages discussed above. A fourth, socio-economic status, includes a method of testing generational cohorts, in addition to indicators we know to be relevant in other advanced industrial countries. Education, employment status, and income are each associated with increased efficacy, satisfaction, and political activity levels. Higher levels of education are typically associated with postmaterialism, as is youth. In Table 8.3, the particular regression coefficients are less important than is the direction of the relationship and whether it is significant or not. If we consider the demographic cleavages mentioned earlier, ethnicity and its linguistic implications appear to be more relevant than region or religion, each of which contains significant predictors for only three variables. Unilingual Inuktitut speakers are more likely to be satisfied with their exposure to land-based activities, while those in Iqaluit are not. Religious denomination appears less relevant than personal religiosity. Most relevant, however, are the types of demographic variables, such as education, employment status, and income, that we know explain political attitudes and behaviours in advanced industrial countries. The relatively low model fit suggests, however, that when we use the demographic predictors to explain

Table 8.3

Predictors of political attitudes

	Political satisfaction	Cynicism	Land satisfaction	Moral traditionalism	Political activity	Postmaterialism
Socio-economic status						
Female					+	
Age					+	−
High School	+	−	−	−		
Employed	−	−	+			+
Income					+	
Ethnicity						
Inuit		−	+		−	
Inuktitut only			+			
Bilingual			−		+	−
Region						
Iqaluit			−			
Kivalliq				+	−	
Religion						
Religiosity		+	+	+		
Anglican						
Catholic						−
Adjusted R²	.04	.11	.25	.05	.15	.05

SOURCE: NuHS 2004, *n* = 900.

political attitudes we are missing a significant part of the story. A different approach provides more helpful information.

Cluster analysis allows us to identify ideologically coherent groups of Nunavummiut. We can then examine these groups to determine whether they contain a higher proportion of younger people, hunters, women, or Iqaluit residents. The interaction between these demographic and political values helps us to identify the salient components of political cleavages within Nunavut. Most important, this approach moves beyond a binary understanding of political debate, for we are less interested in the fact that Inuit believe one thing and non-Inuit believe another. Instead, this allows us to track the simultaneous distribution of multiple demographic indicators.

The cluster analysis relies on five variables created through factor analysis, a four-point postmaterialism scale and a variable concerning gender relations. This last variable appears as a unique factor in factor analysis and so is included as a single item. The five factors are political satisfaction, cynicism, satisfaction with land-based activities, self-sufficient traditionalism, and political activity. Details for the variables, including reliability scores for those created by factor analysis, can be found in the appendix. Together these variables reveal the existence of five ideologically coherent clusters within Nunavut. When we examine these in light of demographic indicators such as place of residence, ethnicity, or educational attainment, we can identify meaningful labels for these clusters.

The five ideologically coherent groups are:

1 Small community modernists
2 Frustrated Iqaluit-based young workers
3 Politically satisfied materialists
4 Cynical spectators
5 Postmaterialist traditionalists.

These groups are divided by statistically significant variations on political values, something that is to be expected given the cluster analysis. At the same time, they hold statistically significant variations on democratic indicators. The attitudinal and demographic characteristics for the different groups are summarized in Table 8.4. By dividing Nunavut into ideologically coherent groups, we have also identified clusters that differ fundamentally in terms of age, ethnicity, income, gender, place of residence, and social and political behaviour. The attitudinal variations reveal the existence of coherent groups possessing distinct behavioural and demographic profiles.

The first group is composed primarily of those living in small communities, particularly in the Kivalliq and Baffin. Group members are most satisfied with access to land-based activities and are most active on the land. The group contains the largest proportion of unilingual Inuit. This is not, however, a group composed solely of full-time hunters; rather, individuals combine paid employment and land-based activities. The group is also active politically, among the most engaged and interested in politics, and it scores highest on the self-sufficient traditionalism factor. This group appears to have best integrated the benefits of small community life: both easy access to

TABLE 8.4

Political and demographic components of political clusters

	1	2	3	4	5
Variable scores†					
Political satisfaction score	−1.10	−.20	.50	.21	.13
Cynicism score	.64	.29	.68	−.66	−.54
Land satisfaction score	−.08	.80	.50	.72	.64
Traditionalism score	−.43	.51	.34	−.47	.05
Political activity score	.39	−.33	−.40	−.05	.37
Postmaterialism score	.44	.58	.56	.49	.48
Men better leaders score	.27	.41	.51	.37	.31
Demographic					
Inuit %	69.9	52.5	59.2	88.3	87.0
Female %	32.5	57.8	29.6	57.6	36.8
Age (mean score)	.37	.29	.40	.21	.31
High school grads %	41.1	60.3	70.6	25.1	32.6
Employed %	62.6	66.2	58.9	35.4	54.2
Harvest frequently %	27.8	8.0	17.7	17.4	23.2
Iqaluit %	22.5	44.9	27.7	16.7	29.3
Community size (mean score)	.45	.63	.55	.47	.49
Inuktitut first language %	64.3	46.8	37.1	80.4	74.4
Unilingual Inuktitut %	11.7	none	9.0	4.7	9.9
Bilingual %	31.5	30.1	21.1	37.4	18.5
Religiosity (mean score)	.71	.50	.60	.83	.54
Anglican	66.2	49.9	45.0	61.9	56.7
Catholic	25.4	30.8	36.9	28.8	31.8
Atheist	2.8	8.4	12.7	2.2	6.2
Canadian identity %	31.5	39.6	23.8	15.9	19.7
Inuit identity %	31.9	32.1	33.2	53.2	49.8
Internet	74.6	87.6	78.7	65.4	80.4
n	110	74	87	100	65

† Results significant at .05 level.

employment and continued engagement in traditional activities. The high levels of political activity point to higher levels of social capital among this first group. In a sense, this group is the success story of Nunavut, securing access to resources in both a more traditional and a contemporary market.

The second group consists of younger employed Nunavummiut and contains a higher than average proportion of Iqaluit residents and women. The members of this group are least satisfied with politics and least satisfied with their participation in land-based activities, including both time on the land and access to country food such as caribou, seal, or Arctic char. Perhaps not surprisingly, this group contains the smallest proportion of frequent harvesters or hunters and scores lowest on self-sufficient traditionalism. Taken together the results suggest a degree of alienation from the land. Debates about whether the government should sponsor hunters to facilitate the sale of country food in community markets or stores are controversial in Nunavut. One side argues that the sale of something so central to traditional life, particularly something governed by sharing practices and obligation, can only reinforce the cultural distance between traditional Inuit society and contemporary settlement life. The other side argues that continued access to country food through typical patterns of distribution is impossible if one is not living in a community close to friends or family who hunt. Frustrated Iqaluit-based Nunavummiut seem most likely to be sympathetic to this second view.

The third group consists of politically satisfied materialists who are least cynical about politics. This group has a higher average age than most, a greater proportion of residents in the Kitikmeot, and is composed primarily of men. Its members are less likely to be bilingual and are most likely to be English speakers. It also contains the largest proportion of atheists. The group members bear a certain resemblance to early political activists, including those integrated into community councils or territorial committees, who viewed full-time education and participation within the existing political system as the key to success.

The fourth group is the most cynical about politics, the least active politically, and the most conservative in its view of gender relations, even though 60 percent of its group members are women. It contains the smallest proportion of individuals who have graduated from high school or who are employed, and it is the least likely group to have members living in Iqaluit. Its members are the most religious and have the lowest average age of any of the clusters. We can imagine that it is this group that is eager to better integrate Inuit traditional knowledge and to better infuse the territory with cultural approaches more relevant to the Christian and Inuit society in the Arctic.

Group five is composed of postmaterialists and those scoring highest on self-sufficient traditionalism. Its members are predominantly from the Baffin, and 10 percent are unilingual Inuktitut speakers. Groups four and five share many characteristics. The proportion of members who prioritize their Inuit identity is similar, as is the ethnic composition of the two groups. Both community size and general geographic distribution are also similar.

And yet the two groups have very different levels of religiosity, bilingualism, and employment status, and their political views – in terms of postmaterialism, cynicism, traditionalism, political activism, and gender relations – are poles apart. This points to different cultural trajectories among Inuit, one less marked by contact with religion but closer to the social values that emerged from precontact Inuit life, the other adopting a form of conservative Inuit traditionalism marked by exposure to Christianity.

These attitudinal clusters are interesting for two reasons. First, they test the assumed compliance of values and beliefs that we witness in other political contexts. Here, postmaterialism is not aligned with liberalism but with traditionalism. Most important, though, the five clusters suggest distinct cultural trajectories within the eastern Arctic population. We can see in the results of this analysis the inheritors of different approaches to political integration, to participation in education or a wage economy, and to Christianity. The complicated nature of economic development is also evident. We can see in these clusters the strains of debate that surfaced earlier in discussions of institutional development that took place between those who viewed economic development as an end in itself (and linked with power) and those who viewed it as a means to the goal of a culturally differentiated political space.

The value of these clusters is that they hint at the consequences of different approaches to the collision of political cultures. Those who have most made the shift to what we might consider to be an unremarkably southern lifestyle appear most frustrated with their access to traditional culture and to the contemporary political system. Those rooted most in the past appear to be most alienated. The cluster that appears most satisfied, both culturally and politically, exhibits markers of a blended culture, with members picking those elements of the different cultural waves that suit them and discarding those that do not. The ramifications of these findings are obvious. Those who have primarily pursued the economic rewards made available by the NLCA are displeased, as are those looking for cultural rewards that appear not to have arrived. The error, it would seem, is in the singular nature of these interests.

We can now draw important conclusions about political attitudes in Nunavut. Theories of postmaterialism, for example, assume that societies are dominated first by materialist concerns and then progress toward postmaterialist concerns. An examination of attitudes in Nunavut suggests, however, that Inuit traditional life was characterized by the simultaneous attention to both materialist and postmaterialist concerns. "Progress," in Nunavut, has served to sever these pursuits rather than to move from one to the other. The trajectory of development is different from what we might expect. There is no normative assessment of postmaterialism. Societies that are predominantly concerned with postmaterialism are not necessarily better than those concerned with more materialist issues. While we can make the same claim about simultaneous attention to materialist and postmaterialist pursuits versus more singular pursuits, this may, in fact, explain dissatisfaction in Nunavut with the progress of the NLCA. The singular attention to either materialist goals or postmaterialist goals denies individuals what earlier generations would have considered a whole and full life, one made meaningful both by a sense of belonging and by the activity required to secure material goods. This notion of separation also surfaces in our examination of the attitudinal clusters.

The results of the cluster analysis suggest that those groups that are most engaged and least cynical are those managing to combine a culture marked by the importance of land with one marked by paid employment. It is worth noting that the results do not lead us to make conclusions about those embracing cultural pluralism versus those adopting more singular pursuits. We cannot conclude that those leading particularly traditional lives are more happy or less engaged than others. We can, however, compare those who are able to successfully combine the benefits of multiple cultures with those who are not.

9
Transforming Political Culture in Nunavut

Despite the tepid support for radical change within the new territory, Nunavut offered claims negotiators and voters the promise of a polity that would be more proximate to regular citizens, more reflective of its predominantly Inuit population, and more concerned with economic and social development in the eastern Arctic. For some, the benchmark against which the success of devolution and the NLCA is judged is embodied in the phrase "Inuit Qaujimajatuqangit," or "that which Inuit have long known." Loosely translated as an Inuit way of doing things, IQ is seen as a central feature of post-devolution life in Nunavut (Henderson 2003d). It stands not only for the better integration of Inuit into public life but also for the better integration of Inuit values, Inuit approaches, and Inuit practices (Nunavut 1999, 2004). Often ill-defined and, thus, hard to integrate easily within the bureaucracy, IQ has become the idée fixe of Nunavut politics, the chief effort to create a shift in the political culture of the eastern Arctic. This is noteworthy, because IQ did not occupy a central role in the deliberations of the Nunavut Implementation Commission (Dahl, Hicks, and Jull 2000; Hicks and White 2000). In part, this stems from the use of the term itself, which gained currency after a Nunavut leaders meeting in Igloolik. Its conceptual equivalent did not occupy in the minds of NIC members the role it has come to play in public debate. This is relevant because it helps us to understand both public expectations of the NLCA and evaluations of public life in Nunavut.

Inuit Qaujimajatuqangit
References to IQ emerged after the signing of the NLCA. The term was not raised in public consultations conducted by the NIC. ITC and TFN documents written in the 1970s refer to the need to ensure that the new territory reflects Inuit needs and wishes, but the assumption at the time was that this referred to additional support for hunters and a bureaucracy that operated in

Inuktitut. Certainly, these were the two elements mentioned most often as key objectives for the new territory.

Before division, the NWT had arranged for traditional knowledge working groups. Typically, these referred to Aboriginal culture as something rooted firmly in the past. After the signing of the NLCA, nascent departments in the Nunavut bureaucracy and organizations such as the Nunavut Social Development Council (NSDC) began exploring the topic of traditional knowledge. At its 1998 Igloolik meeting, the NSDC discussed not only Inuit culture in the past but also contemporary Inuit culture in the eastern Arctic (Arnakak 2001; Irniq and Tester 2006; Nunavut Social Development Council 1998). It was from these discussions that the phrase "Inuit Qaujimajatuqangit" emerged, and it has come to be seen as more than traditional knowledge, encompassing "the Inuit way of doing things: the past, present and future knowledge, experience and values of Inuit society" (Nunavut, IQ Task Force 2002, 4).

Shortly after the first election in 1999, the government convened an elders workshop in an effort to identify how it might incorporate Inuit culture into the political system. Efforts to define IQ in a practical sense reinforced its holistic nature, and suggestions for its implementation proved to be wide-ranging. According to participants, IQ refers to knowledge of the land, kinship patterns, and customary law. Because it is a "philosophy and a way of living and thinking that is difficult to put into a few words," participants deliberately resisted an easy checklist-inspired definition of the concept, something that, while well-intentioned, has proved a considerable stumbling block to those eager to integrate it into bureaucratic daily life (Nunavut, CLEY 2000, 14). One elder noted, for example, that IQ "is respecting and loving" (15). Reaction to these broad definitions, which emphasize an Inuit way of interacting with the world, is mixed. In a 2001 editorial, *Nunatsiaq News* (2001) noted that "in two short years it's degenerated into, well, whatever anyone wants it to mean."

The 1999 workshop provided a wide-ranging list of suggestions for how IQ might be incorporated into the working culture of political life in Nunavut. From the comprehensive list provided by participants, it is possible to identify five areas of interest: communication, research, GN adaptability, monitoring, and cultural contact. In terms of communication, participants called for the creation of resources, including videos and books, and workshops so that individuals could discuss IQ and then make public the content of those discussions. The teaching of IQ, in schools and in workshops to non-Inuit

GN staff, was also discussed. Here, one participant noted that Inuit staff would also benefit from an IQ orientation as "We can't assume that just being born into a culture makes a person an expert in that culture" (Nunavut, CLEY 2000, 6). Emphasis on research was evident in the desire to gather the accumulated knowledge of elders, their "memories, knowledge, stories and skills" (Nunavut, CLEY 2000, 7). Also of interest were the experiences of other governments that had attempted to integrate Aboriginal values and practices into their institutional working cultures. The workshop mentioned the adaptability of the GN. This included greater flexibility for employees, greater flexibility in policy evaluation, and greater attention to the role of elders. Visits from elders were to be encouraged, and elders were to be welcomed when they turned up in government departments. Employees were to be afforded more flexible working hours so that they might hunt caribou, geese, and whales; pick berries; or go clam digging. Participants suggested that these activities are particularly dependent on climate and seasonal variations and that, consequently, a rigid nine-to-five understanding of government hours was inappropriate: government work could be completed after 5:00 PM or on weekends, while hunting could not be rescheduled. Such activities are mentioned not as leisure pursuits but as an essential component of Inuit culture, related not only to the food people eat but also to social gatherings, relationship to the land, and knowledge acquisition. The notion that some Inuit would be hunters while others would be bureaucrats, so prevalent in the 1950s and 1960s federal understanding of divisions among Inuit, is banished by this approach.

Participants also suggested the GN should look beyond the formal "credentials" of potential employees and should prioritize instead practical experience. The importance of monitoring was recognized as workshop participants called for the creation of departmental IQ committees and a monitoring committee for the GN as a whole. Last, participants urged the increased salience of particular components of Inuit culture. This included using Inuktitut in the GN, providing country food to Inuit in hospitals and jails, integrating Inuit counselling methods into the courts, using Inuit patterns of knowledge transmission in the education system, and accepting Inuit healing into the health care system. Together, the recommendations of workshop participants provide concrete examples of how the new territory might emphasize IQ. Some of this is clearly within the purview of the GN and, therefore, provides a blueprint for how the new institutional working culture might better reflect Inuit culture. Other changes suggest wider societal transformation. However manageable this initial list of tasks, the bar has been raised considerably since 1999, and those in charge of various departments have faced increasing pressure to demonstrate that they are integrating IQ beyond providing individuals with time off for hunting, or away days for departments. In 2002, the GN IQ task force suggested that a more appropriate goal would be to integrate government into Inuit culture rather than the other way round (Nunavut, IQ Task Force 2002). In its first review of IQ, the task force called for the creation of a land-bridge between government services and the "primary relationship needs" in Inuit culture: relationships to the land, family, spirit, and organizations (2).

Efforts by the GN legislature and bureaucracy to address IQ have been governed by equal parts enthusiasm and bewilderment. All departments now have an IQ committee or working group as well as an elder to advise on IQ. The government has an interdepartmental IQ task force, and the Department of Culture, Language, Elders and Youth, assumed to be the lead IQ department, convenes an elders' group on the topic, the GN IQ katimajiit. Rhetorically, members of the legislature clearly embrace IQ, deputy ministers affirm their commitment to it, and both suggest it is essential that the political system, its legislature and bureaucracy, reflect it. And yet there is obvious concern that support for IQ seems to be more symbolic than substantive. The challenges of implementation stem from the definitions and role of IQ. IQ plays a functional role, in the sense that it contains components relevant to both process and substance. Thus, IQ is not only about the content of policy decisions – that Inuit receive support if they wish to pursue Inuktitut language education or learn to hunt – but also about the process by which decisions are reached. This functional role is joined by a symbolic role, in which the constituent components of IQ are less relevant than the fact that its emphasis points to a power shift in Nunavut from non-Inuit government authorities to the Inuit population. As the functional components of IQ have been addressed, appetite for the symbolic role of IQ has increased. Methods for attending to this role, however, are less clear.

The functional role of IQ addresses a familiar problem within political culture: the fit between the culture of institutions and the values of a given population. The struggle over IQ, Arnakak (2001, 17) explains, is over "the right to exercise and institute the values and principles of conduct of [Nunavut's] citizenry into its constitution." According to this definition, Nunavut is a success if IQ is incorporated by the territory's political institutions. Early emphasis on IQ prioritized substantive definitions, treating it predominantly as traditional knowledge and behaviour. Knowledge of hunting, climate, land, the use of Inuktitut, the anthropology of Inuit daily life, the perceived tenets of an Inuit cultural approach to social relationships were all incorporated within IQ. This was reinforced by politicians who likened IQ to past practice. The premier, for example, told the 1999 workshop participants that he sometimes asked himself "what my ancestors would have done if they were living in today's world" (Nunavut CLEY 2000, 7). Efforts to integrate these substantive definitions have proved difficult for bureaucrats: "How do you incorporate 'Inuit Qaujimajatuqangit' into the design of a sewage treatment plant?" (*Nunatsiaq News* 2001).

Efforts to ensure that political institutions in Nunavut reflect IQ face four challenges. First there is an obvious translation problem when one seeks to apply values, practices, and knowledge rooted in the past, in lives lived on the land in small family settings, to a contemporary environment, where individuals live in communities within a rights-based polity. Second, it is difficult to apply values and behaviour practised by individuals or small social groups to the culture of institutions. Third, there is the problem of contested notions of Inuit values and knowledge. Fourth, among those notions not contested, there might be a fundamental incompatibility between IQ and the worldviews underpinning Euro-Canadian bureaucratic structures and processes. Each of these problems surfaced in one particular debate, held in 2003 in the Legislative Assembly of Nunavut, on the Human Rights Bill.

In 1999, Nunavut inherited the NWT Fair Practices Act, which functioned as a human rights act. In an effort to introduce a made-in-Nunavut act that also complied with the protections of the Canadian Human Rights Act, Premier Paul Okalik tabled legislation in October 2002. The first reading of the bill occurred, predictably, without incident, in large part because the premier drew parallels between the protection of minorities and the discrimination traditionally suffered by Inuit. As the bill worked its way through the committee stages, however, MLAs began to divide over the inclusion of sexual orientation. Two criticisms emerged, one focused on the protection of individual rights – of any description – and the other focused on sexual orientation. Members alternately noted that the protection of individual rights was anathema to Inuit culture and, thus, inconsistent with IQ and the view that homosexuality or bisexuality either did not exist in traditional Inuit culture or, if they did, they were taboo. The final reading of the bill, on 3 November

2003, saw various attempts to suggest that those who supported it either did not understand IQ or were insufficiently committed to it. The premier, in his defence, brought an elder to the legislature to advise on the IQ compliance of the bill, a move that suggests he was sensitive to such claims. Debate tended to conflate Inuit approaches to sexuality and Arctic Anglicanism. A letter from Andrew Atagotaaluk, the Anglican bishop of the Arctic, was tabled before the debate and summarized his opposition to the bill (Atagotaaluk 2003; see also *Nunatsiaq News* 2003).[1] Arguments that homosexuality is anti-IQ because the bible says it is a sin present the clearest example of Inuit-qua-Christian Qaujimajatuqangit. As two members argued:

> The fundamental law of Canada, the Charter of Rights and Freedoms recognizes ... the supremacy of God in the very first sentence. It begins by stating, "Whereas Canada is founded upon principles that recognize the supremacy of God, and the rule of law." I believe that the laws we pass in Nunavut must also reflect our values and to include Inuit Qaujimajatuqangit in the process as people feel that it is an important tool ... Mr Chairman, we as a society have the right not to be forced by any one group into giving explicit legitimacy and endorsement of anybody's life or their lifestyles. Mr Chairman, I will not support this Bill (Nunavut Hansard, 4 November 2003, 4524).
>
> Who has more say? Do the gays and lesbians? Not us? ... [M]inorities have more rights than the Inuit of Nunavut ... Are we going to change the laws of God? Are we going to accept the same sex marriages and give it a blessing? (Nunavut Hansard, 4 November 2003, 4533)

Attention to IQ, however, relates not just to the content of policy decisions but also to the process by which they are reached, and it represents the first significant effort to ensure that political decision making within the territory subscribes, in some way, to Inuit approaches rather than to Westminster-influenced southern Canadian institutions that have been tailored – with greater or lesser success – to the north.

In an effort to identify the Inuit values animating IQ, Joelie Sanguya conducted interviews with elders. He identified six values that characterized traditional Inuit culture and that continue to be of contemporary relevance. Three of these are related to decision making: conferring or reaching decisions through discussion *(aajiiqatigiingniq)*; finding solutions through resourcefulness, prompted in part by the harsh environment in which Inuit traditionally lived *(quqtuurnunnarniq)*; and learning skills through a hands-on approach *(pilimmaksarniq)*. The remaining three values identify important relationships among Inuit: sound stewardship of the environment *(avatimik kamattiarniq)*, a self-sufficient and nurturing leadership *(pijitsiriq)*, and group collaboration and the equitable distribution of resources *(piliriqatigiingniq)*; (Nunavut Social Development Council 1998; see also Arnakak 2001; Henderson 2004a). Often, the process values are seen to conflict with those prioritized by the GN bureaucracy. *Pilimmaksarniq*, for example, is compared favourably to an unhelpful bureaucratic preoccupation with formal education, degrees, and certificates. In their efforts to pit traditional Inuit values against GN values – and, in so doing, to prove how alien the latter are – such explanations compare the values governing the social interaction of individuals with those governing the functioning of a bureaucracy.

The integration of the process component of IQ has proved more difficult to engineer than has the content component. Concerns over whether the political system reflects the process component of IQ surface frequently in the legislature, where the rules governing behaviour are perceived to conflict with an Inuit approach to governing. The much-vaunted practice of consensus is perceived to be a concession to Inuit decision-making models. Other practices, such as the principle of cabinet solidarity, are seen to conflict with traditional decision making, which allowed those who disagreed with collective decisions to pursue their own path. Frustration at the delayed implementation of IQ has prompted accusations from regular members of insufficient commitment of the legislature. This clash between process values is best seen in a debate, again in 2003, over the removal of Jack Anawak from cabinet.

As part of its decentralization program, the GN decided to relocate jobs in the petroleum products division from the decentralized community of Rankin Inlet to the smaller inland community of Baker Lake. The two MLAs for Rankin Inlet, both of whom were in cabinet, opposed the decision when it was first announced. Once it became cabinet policy, however, only Jack Anawak continued to speak out against it. In punishment, the premier stripped Anawak of his portfolio, but his removal from cabinet could only be engineered by a vote within the Legislative Assembly as a whole. On 7 March 2003, regular member Hunter Tootoo lodged a motion to remove Anawak from cabinet. In defence of his position, Anawak spent relatively little time discussing the decentralized jobs and chose instead to argue that cabinet solidarity was inconsistent with IQ, and that efforts to remove him from cabinet confirmed that the government paid greater attention to the arcane rules and procedures of the legislature than it did to the decision-making processes prioritized by IQ.

> Are they supposed to observe rules that do not fit just for the sake of observing them without even wondering about their suitability? Are Cabinet Members supposed to observe this rather foreign concept of solidarity even when they think they're off the rails that the people's interests are not being well represented? This is not the Inuit way. What are the rules as Inuit know and understand? ... What Inuit values and beliefs are being set aside here are the Inuit values of honesty, listening, respect, acceptance, patience, tolerance, resourcefulness and talking [sic] the long view has not been on display in this situation. At this very moment, the elders of Nunavut do not know what's happening in the proceedings in the House. This is about rules in a style of government that does not fit Nunavut. (Nunavut Hansard, 7 March 2003, 2415)

The bilingual premier, who, when he first became head of government, was still paying off student loans from law school, was accused by older MLAs of not acting like a real Inuk. One elder member suggested that the younger cabinet members "have not even caught up with the concept of what it feels like to be Inuk," in part, because "they have gone through the education [that has] taught [them] about the academics but they have no concept of my traditional unilingual values and principles." Removing Anawak, he added, was unseemly:

> The younger people according to the cabinet members are removing the sole elder in the cabinet. You call this Inuit Qaujimajatuqangit. Those people who say they know about Inuit Qaujimajatuqangit, you don't know what Inuit Qaujimajatuqangit is and I'm trying to explain it to you. (Nunavut Hansard, 7 March 2003, 2422)

This notion of Inuit-ness is not new. Elder interviews from the NRI show that, as children, elders came across Inuit who, they felt, were less influenced by missionaries and traders and who were "real Inuit" compared with those living predominantly on the land but coming into only occasional contact with Qallunaat (IE 113; IE 306). Such an approach risks essentializing the Inuit experience and, in so doing, contradicting explicit attempts to ensure that IQ is viewed as a holistic and contemporary way of life. This notion of a "real Inuk," however, returns to ideals held in the 1950s by the federal government. According to Ottawa, the ideal Inuk spoke English, had some knowledge of primary economic activities, was non-confrontational, and would adapt quickly to the rules and laws employed by federal administrators. In the two examples from 2003, the notion of a "real Inuk" is the reverse of this federal ideal. While the change may be a positive one, in that it points to Inuit control over definitions of authenticity, it is nonetheless damaging in that it suggests that there is one way – and only one way – to be Inuit. This struggle over identity points to the most significant role played by IQ: its symbolic one.

The 1999 workshop report on IQ states that "confirming the value of Inuit Qaujimajatuqangit will restore Inuit pride and increase individual self-esteem. By increasing young Inuit self-esteem, some of today's social problems such as substance and alcohol abuse and even suicide will be eliminated" (Nunavut, CLEY 2000). This function is completely different from that raised earlier. That IQ can serve as a means to address suicide and alcohol abuse is a heavy burden but it suggests that IQ is fundamentally about power, about Inuit taking charge and making positive changes for the future. Seen in this light, it suggests that values relevant to small-group life can make a difference for the better, that they are not irrelevant, that previous governments were not right to engineer the destruction of a way of life grounded in IQ. Power also surfaces in the substantive components of IQ for it is linked to power relations among individuals on the land. The notion that everyone had his or her turn, that power was linked to skill and that skill was linked to practice (and thus power was diffuse), suggests that IQ is the opposite of a rigid hierarchy and credentialism, two hallmarks of the public service. In its symbolic role, though, IQ points to a fundamental shift in political culture, from one grounded in the institutional working culture of a Westminster-inspired system to one rooted in the culture of a predominantly Inuit population.

Views on the functional and symbolic roles of IQ vary among the Inuit and Qallunaat population. Certainly, the Inuit population is divided in its views, which vary according to whether one is from a more traditional or less traditional background, whether one is religious, whether one is living in a decentralized community, whether one hunts to procure country food, and whether one is in the cabinet, the legislature, the bureaucracy, or a land claim organization. An individual's current position within society affects how he or she feels about IQ, and one of the key stumbling blocks is not the notion of disagreement but the fact that IQ is personal as well as collective. In a sense, IQ is large enough to have something for everyone. For some it is about authority and voice, for others it is a pure numbers game related to the employment of Inuit in the public service or the use of Inuktitut in meetings. For still others, it is little more than window dressing, something that allows away days, picnics, and days on the land for a predominantly Qallunaat bureaucracy. In the aggregate, though, attention to IQ points to a vision of politics – and, in particular, the operation of political institutions – that is free from federal or territorial influence. Qallunaat reaction to IQ varies from enthusiastic support to confusion. Contentions that the term should be better defined, that it is inconsistent, that it seems alternately too big or too small to effect meaningful change, that it seems to have nothing to do with politics or public administration can be seen in two lights. First, these contentions might be correct; second, they are an unsurprising reaction to a significant challenge to pre-existing political culture.

Cultural and Economic Predictors of Support

The extent to which the government and civil service integrate IQ is not the only marker of its success. Despite attention to IQ in the Legislative Assembly and in the editorials of *Nunatsiaq News*, Inuit identify different concerns, including community infrastructure, poverty, and housing. Even when we turn to the operation of the bureaucracy, we can see more than enough to occupy attentions, whether the pressures of budget over-runs, program delivery, or policy creation. External assessments of political developments since 1999 have seemed more like laments. Almost forty years after his investigation into the impact of a Mackenzie Valley pipeline in the western Arctic – during the course of which he addressed both social and political development in the NWT – Justice Berger conducted a second examination of political development, this time in the eastern Arctic. Berger's assessment of Nunavut is grim. Its insufficient cultural gains, in particular the fact that the bureaucracy still operates in English, are linked to the dire assessments of demographic reality found in the Irwin Report (Irwin 1989a, see also Tungavik

Federation of Nunavut 1989) as well as to the absence of sufficient resources (Berger 2006). If Inuit are to do better out of the NCLA, the territory requires more resources that are targeted to specific issues. For Berger, financial support and the establishment of a political culture that better reflects Inuit values are necessary bedfellows. Berger's report is even more striking when we consider that it was a conciliator's report whose purpose was to determine how to resolve an impasse in negotiations. That he spoke so forcefully about education in the midst of such a document is indeed telling.

Press accounts concerning Nunavut have suggested that the government is so bedevilled by understaffing and runaway budgets, the population so let down by low levels of education and poverty, that meaningful social development is not the automatic consequence of the NLCA and territory that Nunavummiut had hoped it would be. And yet we know little about how Inuit in Nunavut view their land claim or about how Nunavummiut in general feel about the territory. Indeed, we know little about how Aboriginal Canadians in general feel about their constitutional rights. The public opinion data we have on Aboriginal land claims in Canada tends to track the views of non-Aboriginal Canadians. Much of the existing academic research explores how non-Aboriginal Canadians view the provision of rights or the resolution of treaties for Aboriginal peoples (Gibbins and Ponting 1976; Ponting 2000, 2006; Ponting and Gibbins 1981a, 1981b; Ponting and Langford 1992). What evidence we have suggests that non-Aboriginal Canadians place little emphasis on land claims, providing us with further reason to look elsewhere for answers. Data from Environics, a private polling firm, suggests that a larger proportion of Canadians feel that alcohol and drugs, not land claims, are the most important issues facing Aboriginal Canadians. According to the 1998 Environics data, only 5 percent of Canadians feel that self-government is the most important issue facing Aboriginal peoples. The data also demonstrate that non-Aboriginal Canadians pay inconsistent attention to Aboriginal issues. Although almost three-quarters of respondents knew of the federal apology for the mistreatment of Aboriginal peoples at residential schools, only half that number were aware of the creation of Nunavut.

Attention to the relationship between public opinion and land claims tends to focus on the legitimacy that public support lends to these claims as well as to the factors that might increase that support. A general recognition that a particular band occupied territory to the exclusion of other groups not only is a criterion for comprehensive land claims but is seen as a key element on the public relations front. We have much less data, however, on the expectations that Aboriginal peoples bring to land claims and how they feel about public life following such claims. In Nunavut, however, three surveys asked respondents about their expectations of the NLCA and their assessments of political developments: the 1999 Nunavut add-on to the NWT Labour Force Survey, the 2001 NuHS, and the 2004 NuHS.

The following section addresses two research questions: (1) what are the trends of support for the NLCA and the new territory since 1999? and (2) what is the structure of that support? An analysis of these two questions tells us what to expect with regard to future self-government initiatives in Canada and abroad. It not only allows us to compare Nunavut with other jurisdictions but also serves to highlight potential problems that might be avoided as well as lessons of best practice that might be followed. When evaluating the possible design of the Nunavut government, the Nunavut Implementation Commission warned that expectations, whether too high or too low, could hinder the progress of the land claim and the legislature. Employing data that have not yet been analyzed elsewhere, we can test whether evaluations of progress have met earlier expectations. By examining the structure of support for the NLCA, we are able to test two hypotheses: (1) whether those who benefit materially from the agreement are more supportive of it and (2) whether those who can identity a cultural benefit from the NLCA demonstrate greater support. Initial expectations for the NLCA suggested that there was greater hope for the cultural benefits of reform. It is worth testing whether these cultural benefits are perceived to have arrived.

EXPECTATIONS AND EVALUATIONS

It is useful to determine how northern respondents felt about the impending division in 1999. The results from Table 9.1 indicate the proportion of the population that believed Nunavut would bring positive changes in a number of policy areas.

The results show considerable expectations of improvement in each of the policy areas. For all but one area (the teaching of English and French), over half of all Nunavummiut believed that Nunavut would have a positive impact. This support is most evident, though, when we examine policies related to the vitality of Inuit culture, values, and language rather than those related to the possible economic benefits of the new territory. Over 70 percent believed that the new territory would be good for language, while over

TABLE 9.1

Expectations of Nunavut

Area of improvement	Nunavut	Inuit	Non-Inuit	Significant differences?
Respect for Inuit values	81.2	80.2	85.2	
Teaching of Inuktitut and Inuinnaqtun	76.5	77.1	74.1	**
Inuktitut and Inuinnaqtun	70.8	71.1	69.4	**
Education programs	63.8	68.9	44.1	***
Economic development	63.7	62.9	66.2	*
Environment	63.3	65.4	55.6	***
Community government	61.5	62.8	56.4	**
Justice system	54.9	58.4	42.3	***
Community health	53.3	56.8	40.3	***
Health services	51.5	55.0	38.6	***
Teaching of English and French	37.5	43.0	17.6	***

NOTE: Results are % indicating positive impact.
SOURCE: NWT Labour Force Survey 1999 ($n = 814$). * = $p < .1$; ** = $p < .05$; *** = $p < .01$.

80 percent believed that it would have a positive impact on the integration of Inuit values. This can be seen as a precursor to the public and bureaucratic attention paid to the integration of IQ.

Equally striking are differences between the expectations of Inuit and non-Inuit residents in Nunavut. In all but two cases, Inuit expectations were higher than were those of non-Inuit. The exceptions include economic development and, interestingly, the incorporation of Inuit values. On the whole, though, the results show that hopes were higher among Inuit than among non-Inuit. Differences between the two groups are statistically significant at either the .1, .05, or .01 level for ten of the eleven policy fields. Only on expectations of the integration of Inuit values were Inuit and non-Inuit assessments similar. These results suggest that if expectations were not met it would be the higher hopes of Inuit that would be disappointed. Among the non-Inuit population, fewer than half believed there would be positive improvements in five of the eleven policy areas.

If questions about expectations suggest that the NLCA and Nunavut would be judged on their treatment of Inuit language, culture, and values, evaluations suggest that Nunavummiut were also aware of the financial benefits of the new territory. The GN introduced hundreds of stable, well-paying jobs, which provided an economic opportunity unprecedented in the eastern Arctic. The 2004 NuHS asked respondents about their views of these jobs. The results show that individuals had positive assessments of employment with the GN. These were not, it should be noted, uninformed opinions as by 2004 many of the respondents had either worked for the GN or had learned of the trials faced by GN employees through media sources or word of mouth. With this in mind, the results show that over 80 percent believed that the pay and benefits enjoyed by GN employees, along with the stress levels they encountered, were better or equal to those encountered in other jobs. In terms of worker satisfaction, fewer than one-fifth of respondents believed morale and happiness to be lower among GN employees than among other workers. This suggests that respondents were well aware of the economic as well as the cultural benefits made available by the NLCA and Nunavut. A more robust understanding of evaluations, however, surfaces in the available time series data.

THE STRUCTURE OF SUPPORT

Since 1999, each survey has sought responses to five evaluations of public life. The first probes attitudes toward the NLCA, while three probe Nunavut's impact on all who live there, on the respondent's community, and on the respondent. A fifth question asks about the government's ability to function, given the current financial situation.

Table 9.2 tracks support for these questions across the three datasets. Two things are worth identifying here. First, the questions distinguish between the land claim in general and the creation of the government of Nunavut, provisions for which were contained within the NLCA. The data suggest that respondents attribute a greater impact to the territorial legislature and its civic service rather than the land claim. Second, the questions distinguish between the past and future. A greater number believe that some

TABLE 9.2

Support for the NLCA and Nunavut, percent agreeing

	1999	2001	2004
Implementation of NLCA positive impact on me	51.4	56.7	57.6
Nunavut positive impact for me personally	62.9	67.2	65.0
Nunavut opportunity for all to govern lives better	85.9	79.3	76.5
Nunavut positive impact on my community	80.5	74.4	73.3
Difficult time maintaining existing programs	74.8	80.2	83.2

SOURCES: 1999 NWT Labour Force Survey (n = 814); 2001 NuHS (n = 5816); 2004 NuHS (n = 900).

form of positive impact will eventually result from the government than believe that one has already occurred. A considerable reserve of support and optimism remains, even if assessments to date have been tepid.

In terms of trends over time, we see a clear decrease in the belief that the new territory will allow Nunavummiut to govern their lives better, a steady decrease in the impact of Nunavut on the respondent's community, and a steady increase in the perceived problem of funding and maintaining programs. The perceived benefit of the NLCA and Nunavut on individuals, however, does not follow these trends. Although there has been an increase in personal assessments of impact, 2001 seemed to be a particularly bad year for the land claim, with fewer than half of respondents indicating it would have a positive impact. That same year, however, assessments of the territory increased dramatically. It is possible that individuals shifted their attention away from the land claim and toward the territory as a way of retaining positive feelings about political developments. The motivations behind different responses become clear, however, when we start to disaggregate responses by social characteristics.

Table 9.3 tracks support for the NLCA and Nunavut by ethnicity, and here some interesting findings emerge. First, Inuit and non-Inuit do not necessarily share parallel assessments of political developments. Certainly, there is evidence of similar thinking. Inuit and non-Inuit have both become increasingly convinced of the financial troubles facing Nunavut, with more than 80 percent of Inuit and more than 90 percent of non-Inuit believing

TABLE 9.3

Support for the NLCA and Nunavut, by ethnicity, percent agreeing

	1999 Inuit	1999 Non-Inuit	2001 Inuit	2001 Non-Inuit	2004 Inuit	2004 Non-Inuit
Implementation of NLCA positive impact on me	57.2	31.0	60.6	36.2	61.9	39.4
Nunavut positive impact for me personally	68.2	42.8	68.3	61.3	63.4	72.0
Nunavut opportunity for all to govern lives better	86.5	83.8	78.8	81.5	74.0	86.9
Nunavut positive impact on my community	79.6	84.0	73.0	82.1	69.7	89.0
Difficult time maintaining existing programs	73.2	80.7	79.1	86.6	81.2	91.6

NOTE: Results in bold represent statistically significant differences between Inuit and non-Inuit at the .05 level.
SOURCES: 1999 NWT Labour Force Survey ($n = 814$); 2001 NuHS ($n = 5816$); 2004 NuHS ($n = 900$).

that the territory will have a difficult time maintaining existing programs. Non-Inuit, however, seem increasingly convinced that the territory will have a positive effect on them personally, while Inuit views are relatively static in this regard. Inuit have become less convinced that the territory provides an opportunity for Nunavummiut to govern their lives better, while non-Inuit views are unchanged over time. A first conclusion, then, is that we see different trends at work among Inuit and non-Inuit respondents.

Second, the differences between Inuit and non-Inuit respondents have grown over time. In 1999, ethnicity produced statistically significant variations in responses to assessments of the NLCA, the personal impact of the territory, and the capacity to maintain programs. By 2001, Inuit and non-Inuit held statistically significant views on four of the five indicators, and by 2004 Inuit and non-Inuit do not have similar responses to any of the indicators.

Clearly, ethnicity has an impact on support for the NLCA and Nunavut. It is worth determining whether other characteristics, such as age, level of education, community size, and gender also have an impact. One tactic would be to examine each of these as predictors of support for the NLCA and Nunavut and determine which characteristics prompt individuals to feel greater or lesser support for political developments. We know, however, that expectations were highest among Inuit and that expectations of cultural change were far higher than were expectations of economic developments. If we know that some individuals are supportive of the NLCA and Nunavut and that others are not, it is worth determining whether political developments have a differential impact among the population.

The remainder of this chapter pits two hypotheses against each other. The first, which stems from data discussed earlier, suggests that those who have benefited culturally from the NLCA and Nunavut will be more supportive than will those who have not. If this is true, we would expect positive evaluations of the NLCA and the territory from those who are currently benefiting culturally, through their ability to speak Inuktitut or Inuinnaqtun at home or at work, those who have positive assessments of the strength of the Inuit languages, and from those who are happy with the frequency with which they go hunting or eat country food. A second hypothesis suggests that those who have benefited materially from developments will hold more positive views than will those who have not. These respondents would include those with higher levels of education, those with sufficient employment (including employment with the government), and those with higher incomes. These two hypotheses test whether residents see in Nunavut a cultural renaissance for Inuit or a stepping stone for economic emancipation. This, in turn, allows us to determine whether Nunavut is presently a tiered society, one in which some are benefiting from the NLCA while others are not. To test this, I rely on a series of regression analyses, with each of the questions about Nunavut serving as dependent variables.

The analysis presents three models. The first model includes measures of cultural vitality, including access to the land, knowledge of Inuktitut, use of Inuktitut at home, frequency of harvesting activity, creation of Inuit crafts, and access to country food. If individuals possessing these characteristics are more supportive of the NLCA or Nunavut then this will confirm that Nunavut is being judged primarily on the improvements it has made to Inuit vitality. The second model posits another hypothesis and includes measures of economic vitality. Variables such as income, employment status, dwelling conditions, and whether the respondent has ever worked or is currently working for the GN will help us to determine whether economic considerations are driving assessments of political developments. The third model, the fully specified model, includes a number of control variables such as ethnicity, gender, age, whether the respondent has graduated from high school, willingness to move for jobs, exposure to the internet, and whether the respondent lives in Iqaluit. These allow us to speak to the varied circumstances of Nunavummiut. If the primary economic benefits are perceived to be found in Iqaluit rather than in the smaller communities, for example, residence in Iqaluit could appear as a predictor of positive evaluations.

The results from the regression analysis appear in Tables 9.4 through 9.7. Four findings emerge. First, there appears to be clear evidence that cultural vitality does a better job of explaining expectations and evaluations than does personal economic success. In other words, respondents who are able to eat country food, spend time on the land, speak Inuktitut at home, or participate in harvesting activities frequently are more likely to be pleased with the NLCA and with the impact of Nunavut on their community or themselves. They are also more likely to believe that the territory allows all Nunavummiut to better govern their lives. This finding should not be taken lightly. Employment status and income, for example, appear irrelevant to evaluations of public life post-1999. Individuals are not happier with progress in Nunavut if they have a job or if they have a higher income. The sole measure of economic vitality that is a consistent predictor of positive evaluations is dwelling condition. Individuals view the NLCA and Nunavut more favourably if they are satisfied with the condition of their homes. These findings

TABLE 9.4

Impact of NLCA on individual, 2001 and 2004

		2001			2004		
		Model 1	Model 2	Model 3	Model 1	Model 2	Model 3
Constant		.514 (.03)***	.432 (.04)***	.383 (.05)***	.231 (.07)***	.159 (.09)*	-.037 (.124)
Cultural vitality	Country food	.110 (.03)***	.104 (.03)***	.096 (.03)***	.149 (.09)	.121 (.09)	.143 (.09)
	Time on land	n/a	n/a	n/a	.127 (.07)*	.129 (.07)*	.161 (.07)**
	Crafts	.024 (.02)	.024 (.02)	.014 (.02)	-.026 (.04)	-.014 (.04)	-.018 (.04)
	Inuktitut first language	.027 (.02)	.041 (.02)*	.002 (.04)	-.009 (.06)	.022 (.06)	-.003 (.08)
	Inuktitut at home	.011 (.02)	.016 (.02)	.016 (.02)	.079 (.05)	.092 (.05)*	.069 (.05)
	Harvest frequently	.024 (.02)	.030 (.02)	.028 (.02)	.173 (.06)***	.170 (.06)***	.136 (.06)**
Economic vitality	Income		-.002 (.03)	-.016 (.03)		.022 (.07)	-.006 (.08)
	Employed		.002 (.02)	.004 (.02)		-.001 (.04)	-.002 (.04)
	Dwelling condition		.103 (.02)***	.102 (.02)***		.172 (.06)***	.149 (.06)**
	Work for GN		.019 (.01)	.013 (.02)		-.067 (.04)*	-.059 (.04)
Control variables	Inuit			.056 (.04)			.100 (.08)
	Female			.013 (.01)			-.009 (.04)
	Iqaluit			.032 (.02)			.117 (.05)**
	Education			-.019 (.02)			.031 (.05)
	Age			.099 (.03)***			.160 (.07)**
	Willing to move			.007 (.01)			.083 (.04)**
	Internet use			.019 (.02)			-.017 (.04)
Adjusted R²		.02	.04	.05	.09	.10	.12

NOTES: Data are unweighted. DV: Impact of NLCA on respondent. Results are unstandardized coefficients for OLS regression with standard errors in parentheses. * = $p < .1$; ** = $p < .05$; *** = $p < .01$.
SOURCE: NuHS 2001, 2004.

TABLE 9.5

Impact of Nunavut on individual, 2001 and 2004

		2001			2004		
		Model 1	Model 2	Model 3	Model 1	Model 2	Model 3
Constant		.633 (.03)***	.567 (.04)***	.529 (.04)***	.694 (.06)***	.583 (.08)***	.478 (.10)***
Cultural vitality	Country food	.074 (.03)**	.076 (.03)**	.087 (.03)***	.070 (.08)	.060 (.08)	.100 (.08)
	Time on land	n/a	n/a	n/a	-.014 (.06)	-.012 (.06)	.011 (.06)
	Crafts	.064 (.02)***	.067 (.02)***	.065 (.02)***	-.058 (.03)*	-.047 (.03)	-.042 (.03)
	Inuktitut first language	.026 (.02)	.045 (.02)*	.026 (.03)	-.185 (.05)***	-.170 (.05)***	-.088 (.06)
	Inuktitut at home	-.028 (.02)	-.021 (.02)	-.018 (.02)	.053 (.04)	.065 (.04)	.070 (.04)*
	Harvest frequently	-.024 (.02)	-.022 (.02)	-.026 (.02)	.157 (.05)***	.159 (.05)***	.160 (.05)***
Economic vitality	Income		.056 (.03)*	.025 (.03)		-.007 (.06)	-.065 (.06)
	Employed		-.016 (.02)	-.015 (.02)		.051 (.03)*	.030 (.03)
	Dwelling condition		.060 (.02)***	.055 (.02)**		.089 (.05)*	.060 (.05)
	Work for GN		.006 (.01)	.007 (.02)		.032 (.03)	.035 (.03)
Control variables	Inuit			.041 (.04)			-.066 (.07)
	Female			-.013 (.01)			-.011 (.03)
	Iqaluit			.047 (.02)**			.090 (.04)**
	Education			-.003 (.01)			.040 (.04)
	Age			.041 (.03)			.038 (.06)
	Willing to move			-.014 (.01)			.037 (.03)
	Internet use			.031 (.02)*			.036 (.04)
Adjusted R²		.01	.02	.03	.05	.06	.07

NOTES: Data are unweighted. DV: Impact of Nunavut on individual. Results are unstandardized coefficients for OLS regression with standard errors in parentheses. * = $p < .1$; ** = $p < .05$; *** = $p < .01$.
SOURCE: NuHS 2001, 2004.

TABLE 9.6

Impact of Nunavut on ability to govern better, 2001 and 2004

		2001			2004		
		Model 1	Model 2	Model 3	Model 1	Model 2	Model 3
Constant		.666 (.03)***	.553 (.05)***	.535 (.05)***	.653 (.06)***	.554 (.08)***	.596 (.10)***
Cultural vitality	Country food	.058 (.04)	.054 (.04)	.050 (.04)	-.010 (.08)	-.028 (.08)	-.018 (.08)
	Time on land	n/a	n/a	n/a	.155 (.06)***	.151 (.06)***	.153 (.06)***
	Crafts	.034 (.02)	.037 (.02)*	.032 (.02)	.000 (.03)	.009 (.03)	.014 (.03)
	Inuktitut first language	-.075 (.03)***	-.048 (.03)	-.034 (.04)	-.113 (.05)**	-.106 (.05)**	-.111 (.06)*
	Inuktitut at home	-.002 (.02)	.010 (.02)	.005 (.02)	.012 (.04)	.021 (.04)	.008 (.04)
	Harvest frequently	-.005 (.02)	.001 (.02)	-.010 (.03)	.000 (.05)	.006 (.05)	-.013 (.05)
Economic vitality	Income		.052 (.03)	.044 (.04)		-.047 (.06)	-.034 (.06)
	Employed		-.026 (.02)	-.027 (.02)		.026 (.03)	-.022 (.03)
	Dwelling condition		.145 (.03)***	.147 (.03)***		.116 (.05)**	.121 (.05)**
	Work for GN		.010 (.02)	.016 (.02)		.058 (.03)*	.039 (.03)
Control variables	Inuit			-.010 (.05)			-.008 (.06)
	Female			-.018 (.02)			-.025 (.03)
	Iqaluit			.019 (.03)			.043 (.04)
	Education			-.015 (.02)			-.023 (.04)
	Age			.086 (.04)**			-.004 (.06)
	Willing to move			.025 (.02)			.049 (.03)
	Internet use			-.008 (.02)			-.068 (.04)*
Adjusted R^2		.01	.03	.04	.02	.04	.04

NOTES: Data are unweighted. DV: Impact of Nunavut on ability to govern better. Results are unstandardized coefficients for OLS regression with standard errors in parentheses. * = $p < .1$; ** = $p < .05$; *** = $p < .01$.

SOURCE: NuHS 2001, 2004.

TABLE 9.7

Nunavut will face financial troubles, 2001 and 2004

		2001			2004		
		Model 1	Model 2	Model 3	Model 1	Model 2	Model 3
Constant		.825 (.03)***	.777 (.05)***	.752 (.05)***	.811 (.06)***	.886 (.08)***	.745 (.10)***
Cultural vitality	Country food	-.074 (.04)*	-.066 (.04)*	-.073 (.04)*	.020 (.07)	.035 (.07)	.057 (.08)
	Time on land	n/a	n/a	n/a	-.082 (.05)	-.081 (.05)	-.058 (.05)
	Crafts	-.049 (.02)**	-.043 (.02)**	-.043 (.02)**	.012 (.03)	.002 (.03)	-.009 (.03)
	Inuktitut first language	-.014 (.03)	-.002 (.03)	-.059 (.04)	-.120 (.04)***	-.130 (.05)***	-.136 (.06)**
	Inuktitut at home	-.073 (.02)***	-.068 (.02)***	-.069 (.02)***	-.016 (.04)	-.024 (.04)	-.032 (.04)
	Harvest frequently	.013 (.02)	.013 (.02)	.009 (.02)	.079 (.05)*	.079 (.05)*	.085 (.05)*
Economic vitality	Income		.073 (.03)**	.071 (.04)*		.021 (.06)	.021 (.06)
	Employed		.007 (.02)	.008 (.02)		-.014 (.03)	-.009 (.03)
	Dwelling condition		.006 (.03)	.005 (.03)		-.108 (.05)**	-.118 (.05)**
	Work for GN		-.026 (.02)	-.024 (.02)		-.017 (.03)	-.013 (.03)
Control variables	Inuit			.094 (.04)**			.034 (.06)
	Female			-.009 (.02)			.061 (.03)**
	Iqaluit			.001 (.03)			.078 (.04)*
	Education			.018 (.02)			.025 (.04)
	Age			.01 (.04)			.052 (.05)
	Willing to move			-.019 (.02)			.049 (.03)
	Internet use			.008 (.02)			-.03 (.03)
Adjusted R²		.03	.03	.03	.03	.04	.05

NOTES: Data are unweighted. DV: Nunavut will face financial troubles. Results are unstandardized coefficients for OLS regression with standard errors in parentheses. * = p < .1; ** = p < .05; *** = p < .01.
SOURCE: NuHS 2001, 2004.

hold not only when we are examining attitudes toward the NLCA but also when we are examining attitudes toward the government. Evaluations of housing are likely tied as much to social phenomena such as overcrowding as they are to evaluations of the physical infrastructure of the house itself. In his study of housing in Cape Dorset, Frank Tester (2006) identifies the web of relationships among housing quality, overcrowding, economic well-being, social well-being, and health.

Second, when we examine control variables, ethnicity appears to be irrelevant. Inuit are not happier with territorial developments than are non-Inuit. Similarly, if we compare these results to those found in the first and second models mentioned above, we find that hunting or eating country food is a positive predictor, regardless of ethnicity. Non-Inuit who hunt and eat country food are happier with political developments than are those who do not participate in these activities. Although more likely among longer-term residents, this suggests that a higher level of engagement with land-based activities, what some might see as traditional Inuit culture, is a predictor of support.

Third, we see some interesting differences over time. In 2001, for example, assessments of the NLCA depend on ability to eat country food, condition of dwelling, and age. By 2004, however, a broader range of variables became statistically significant predictors of views. Spending time on the land, harvesting frequently, living in Iqaluit, and a willingness to move for work all serve as positive predictors of support for the NLCA. These patterns hold for the impact of Nunavut on respondents and their improved ability to govern their lives. Over time, then, the hypothesis of cultural vitality has become stronger, not weaker. This is reflected not only in the wider range of statistically significant predictors but also in the improved adjusted R^2 scores for the regression models.[2] We should note, however, that the scores are, in general, very low and that much of the variation in the dependent variables remains unexplained.

Fourth, we see different patterns of results across questions. Control variables such as age, gender, or place of residence are relevant to some questions but not to others. Control variables such as ethnicity, place of residence, and age are relevant to assessments of the NLCA but perform less well as predictors of support for Nunavut. In general, though, those living in Iqaluit and those willing to move for work are more supportive of the NLCA and Nunavut, while older respondents are happier with the NLCA. There are two occasions when economic predictors other than dwelling condition prove useful. Income is a positive predictor of perceived financial troubles in the 2001 data and, in the 2004 data, working for the GN serves, not surprisingly, as a positive predictor of improved governance, though not in the fully specified model.

This is most striking when we turn to assessments of financial troubles. The other dependent variables under examination measure positive feelings. The final dependent variable, however, measures pessimism regarding the future of Nunavut. Here we see that women and those living in Iqaluit, are among the most likely to believe that financial troubles will make meeting program goals difficult. Those who learned Inuktitut as a first language and those happy with the condition of their dwelling are more likely to be optimistic about the future.

What, then, can we take from these results? On the one hand, the data clearly show that Nunavummiut are judging Nunavut and the NLCA on their cultural merits rather than on their economic merits. Not only are economic variables useless as positive predictors of developments, but they are also absent as negative predictors. It is not that income causes one to have significantly higher or significantly lower assessments of political developments – it is largely irrelevant. Respondents are not, for the most part, basing their assessments of Nunavut on their material surroundings, although dwelling condition is a consistent and important factor. In all other respects, though, "doing well out of Nunavut" has nothing to do with money and everything to do with the ability to lead a life grounded in what might be considered traditional practice. If government officials understand the basis upon which Nunavummiut are framing their evaluations of public life, then it is likely that they will be able to improve upon existing assessments. On the other hand, there is clear evidence that Nunavummiut see economic rather than cultural challenges ahead for the territory. This suggests a certain temporal order to things. Individuals who are *currently* happy with the NLCA and Nunavut tend to exhibit signs of cultural vitality, but assessments of expectations of *future* happiness clearly depend on the territory's ability to meet economic expectations.

10
Cultural Pluralism and Political Culture

Nunavut: Rethinking Political Culture clarifies certain misconceptions about political life in the north. I demonstrate, for example, that consensus politics was not a conscious effort to integrate Aboriginal decision-making practice. Until recently, both territorial and federal officials viewed the arrival of political parties as inevitable. Continued federal influence delayed the establishment of responsible government until the 1980s, at which point consensus politics seemed so entrenched that there was little appetite for reform. In my investigation of consensus politics, I also show that the absence of parties does not significantly alter the behaviour of legislators. Although campaigning is more expensive for individuals, and the tenor of campaigns is different than would otherwise be the case, legislative members mimic remarkably faithfully the roles they would occupy in a partisan system. During campaigns, when the absence of parties is most noticeable, it is candidates rather than voters who portray political debate through a local rather than a territorial lens. Consensus politics in Nunavut is remarkable for what it has not produced rather than for what it has.

The analysis of political participation similarly corrects earlier assumptions. Voter turnout in territorial contests does not reflect the flurry of participation we have come to expect. The system of enumeration has excluded from the territorial rolls over five thousand Nunavummiut who appear on the federal list. Our assessments of participation have been drastic overestimations. Although rates of political participation among "spectators" may appear unremarkable, the distribution of electoral posts across the territory – in both public and Inuit organizations – ensures that there are elected positions for a far greater proportion of the population than is the case in southern Canada.

Beyond correcting misconceptions, *Nunavut: Rethinking Political Culture* explores topics not yet mined by other scholars. It identifies in precontact and contact Inuit society approaches to resource distribution and social control that can be seen as the foundation of a political culture, even in the absence of formal institutions. It demonstrates that attitudes toward deference and efficacy are different from those exhibited in southern Canada. It distinguishes between substantive and symbolic aspects of Inuit Qaujimajatuqangit and unpacks the nature of support for the current territory. The Nunavut case study is a rich one, and it provides enough evidence – both qualitative and quantitative – to keep political scientists both happy and busy for many years.

The appeal of the case study, though, is in its ability to contribute to our conceptual understanding of political culture. In general, the population of Nunavut is similar to that of the rest of Canada. Health and economic statistics suggest Nunavummiut are in a more vulnerable position than the rest of the Canadian electorate, but there are clearly common Canadian denominators. The pace of change that delivered this eastern Arctic population to its *relatively* equivalent position is, however, remarkable. A contemporary electorate that was excluded from the political system until the 1960s provides us with the sort of empirical test case that enables us to stretch and bend elements of theory to determine whether they can still explain why people vote, what people think, and how institutions reflect and influence culture.

Both the speed and content of transformations are important. At the end of the Second World War, the Canadian state was virtually absent from the lives of eastern Arctic residents, its presence limited to military bases. Over the next twenty years, the process of religious conversion that had begun following the First World War accelerated, the economic transformation from hunting to wage capitalism began in earnest, and Inuit were integrated as political citizens into a network of institutions that alternately ignored them, viewed them as objects, or treated them as desperately in need of assistance. Consistent federal attention to democracy at the local level caused councils and committees, both public and ethnic, to flourish so that when federal policy was forced to acknowledge the legitimacy of a land claim, Inuit were already primed for action. The case study is sufficiently different from those that we normally encounter in advanced industrial states to allow us to confirm or refute certain theories intended to describe a general reality. If these theories still explain political operations in Nunavut, then we can lend them additional weight. If they do not, then we can refine them in an effort to better explain the interactions between and among citizens and the state.

The research presented in *Nunavut: Rethinking Political Culture* calls for minor modifications in conceptual approaches to political development. It suggests that the hierarchy of needs cannot describe the simultaneous pursuit of higher- and lower-order needs. This has an obvious impact on the ability of the scarcity thesis to account for postmaterialist attitudes. In Nunavut, it appears that postmaterialism is not the result of a linear pattern of progress but that it stems instead from a developmental process that has produced a specialization of interests, from mixed to material, and mixed to postmaterial.

The three research questions posed at the beginning of the book contribute to wider theoretical debate. The impact of traditional Inuit political culture within the current territory helps us to understand how distinct cultural fragments can affect a wider political culture. The impact of federal and territorial institutional development allows us to explore the interaction among separate elements of political culture. Asking whether there is a distinct political culture in Nunavut allows us to determine whether or not the state serves as a homogenizing influence. The main conclusions address the interaction of cultural fragments and institutions within political culture and offer lessons that are relevant to students of cultural pluralism.

Political culture in Nunavut bears the marks of three cultural influences: (1) a traditional Inuit approach to resource distribution and social control, (2) a liberal Canadian political culture into which Inuit were integrated, and (3) the institutional development of the NWT. These three distinct cultural influences have not exerted equal influence. Temporally, the federal culture was more dominant than were the other two, although contemporary culture is the product not only of federal influence but of negotiations between federal and territorial authorities concerning political development in the Arctic. Traditional Inuit approaches to social control and decision making have, in many ways, assumed a more minimal role in Nunavut. As the first review of IQ noted, Nunavut now faces the task of integrating Inuit approaches to political life into an established government system rather than the other way around. If a relatively coherent Inuit political culture existed in the eastern Arctic before the integration of Inuit, why was it not more dominant? The answer, in part, lies in the inequality of political cultures and notions of institutional "congealment."

Political cultures are bounded by political borders or, in stateless nations, by the boundaries of an identity group or imagined community. They distinguish themselves by the attitudinal and behavioural norms in place within the political sphere, rules of interaction between citizen and state that are clarified by political institutions. Altering any of these elements – whether attitudes, behaviours, or institutions – is not particularly easy. Research on Communist political culture has consistently shown the inability of top-down changes to instil the desired complement of attitudes and behaviours (Brown and Grey 1979), while more recent institutional changes in advanced industrial states prove no match for already established patterns of behaviour and approaches to political life. Canadian research on political culture, however, has focused primarily on the capacity for change that was made possible by coherent and distinct cultural approaches, marked either by the arrival of a political class that had distinct approaches to political life or the imposition of new colonial masters. Influence was not guaranteed, however. Settlers had to arrive en masse, had to constitute a significant proportion of the population, and their views had to be relatively coherent. The eastern Arctic has never seen the type of migration that occurred in New France or post-Conquest British North America. And yet there is obvious evidence that, in Nunavut, rapid cultural change was facilitated by discrete waves of incomers, each of which had very clear attitudes toward resource distribution, social control, civic engagement, and the role of the state. If we think of some of these groups, for example, missionaries or northern service officers, their influence far exceeded their demographic weight. Part of this influence stems from the culture that they encountered. Although contested, the impact of the United Empire Loyalists on early Canadian political culture was attributed not just to their number and ideological coherence but also to the point at which they arrived. Political cultures that are not sustained through formal institutions but through informal interaction among individuals will be more malleable, more subject to outside interference, than will others. We have reason to believe that this explains political culture in Nunavut. The capacity to alter a political culture decreases after the "point of congealment."

Although Horowitz (1966) and Lipset (1968) identified different markers of congealment, political developments in the Arctic suggest two developmental stages. If political culture is composed of attitudinal, behavioural, and institutional elements, then institutions provide the surest guarantee of future cultural socialization. Behaviour can be changed relatively easily if one changes the rules of political interaction. We can, for example, introduce compulsory voting and, in so doing, transform middling rates of turnout into those that rank among the highest in the world. Attitudes are far less malleable. Forcing a citizen to vote provides no guarantee that her attitudes toward civic duty will change. We know, however, that attitudes alter over the course of an individual's lifetime and that economic conditions and status affect personal outlooks and views of the state. Institutions, by contrast, provide political culture with a certain rigidity. This is not to suggest that institutions never change. A legislature can alter constituency boundaries, change the number of representatives, shed old jurisdictional responsibilities, and acquire new ones, but it remains throughout an agent of socialization with an institutional memory that functions as a conservative force within a given political culture. The first form of congealment, then, is the presence of political institutions.

Inuit political culture identified ideal behaviours that governed the distribution of resources, collective decision making, and leadership. It developed mechanisms of social control to ensure compliance with those ideal behaviours. However widespread those practices, Inuit society lacked an institutional bedrock for its political culture. This is not a normative statement about the value of Inuit culture or its state of development; rather, it merely indicates that the absence of political institutions denied Inuit culture a buffer against the successive influences of missionaries and government officials. This absence prevented what Breton (1964) might term a "completeness" to Inuit *political* culture. Rules in Inuit society were sustained not by laws or organizations designed to ensure adherence but solely by a compliant Inuit population. The very moment when such rules no longer appealed to the population, they evaporated as agents of socialization. This is not to say that the Christianization of the population completely eradicated the practice of shamanism but that the mechanism of social control was supplanted by an authority that was external to Inuit political culture. That shift was significant for it so altered the structure of Inuit life that successive changes in the rules were far more invasive. Denied the ability to establish rules of behaviour, Inuit political culture lacked a key agent of socialization. When government officials arrived, with their own rules about residential education or political participation, they perceived a blank canvas, and, because of earlier developments, they were more correct than they might have been. The moral authority of their activities is another matter, as the cultural vulnerability of Inuit would have seemed, at the time, to be part of the appeal, but the impact on Inuit political culture is obvious.

Whatever normative evaluations we might make about the federal government, its empirical assumptions were wrong in at least one sense: it assumed that Inuit were leading pre-political lives. Inuit political culture existed, but the absence of institutions made it pre-institutional rather than pre-political. Inuit political culture was thus far more malleable than any of the societies typically examined by political culture scholars. That efforts to integrate Inuit into the Canadian political system occurred on the heels of significant cultural and economic conversion only heightened their influence. From that point on, the establishment of political institutions in the eastern Arctic proceeded in the interests of federal and, later, territorial authorities. Values about responsible government, a strong executive, and cabinet solidarity can all be found in the north, the minority status of the executive proving no match for the behavioural norms that guarantee a docile opposition. The role of the state as an economic engine appears to have had a similar impact on citizen expectation. Obviously, this was not the final stage of political development for the territory. Those working in Yellowknife had within their sights one political goal: the attainment of provincial status. A second possible goal, however, offers a second form of congealment: the congruence of institutions, attitudes, and behaviour.

Political cultures possessing institutions that establish behavioural rules will find themselves less permeable than those lacking durable agents of socialization. And yet we know that experiments in institutional design sometimes graft foreign constitutions or methods of bureaucratic organization onto cultures that prioritize different values. Sometimes these experiments work well. The newly established devolved legislatures in Scotland and Wales adopted variants of the German electoral system and, thus far, the electorate has not rejected the change in favour of the more traditional first-past-the-post system. In New Zealand, however, where a similar system was adopted, public reaction to the new structures was mixed. The coalition government made possible by the mixed proportional system seemed at odds with the public preference for strong single-party government. In the eastern Arctic, the population had not yet identified ideals regarding institutions. Among Inuit, there was no pre-existing preference for strong single-party government. Collective decision making does provide us with certain suggestions about the ideal polity, one founded on deference and the inevitability of dissent. Inuit reaction to government activities does not suggest automatic support for the changes imposed on their lives. Discussions in local councils and committees concerning the introduction of formal education suggest that a more proximate solution would have been preferred. As the federal government and territorial council sought to integrate Inuit into the political system, possible divisions between the values promoted by institutions and those held by Inuit suggested that the institutions governing political life in the Arctic and the attitudes and behaviour of its electorate were not a perfect match. And yet the campaign for a land claim in no way stemmed from a desire to homogenize the constituent elements of political culture. It was, primarily, a bid for access to resources. In part, this stems from the treatment of rules.

When attempting to convert Inuit, missionaries emphasized the similarities between traditional Inuit mechanisms of social control and Christianity. By emphasizing behavioural norms that governed reactions to authority, missionaries ensured that the elements of Inuit political culture that survived were those that emphasized deference. As a result, Inuit were conditioned to integrate well into any political system that later sought to include them. That the mediating agents between Inuit society and the Canadian political system were first the Church and then agents of the state only served to heighten the importance of rules. By the 1970s, when Inuit began questioning those rules, it was not out of a desire to challenge their existence but to make them work for Inuit; the point was not to supplant the existing political system but to assume a position of power within it. This explains why predictors of political behaviour in Nunavut, and why the roles adopted by Nunavut legislators, are so typical of those exhibited by other Canadians. Only now, upon the attainment of a new territory, are the existing rules about political culture being rewritten.

After the signing of the NLCA, the eastern Arctic became, yet again, a battleground for supremacy among different approaches to political life. It therefore has much to teach us about the operation of cultural pluralism. Here we see an effort to alter the pre-existing territorial political culture so that it is better grounded in traditional Inuit approaches at the same time as these approaches are being contested and debated within Nunavut society. Efforts to integrate IQ into the institutional working culture can be seen as the final stage in the establishment of a coherent political culture in the eastern Arctic, one in which the institutions reflect, and therefore sustain, the attitudinal and behavioural norms of a predominantly Inuit population. We can see these goals when we look at predictors of support for the NLCA and for the territory, and when we identify those doing well thanks to political developments. Perhaps most important, studying political culture in Nunavut at this particular point in its political development allows us to better understand not only what it looks like when rival approaches to politics are in conflict but also the process by which one culture begins to dominate another.

Appendix

Variables Used in Cluster Analysis in Chapter 8

Political satisfaction (Cronbach's alpha = .554)
Variable created through factor analysis composed of two questions and one statement:

1. How satisfied are you with the way democracy works in Canada? (0-1)
2. How satisfied are you with the way democracy works in Nunavut? (0-1)
3. The national political parties generally try to look after the best interests of everybody and not just the interests of those who vote for them. (0-1)

Cynicism (Cronbach's alpha = .541)
Variable created through factor analysis composed of three statements:

1. People elected to Parliament in Ottawa soon lose touch with the people. (0-1)
2. People like me don't have any say about what the government does. (0-1)
3. Political parties do more to divide the country than to unite it. (0-1)

Satisfaction with land-based activities (Cronbach's alpha = .578)
Variable created through factor analysis composed of two questions:

1. How satisfied are you with your ability to eat as much country food as you would like? (0-1)
2. How satisfied are you with your ability to spend as much time on the land – hunting, fishing, camping, etc. – as you would like to? (0-1)

Self-sufficient traditionalism (Cronbach's alpha = .415)
Variable created through factor analysis composed of three statements:

1. The welfare state makes people less willing to look after themselves. (0-1)
2. Canada would have fewer problems if there was more emphasis on the traditional family. (0-1)
3. Sometimes politics and government seem so complicated that a person like me can't really understand what's going on.

Political activity (Cronbach's alpha = .383)
Variable created through factor analysis composed of two items:

1. How interested would you say you are in politics? (0-1)
2. Political activity index (0-5) based on types of participation:
   - Contacted a politician or government official, either in person, in writing or some other way
   - Signed a petition, made a statement on the radio or wrote a letter to the newspaper
   - Attended a meeting
   - Attended a rally or demonstration
   - Worked together with other people who shared your concerns.

Postmaterialism
Index (0-1) composed of two questions:

1. Here's a list of four social goals. Which of these goals is most important to you personally?
2. And which of these goals is the second most important to you?
   - Fighting crime
   - Giving people more say in important government decisions
   - Maintaining economic growth
   - Protecting freedom of speech.

Notes

CHAPTER 1: INTRODUCTION
1. For research on the collision of cultures within the legislature and claims boards, see White (2005, 2006).

CHAPTER 2: POLITICS IN NUNAVUT
1. Created by royal charter in 1670, the Hudson's Bay Company owned the land on which it operated until 1869, at which point all lands were transferred to the Government of Canada.
2. A declining market in furs and pressure from animal rights activists prompted the HBC to close its trading posts and fur auction in 1991. Until that point, the HBC continued to send Scottish employees to the Arctic, although by then their men were employed to manage the already developed network of northern stores throughout the territory.
3. For more information on the Arctic relocations see Irwin (1989); Tester and Kulchyski (1994).
4. Nationalist groups in Scotland, Quebec, and Catalonia each enjoyed breakthroughs in the form of electoral success in the 1970s.
5. This quotation refers to politics in the NWT. For a response to this view see White (1999b).
6. See also Kirmayer, Boothroyd, and Hodgins (1998); Kirmayer, Fletcher, and Boothroyd (1998); Kirmayer, Malus, and Boothroyd (1996).
7. For some, this suggests that adults have lost the ability to parent effectively, and certainly there is evidence that some children feel let down by parents who do not push them to complete their formal education (Kivalliq Consulting 1986). The greater disconnect between men's roles in traditional and contemporary society and women's roles can explain, in this view, the higher rate of suicide among men.(Brooke 2000).
8. Inuit from other jurisdictions, such as Nunavik or Greenland, are not beneficiaries of the Nunavut land claim.

9 The Committee of the Whole is similar to a standing committee comprised of all members of the legislature and examines legislation with the same attention to detail one might expect of committee proceedings.

CHAPTER 3: INUIT POLITICAL CULTURE

1 Those in the north Baffin, for example, employed sod huts that provided more permanent structures than were used by Inuit farther south (Trott 2001).
2 Briggs (1982, 123) notes, for example, that "having" "is valued negatively by society but positively by individuals; we ought not to want it but we do."
3 The specific reference here was to ptarmigan feathers and caribou bones, respectively (IE 070).

CHAPTER 4: POLITICAL INTEGRATION IN THE EASTERN ARCTIC

1 This quotation was drawn from the 1958 first session of the territorial council.
2 Or, put another way by Minister Laing in his 1964 letter to Lester Pearson: "the dangers of a predominantly Eskimo population being exploited by those who would seek office only for their own purposes" had long justified the disenfranchisement of residents in the eastern Arctic. It is worth noting that Laing was writing to the prime minister in an effort to outline the extent of the problem; he estimated that 6,000 Inuit and 2,000 Qallunaat were excluded from the territorial franchise and that a divided territory, which extended the right to vote for those in the western half, would still have denied 3,000 adults the franchise (Laing 1964).
3 The recent Aboriginal Peoples Survey identified a median income for Inuit in Nunavut of $13,190.
4 The southern migration of Inuit remained a federal concern for decades (Government of Canada, Department of Indian and Northern Affairs 1982).
5 Even though the commissioner begins the letter by questioning federal funding of organizations, he ends it by suggesting that, if the organizations are given enough money, then they will calm down and "become responsible bodies."

CHAPTER 5: INSTITUTIONAL DESIGN IN THE EASTERN ARCTIC

1 The executive head was referred to as a governor in British colonies, as a lieutenant governor in substate units, and as a commissioner in the Yukon and Northwest Territories.
2 Attempts to maintain this distinction in Chapters 3 and 4 prove how difficult such an exercise can be, as events in both chapters rely on the same fundamental chronology and involve the same federal officials.
3 From 1950 to 1966, the administration of Indian affairs was the responsibility of the Department of Citizenship and Immigration.

4 According to one manifest, the DC4 cargo load included 4 dogs, 1 hamster, 12 goldfish, 1 budgie, and 1 pet skunk. Staff travelled one week later in a DC7C.
5 Some of the Drury staff appeared to believe that this situation suited the commissioner, who was then able to exert greater control than he might have done in a political system in which council members assumed greater responsibility: "It is my long held view and belief that the Commissioner and Deputy Commissioner do not want good intelligent people running for Council. They do not want young people with young dynamic ideas that may not agree with the 'old boy system' prevalent on the 6th floor. They would rather want to continue getting the stumble bums so they can control, manipulate, intimidate, cajole and teach those poor ignorant elected people" (Barnabé 1979b).
6 As the NIC assumed a purely advisory role, the Nunavut Act also created the Office of the Interim Commissioner, which had the authority to establish government systems and processes and to enter into contracts, including with regard to the new government's first employees and leases for government offices.

CHAPTER 6: CONSENSUS POLITICS

1 This is similar to patterns of participation in the NWT, where sixty-five and fifty-eight candidates presented themselves in the 1999 and 2003 elections, respectively, with five acclamations in a 2003 contest. The acclaimed seats, which represent an unusually high number, should not be attributed to a lack of political participation in particular constituencies but to individuals not wishing to run against, or not favouring their electoral chances against, a declared candidate.
2 There were, for example, 11,285 registered voters in the 2004 Nunavut election and 21,153 registered voters in the 2003 NWT election. By contrast, the 2004 Canadian election saw 1,684 candidates compete in an electorate consisting of 22,466,621 registered voters.
3 Voters in Nunavut are no doubt aware that, even in a partisan system, their ability to send one MP to the House of Commons offers them little in the way of influence over who forms the government.
4 There are, of course, exceptions to the general rule of higher imposed burdens. The current premier of the NWT was acclaimed in his constituency during the 2003 election and was unopposed in his bid to become premier. As a result, Joe Handley has become head of government without ever winning a single vote.
5 Before division, four cabinet seats were set aside for eastern MLAs and four for western MLAs.
6 One other cabinet minister, Manitok Thompson, had been critical of the proposal before it was announced, but once it became a cabinet decision the then minister ceased to criticize the proposal.

7 Interestingly, when representatives turned their attention to policy, structural differences served to divide them, whereas cultural divisions were what accounted for differing normative visions of the polity.
8 The current premier appears to operate within the orbit of the NDP, his personal staff and deputy ministers often being former NDP staff or civil servants in the former NDP Yukon administration.
9 Since 1999, however, the GN and NTI have reached a formal cooperation protocol, an agreement that they renewed during the second legislature.

CHAPTER 7: POLITICAL PARTICIPATION IN NUNAVUT

1 It is possible that the popularity of the Legion and Elks stems from their role as eating and drinking establishments.
2 Any Inuk in the Baffin may in fact stand for four of those positions: the three executive positions and the position of general board member from his or her particular community.
3 In contrast, turnout for the first election in the post-division NWT was 71 percent, ranging from 55 percent in Frame Lake to 91 percent in Hay River North.
4 The two Rankin Inlet constituencies are excluded from this analysis because the acclamation in Rankin Inlet North skews participation rates in the communities.
5 Analysis of variance (ANOVA) tests, using season as a grouping variable and turnout as the dependent variable, produce non-significant findings. ANOVA examines the impact of a categorical independent variable on an interval-level dependent variable. In this case, we can see whether turnout (the dependent variable) is significantly higher or lower in, for example, autumn or spring.
6 It is worth noting that the Canadian Alliance attempted to field a candidate but was prevented from doing so by Elections Canada because the appropriate papers were filed thirty minutes late. See *Nunatsiaq News*, 17 November 2000.
7 OLS regression tests the independent impact of predictor variables on a dependent variable. Here the dependent variable is voter turnout. Positive coefficients mean that an increase in the independent variable has a positive impact on turnout levels.
8 Factor analysis identifies the underlying latent variable behind the variables that we have in our dataset. It allows us to see the links among different groups of variables and to measure the impact of the single latent variable rather than the impact of several individual variables.
9 This includes eight city councillors, one mayor, one member of the provincial parliament, and one MP in Ottawa.

CHAPTER 8: IDEOLOGICAL DIVERSITY IN NUNAVUT

1 The Canadian respondents include only those living in provinces.

2 Individuals identifying two materialist options were given a score of 0, those who identified a materialist option first and a post-materialist option second were given a score of .33, and so on.

CHAPTER 9: TRANSFORMING POLITICAL CULTURE IN NUNAVUT

1 The Anglican diocese of the Arctic and its bishop are more conservative about sexual orientation than is the general synod of the Anglican Church of Canada. In June 2005, the diocese indicated that it would not employ "anyone having pre-marital sex, homosexuals, lesbians and bisexuals," pedophiles, or "anyone who 'supports and promotes such behaviour, lifestyle or teaching'" (Sison 2005, 8).

2 The adjusted R^2 provides a measure of the model fit. It identifies the proportion of the variation in the dependent variable explained by the presence of the independent variables. An R^2 of .345, for example, would mean that 34.5 percent of the variation in the dependent variable can be explained by the independent variables.

References

Abadian, Sousan. 1999. "From Wasteland to Homeland: Trauma and the Renewal of Indigenous Peoples and Their Communities." PhD diss., Harvard University.

Abele, Francis. 1997. "Understanding What Happened Here: The Political Economy of Indigenous Peoples." In *Understanding Canada: Building on the new Canadian Political Economy*, ed. Wallace Clement, 118-41. Montreal-Kingston: McGill-Queen's University Press.

Adams, Michael. 2003. *Fire and Ice: The United States, Canada and the Myth of Converging Values*. Toronto: Penguin.

Alfred, Taiaiake. 1999. *Peace, Power, Righteousness: An Indigenous Manifesto*. Oxford: Oxford University Press.

Alia, Valerie. 1990. "Aboriginal Peoples and Campaign Coverage in the North." In *Aboriginal Peoples and Electoral Reform in Canada*, ed. R.A. Milen, 105-52. Toronto: Dundurn Press.

–. 1994. *Names, Numbers and Northern Policy: Inuit, Project Surname and the Politics of Identity*. Halifax: Fernwood Publishing.

Almond, Gabriel, and Sidney Verba. 1963. *Civic Culture*. Princeton: Princeton University Press.

Amagoalik, John. 1978. Letter to OSR Commissioner E.H. Drury, 1 May.

Andersen, Thomas, Jack Kruse, and Birger Poppel. 2002. "Survey of Living Conditions in the Arctic: Inuit Saami and the Indigenous Peoples of Chukotka." *Arctic* 55 (3): 310-17.

Andersen, Thomas, and Birger Poppel. 2002. "Living Conditions in the Arctic." *Social Indicators Research* 58: 91-216.

Anderson, Christopher J. 1998. "Parties, Party Systems, and Satisfaction with Democratic Performance in The New Europe." *Political Studies* 46: 572-88.

Armstrong, Brian. 1999. "The Election of Nunavut's First Legislative Assembly." *Canadian Parliamentary Review* 22 (2): 16-18.

Arnakak, Jaypeetee. 2001. "Northern IQ." *Management* 12 (1): 17-19.

Atagotaaluk, Andrew. 2003. Letter to Premier Paul Okalik. Tabled before the Nunavut Legislative Assembly, 31 October.

Bakvis, Herman. 1991. *Regional Ministers: Power and Influence in the Canadian Cabinet.* Toronto: University of Toronto Press.
Barnabé, Claire. 1979a. Report of 15 January meeting with Joe Tigullaraq. 5 February.
–. 1979b. Memo to Wendy Porteous re 27 February letter from John Parker. 5 March.
–. 1979c. Memo to Barbara Darling re sections 3 and 4 of final report. 10 August.
Bell, David V.J. 1970. "The Loyalist Tradition in Canada." *Journal of Canadian Studies* 5 (2): 22-33.
Bennett, John, and Susan Rowley. 2004. *Uqalurait: An Oral History of Nunavut.* Montreal-Kingston: McGill-Queen's University Press.
Berger, Thomas R. 2006. *The Nunavut Project: Conciliator's Final Report of the Nunavut Land Claims Agreement Implementation Contract Negotiations for the Second Planning Period 2003-2013.* Ottawa.
Berrington, Hugh. 2003. "Role of Political Parties." Politics Student: news.bbc.co.uk.
Billson, Janet Mancini. 2001. "Inuit Dreams, Inuit Realities: Shattering the Bonds of Dependency." *American Review of Canadian Studies* 31 (1/2): 283-300.
Blais, André. 2000. *To Vote or Not to Vote? The Merits and Limits of Rational Choice Theory.* Pittsburgh: University of Pittsburgh Press.
Blais, André, and Agniewska Dobrzynska. 1998. "Turnout in Electoral Democracies." *European Journal of Political Research* 33: 239-61.
Bourdieu, Pierre. 1986. "Forms of Capital." In *Handbook of Theory and Research for the Sociology of Education,* ed. J.C. Richardson, 241-55. New York: Greenwood Press.
Boyce, John R., and Diane P. Bischak. 2002. "The Role of Political Parties in the Organization of Congress." *Journal of Law, Economics and Organization* 18 (1): 1-38.
Breton, Raymond. 1964. "Institutional Completeness of Ethnic Communities and the Personal Relations of Immigrants." *American Journal of Sociology* 70 (2): 193-205.
Briggs, Jean L. 1982. "Living Dangerously: The Contradictory Foundations of Value in Canadian Inuit Society." In *Politics and History in Band Societies,* ed. Eleanor Leacock and Richard Lee, 109-31. Cambridge: Cambridge University Press.
Brooke, James. 2000. "Canada's Bleak North Is Fertile Ground for Suicide." *New York Times,* 28 June.
Brown, Archie, and Jack Gray, eds. 1979. *Political Culture and Political Change in Communist States.* London: Macmillan.
Cairns, Alan. 2000. *Citizens Plus: Aboriginal Peoples and the Canadian State.* Vancouver: UBC Press.
Calder v. Attorney General of British Columbia (1973), 34 D.L.R. (3d) 145.
Cameron, Kirk, and Graham White. 1995. *Northern Governments in Transition: Political and Constitutional Development in the Yukon, Nunavut and the Western Northwest Territories.* Montreal: Institute for Research on Public Policy.
Canada. Department of Indian Affairs and Northern Development (DIAND). 1967. "Power of Community Councils." Note to Commissioner of the Northwest Territories. 10 October.

Canada. Department of Indian and Northern Affairs. 1982. *Living in the South*. Ottawa: Indian and Northern Affairs Canada.

Canada. Department of Northern Affairs and National Resources. 1959. "Human Problems in the Canadian Arctic." *Department of Northern Affairs and National Resources 1958-1959 Annual Report*. Ottawa: Department of Northern Affairs and National Resources.

Canada. Royal Commission on Aboriginal Peoples (RCAP). 1996. Report of the Royal Commission on Aboriginal Peoples. Ottawa: RCAP.

Canada. Special Representative on Constitutional Development. 1980. *Constitutional Development and the Northwest Territories: Report of the Special Representative*. Ottawa: Supply and Services.

Carty, R. Kenneth. 2002. "Canada's Nineteenth-Century Cadre Parties at the Millennium." In *Political Parties in Advanced Industrial Democracies*, ed. Paul Webb, David Farrell, and Ian Holliday, 245-378. Oxford: Oxford University Press.

Carty, R. Kenneth, William Cross, and Lisa Young. 2000. *Rebuilding Canadian Party Politics*. Vancouver: UBC Press.

Carty, R. Kenneth, and David K. Stewart. 1996. "Parties and Party Systems." In *Provinces: Canadian Provincial Politics*, ed. C Dunn, 63-94. Peterborough: Broadview Press.

CBC. 2005a. "'No Longer a Rubber Stamp Legislature': Nunavut MLAs Defeat Budget Item." 9 March. Web posting.

–. 2005b. "Again, Regular MLAs Strike Budget Item." 22 March. Web posting.

–. 2005c. "Regular MLAs Vote to Have Another Budget Item Deleted." 22 March. Radio item.

Chrétien, Jean. 1972. *Report to the Standing Committee on Indian Affairs and Northern Development on the Governments Northern Objectives, Priorities and Strategies for the 70s*. Ottawa: Department of Indian and Northern Development.

Clancy, Peter. 1987. "The Making of Eskimo Policy in Canada, 1952-62: The Life and Times of the Eskimo Affairs Committee." *Arctic* 40 (3): 191-97.

–. 1994. *Contours of the Modern State in the Territorial North: Policies, Institutions and Philosophies*. Research study prepared for the Royal Commission on Aboriginal Peoples. Ottawa.

Coates, Kenneth, and William Morrison. 1992. *The Forgotten North: A History of Canada's Provincial Norths*. Toronto: James Lorimer and Company.

Coleman, J.C. 1988. "Social Capital in the Creation of Human Capital." *American Journal of Sociology* 94: 95-120.

Condon, Richard G., Julia Ogina, and the Holman Elders. 1996. *The Northern Copper Inuit: A History*. Norman, OK: University of Oklahoma Press.

Crewe, I., T. Fox, and J. Alt. 1977. "Non-Voting in British General Elections, 1966-October 1974." In *British Political Sociology Yearbook 3*, ed. C. Crouch, 38-110. London: Croom Helm.

Curtice, John. 2003. "Turnout, Electoral Behaviour and Fragmentation of the Party System." In *Election 2003: Scottish Parliament Information Centre (SPICE) Research Report*, ed. R. Burnside, S. Herbert, and S. Curtis, 12-13. Edinburgh: Scottish Parliament.

Dacks, Gurston. 1980. "The Drury Report: Constitutional Development for Whom?" *Canadian Public Policy* 6 (2): 384-99.

–. 1986. "Politics on the Last Frontier: Consociationalism in the Northwest Territories." *Canadian Journal of Political Science* 19 (2): 345-61.

–. 1993. "Nunavut: Aboriginal Self-Determination through Public Government." Ottawa: RCAP.

Dahl, Jens. 1997. "Gender Parity in Nunavut?" *Indigenous Affairs*. July/December: 42-47.

Dahl, Jens, Jack Hicks, and Peter Jull, eds. 2000. *Nunavut: Inuit Regain Control of Their Lands and Their Lives*. Copenhagen: IWGIA.

Dalton, Russell. 2002. *Citizen Politics*. 3rd ed. New York: Chatham House, Seven Bridges.

Dickerson, Mark. 1992. *Whose North? Political Change, Political Development, and Self-Government in the Northwest Territories*. Vancouver: UBC Press.

Dinsdale, Walter. 1961. Letter to Barrister and Solicitor Mark H. de Weerdt. 1 February.

–. 1963. Letter to NWT Commissioner R.G. Robertson. 2 January.

Duverger, Maurice. 1954. *Political Parties: Their Organization and Activity in the Modern State*. London: Methuen.

Faulkner, Hugh. 1979. Letter to Eric Tagoona.

Flumian, M. 1999. "Redesigning Government around the Citizen: The Creation of Nunavut." In *Collaborative Government: Is There a Canadian Way?* ed. Susan Delacourt and Donald G. Lenihan, 92-98. Toronto: Institute for Public Administration of Canada.

Franklin, Mark. 1999. "Electoral Engineering and Cross-National Turnout Differences: What Role for Compulsory Voting?" *British Journal of Political Science* 29: 205-24.

–. 2002. "Electoral Participation." In *Comparing Democracies 2: New Challenges in the Study of Elections and Voting*, ed. L. Leduc, R.G. Niemi, and P. Norris, 148-68. London: Sage.

Freeman, Milton. 1967a. Letter to Chief Electoral Officer, Ottawa. 15 April.

–. 1967b. Letter to Peter S. Jull, Staff Officer GNWT. 5 July.

Frideres, James S. 1991. "From the Bottom Up: Institutional Structures and the Indian People." In *Social issues and Contradictions in Canadian Society*, ed. B. Singh Bolaria, 108-32. Toronto: Harcourt Brace.

Gibbins, Roger. 1990. "Electoral Reform and Canada's Aboriginal Population: An Assessment of Aboriginal Electoral Districts." In *Aboriginal Peoples and Electoral Reform in Canada*, ed. R.A. Milen, 153-84. Toronto: Dundurn Press.

Gibbins, Roger, and J. Rick Ponting. 1976. "Public Opinion and Canadian Indians." *Canadian Ethnic Studies* 8 (2): 1-17.

Gombay, Nicole. 2000. "The Politics of Culture: Gender Parity in the Legislative Assembly of Nunavut." *Études/Inuit/Studies* 24 (1): 125-48.

Gray, M., and M. Caul. 2000. "Declining Voter Turnout in Advanced Industrial Democracies." *Comparative Political Studies* 33: 1091-122.

Green, Joyce. 2003. "Decolonization and Recolonization in Canada." In *Changing Canada: Political Economy as Transformation*, ed. Wallace Clement and Leah Vosko, 51-78. Montreal-Kingston: McGill-Queen's University Press.

Gunther, Richard, and Larry Diamond. 2001. "Types and Functions of Parties." In *Political Parties and Democracy*, ed. Larry Diamond and Richard Gunther, 3-39. Baltimore: Johns Hopkins University Press.

Hamilton, Alvin. 1960. Personal correspondence, 18 January.

Hartz, Louis. 1964. *The Founding of New Societies: Studies in the History of the United States, Latin America, South Africa, Canada and Australia*. New York: Harcourt Brace.

Henderson, Ailsa. 1999. "Territorial Political Culture and the Creation of Nunavut." Paper presented to the Nordic Association of Canadian Studies, Reykjavik.

–. 2001. "Northern Jurisdiction: Government Structures in Nunavut" *Hemisphere* 9 (3): 31-34.

–. 2003a. *Suicide and Community Wellness in Nunavut: A Report Prepared for the Nunavut Task Force on Suicide Prevention and Community Healing*. Iqaluit: Department of Health and Social Services.

–. 2003b. *Best Practices in Suicide Prevention and the Evaluation of Suicide Prevention Programs in the Arctic*. Iqaluit: Department of Executive and Intergovernmental Affairs.

–. 2003c. "Identity as a Label or Process?: Measuring Belonging." In *The Politics of Contesting Identity*, ed. C.J.A. Stewart, K.G. Francis, and A.K. Dorman-Jackson, 227-49. Edinburgh: University of Edinburgh Press.

–. 2003d. "Inuit Qaujimajatuqangit." In *Encyclopedia of the Arctic*, ed. Mark Nuttall. London: Fitzroy Dearborn.

–. 2004a. *Social Well-Being in Nunavut*. Iqaluit: Department of Executive and Intergovernmental Affairs.

–. 2004b. *Nunavut Election 2004*. Iqaluit: CBC.

–. 2004c. "Northern Political Culture? Political Behaviour in Nunavut." *Études/Inuit/Studies* 28 (1): 133-53.

–. 2004d. "Regional Political Cultures in Canada." *Canadian Journal of Political Science* 37 (3): 595-615.

Hicks, Jack. 2004. "On the Application of Theories of 'Internal Colonialism' to Inuit Societies." Paper presented to the Canadian Political Science Association, Winnipeg.

Hicks, Jack, and Graham White. 2000. "Nunavut: Inuit Self-Determination through a Land Claim and Public Government?" In *Nunavut: Inuit Regain Control of Their Lands and Their Lives*, ed. Jens Dahl, Jack Hicks, and Peter Jull, 30-115. Copenhagen: IWGIA.

–. 2005. "Building Nunavut through Decentralization or Carpet-Bombing It into Near-Total Dysfunction? A Case Study in Organizational Engineering." Paper presented to the Canadian Political Science Association, London.

Hillson, John D. 1968. Memo: *The Achievement of Responsible Government*, 25 November.

Hodgson, Stuart. 1969a. Letter to John A. MacDonald, Deputy Minister, DIAND. 21 February.

–. 1969b. Letter to Jean Chrétien, Minister of Indian Affairs and Northern Development, 28 January.

–. 1974. *Goals of the Government of the NWT.* Yellowknife.

–. 1977. Letter to OSR Commissioner E.H. Drury. 22 April.

–. 1979a. Letter to OSR Commissioner E.H. Drury. 27 February.

–. 1979b. Letter to OSR staff member George Braden. 26 February.

Honigmann, John J., and Irma Honigmann. 1965. "Eskimo Learn to Run Their Own Affairs." *Dalhousie Review* 45: 289-98.

Horowitz, Gad. 1966. "Conservatism, Liberalism and Socialism in Canada: An Interpretation." *Canadian Journal of Economics and Political Science* 32: 143-70.

Horton, E.R. 1968. Statement in connection with Frobisher Bay visit.

Hough, Dan, and Charlie Jeffery, eds. 2006. *Devolution and Electoral Politics: A Comparative Exploration.* Manchester/New York: Manchester University Press/Palgrave.

Howard, Albert, and Frances Widdowson. 1999. "The Disaster of Nunavut." *Policy Options* (July/August): 58-61.

Howe, Paul, and Joseph F. Fletcher. 2001. "The Evolution of Charter Values." In *Canada: The State of the Federation 2001*, ed. Hamish Telford and Harvey Lazar, 265-92. Montreal-Kingston: McGill-Queen's University Press.

Inglehart, Ronald. 1977. *Silent Revolution: Changing Values and Political Styles among Western Publics.* Princeton: Princeton University Press.

–. 1990. *Culture Shift in Advanced Industrial Society.* Princeton: Princeton University Press.

Inuit Land Claims Commission. 1977. *Proposal: Agreement-in-Principle for the Establishment of Inuit Rights between the Inuit of Nunavut and the Government of Canada.* Frobisher Bay: ILCC.

Inuit Tapiriit Kanatami. 2004. *The Case of Inuit Specific: Renewing the Relationship between the Inuit and Government of Canada.* Ottawa: ITK.

Inuit Tapirisat of Canada (ITC). 1974. *An Introduction to the Eskimo People of Canada and Their National Organization.* Ottawa: ITC.

–. 1976. *Nunavut: Agreement-in-principle as to the Settlement of Inuit Land Claims in the Northwest Territories and Yukon Territory between the Government of Canada and the Inuit Tapirisat of Canada.* Ottawa: ITC.

–. 1977. *Speaking for the First Citizens of the Canadian Arctic.* Ottawa: ITC.

–. 1978. "Constitutional and Political Development as It Affects the Inuit of Canada." Letter sent to the Office of the Special Representative.

–. 1979. *Political Development in Nunavut.* Ottawa: ITC.

–. N.d. *Building a Future from Our Past*. Ottawa: ITC.

Irlbacher Fox, Stephanie. 2004. "Governance in Canada's Northwest Territories: Emerging Institutions and Governance Issues." Paper presented at Northern Research Forum Open Meeting, Yellowknife.

Irniq, Peter, and Frank James Tester. 2006. "Inuit Qaujimajatuqangit: Community History, Politics and the Practice of Resistance." Paper presented at the Coastal Zone Canada Conference, Tuktoyaktuk.

Ironside, R.G. 2000. "Canadian Northern Settlements: Top-Down and Bottom-Up Influences." *Geografiska Annaler Series B Human Geography* 82 (2): 103-14.

Irwin, Colin. 1989a. *Lords of the Arctic, Wards of the State: The Growing Inuit Population, Arctic Resettlement and Their Effects on Social and Economic Change*. Ottawa.

–. 1989b. "Irwin Report – Lords of the Arctic: Wards of the State." *Northern Perspectives* 17 (1): 2-12.

Ittinuar, Peter. 1981. "Inuit Participation in Politics." In *A Century of Canada's Arctic Islands, 1880-1980*, ed. Morris Zaslow, 291-98. Ottawa: Royal Society of Canada.

Jenness, Diamond. 1922. The Life of the Copper Eskimos. Report of the Canadian Arctic Expedition 1913-18. Ottawa: F.A. Acland, King's Printer.

Johnston, Richard. 1980. "Federal and Provincial Voting: Contemporary Patterns and Historical Evolution." In *Small Worlds: Provinces and Parties in Canadian Political Life*, ed. D.J. Elkins and R. Simeon, 131-78. Toronto: Methuen.

Jull, Peter S. 1966. Personal correspondence to NWT Commissioner Stuart Hodgson, 15 December.

Jull, Peter. 1994. "A Personal Response to Frank J. Tester and Peter Kulchyski, *Tammarniit (Mistakes): Inuit Relocation in the Eastern Arctic, 1939-63*." *Northern Review* 12/13 (Summer/Winter): 197-202.

–. 2001a. "'Nations with Whom We Are Connected': Indigenous Peoples and Canada's Political System, Part 1." *Australian Indigenous Law Reporter* 6 (2): 1-16.

–. 2001b. "'Nations with Whom We Are Connected:' Indigenous Peoples and Canada's Political System, Part 2." *Australian Indigenous Law Reporter* 6 (3): 1-15.

–. 2001c. Negotiating Nationhood, Renegotiating Nationhood: Canada's Nunavut and Nunavut's Canada." *Balayi Culture, Law and Colonialism* 3: 67-86.

Kamingoak, Peter. 1966. Letter to NWT Commissioner Stuart Hodgson, 25 August.

Karetak, Elisapee. 2000. *Kikkik* (DVD). Iqaluit: Elisapee Karetak and Ole Gjerstad.

Kattu, Peter. 1979. Letter to OSR Commissioner E.H. Drury, 29 January.

Katz, Richard S., and Peter Mair. 1995. "Changing Models of Party Organization and Party Democracy: The Emergence of the Cartel Party." *Party Politics* 1: 5-28.

Keewatin Regional Eskimo Advisory Conference. 1969. Minutes of the 12-16 May meeting, Churchill.

Kellough, Gail. 1980. "From Colonialism to Economic Imperialism: The Experience of the Canadian Indian." In *Structured Inequality in Canada*, ed. C. John Harp and John Hofley, 344-65. Scarborough: Prentice Hall.

Kernerman, Gerald. 2005. *Multicultural Nationalism: Civilizing Difference, Constituting Community*. Vancouver: UBC Press.

Key, V.O. 1949. *Southern Politics: In State and Nation*. New York: Knopf.

Kirmayer, L.J. 1994. "Suicide among Canadian Aboriginal Peoples." *Transcultural Psychiatry* 31: 3-58.

Kirmayer, L.J., L.J. Boothroyd, and S. Hodgins. 1998. "Attempted Suicide among Inuit Youth: Psychosocial Correlates and Implications for Prevention." *Canadian Journal of Psychiatry* 43: 816-27.

Kirmayer, L.J., C. Fletcher, and L.J. Boothroyd. 1998. "Suicide among the Inuit of Canada." In *Suicide in Canada*, ed. A. Leenars and R. Bland, 189-211. Toronto: University of Toronto Press.

Kirmayer, L.J., M. Malus, and L.J. Boothroyd. 1996. "Suicide Attempts among Inuit Youth: A Community Survey of Prevalence and Risk Factors." *Acta Psychiatrica Scandinavica* 94: 8-17.

Kitschelt, Herbert. 1989. *The Logics of Party Formation: Ecological Politics in Belgium and West Germany*. Ithaca: Cornell University Press.

Kivalliq Consulting, Management and Training Services. 1986. *Keewatin Suicide Prevention and Intervention Study*. Rankin Inlet: Keewatin Regional Council.

Kornberg, A., W. Mishler, and H.D. Clarke. 1982. *Representative Democracy in the Canadian Provinces*. Scarborough: Prentice-Hall.

Kral, Michael, Meeka Arnakaq, Naki Ekho, Okee Kunuk, Elisapee Ootoova, Malaya Papatsie, and Lucien Taparti. 1998. "Stories of Distress and Healing: Inuit Elders on Suicide." In *Suicide in Canada*, ed. Antoon A. Leenaars, Susanne Wenckstern, Isaac Sakinofsky, Ronald J. Dyck, Michael J. Dral, and Roger C. Bland, 179-88. Toronto: University of Toronto Press.

Kral, Michael, and J. Bruce Minore. 1999. "Arctic Narratives: Participatory Action Research on Suicide and Wellness among the Inuit." Paper presented at the Society for Community Research and Action Conference, New Haven. June.

Kreelak, Martin. 2002. *Kikkik E1-472* (DVD). Ottawa: Inuit Broadcasting Corporation and Ole Gjerstad.

Kusugak, Jose. 2000. "The Tide Has Shifted." In *Inuit Regain Control of Their Lands and Their Lives*, ed. Jens Dahl, Jack Hicks, and Peter Jull, 20-28. Copenhagen: IWGIA.

Kymlicka, Will. 1995. *Multicultural Citizenship: A Liberal Theory of Minority Rights*. Oxford: Oxford University Press.

Ladner, Kiera. 2001. "Negotiated Inferiority: The Royal Commission on Aboriginal People's Vision of a Renewed Relationship." *American Review of Canadian Studies* 31 (1/2): 241-65.

Laing, Arthur. 1964. Letter to Prime Minister Lester B. Pearson, 27 July.

–. 1967. Letter to NWT Commissioner Stuart Hodgson.

Langlois, Stéphanie, and Peter Morrison. 2002. "Suicide Deaths and Suicide Attempts." *Health Reports* 13 (2): 9-22.

Laski, Harold J. 1938. *Grammar of Politics*. 4th ed. New York: Macmillan.
Laugrand, Frédéric. 1997. "Le *siqqitiq*: Renouvellement religieux et premier ritual de conversion chez les Inuit du nord de la Terre de Baffin." *Études/Inuit/Studies* 21 (1/2): 101-40.
Légaré, André. 1996. "The Process Leading to a Land Clams Agreement and Its Implementation: The Case of the Nunavut Land Claims Settlement." *Canadian Journal of Native Studies* 16 (1): 139-63.
–. 1997. "The Government of Nunavut (1999): A Prospective Analysis." In *First Nations in Canada: Perspectives on Opportunity, Empowerment and Self-Determination*, ed. J. Rick Ponting, 404-31. Toronto: McGraw-Hill Ryerson.
–. 1998. "An Assessment of Recent Political Development in Nunavut: The Challenges and Dilemmas of Inuit Self-Government." *Canadian Journal of Native Studies* 18 (2): 271-99.
–. 1999. *Nunavut: A Bibliography, 1976-1999*. Quebec: Université Laval.
–. 2002. "Nunavut: The Construction of a Regional Collective Identity in the Canadian Arctic." *Micazo Sa Review* 12 (2): 65-89.
Lipset, Seymour Martin. 1968. *Revolution and Counterrevolution: Change and Persistence in Social Structures.* New York: Basic Books.
–. 1986. "Historical Traditions and National Characteristics: A Comparative Analysis of Canada and the United States." *Canadian Journal of Sociology* 11 (2): 113-55.
–. 1990. *Continental Divide: The Values and Institutions of the United States and Canada.* New York: Routledge.
Loukacheva, Natalia. 2004. "Comparative Arctic Governance: The Jurisdiction of Greenland and Nunavut Re-Examined." In *Arctic Governance*, ed. Timo Koivurova, Tanja Joona, and Reija Shnoro, 114-37. Rovaniemi: Oy Sevenprint.
Macaulay, Alexander. 2002. "Mortality in the Kivalliq Region of Nunavut, 1987-1996." PhD diss., University of Manitoba.
Macaulay, Alexander, Pamela Orr, Sharon Macdonald, Lawrence Elliott, Rosemary Brown, Anne Durcan, and Bruce Martin. 2003. "Mortality in the Kivalliq Region of Nunavut, 1987-1996," *Circumpolar Health* 63 (2): 80-85.
MacDonald, John. 1998. *The Arctic Sky: Inuit Astronomy, Star Lore, and Legend*. Toronto: Royal Ontario Museum and Nunavut Research Institute.
Macdonald, Mark R. 2000. "Re-Learning Our ABCs? The New Governance of Aboriginal Economic Development in Canada." In *How Ottawa Spends: 2000-2001*, ed. Leslie Pal, 161-84. Toronto: Oxford University Press.
Malone, Marc. 1989. "The View from Yellowknife." *Northern Perspectives* 17 (1): 13-14.
Mamadouh, Virginie. 1997. "Political Culture: A Typology Grounded on Cultural Theory." *Geojournal* 43: 17-25.
Maslow, Abraham. 1943. "A Theory of Human Motivation." *Psychological Review* 50: 370-96.

Matthiasson, John S. 1992. *Living on the Land: Northern Baffin Inuit Respond to Change.* Peterborough: Broadview.

Mayes, Roger G. 1982. "Contemporary Inuit Society." *Musk-Ox* 30: 36-47.

McEwen, Nicola. 2003. "Is Devolution at Risk? Examining Attitudes towards the Scottish Parliament in Light of the 2003 Election." *Scottish Affairs* 44: 54-73.

McRae, K.D. 1978. "Louis Hartz's Concept of the Fragment Society and Its Applications to Canada." *Canadian Studies* 5: 17-30.

Merritt, John. 1993a. "Nunavut: Canada Turns a New Page in the Arctic." *Canadian Parliamentary Review* (Summer): 2-6.

–. 1993b. "Nunavut: Preparing for Self-Government." *Northern Perspectives* 21 (1): 3-6.

–. 1993c. *Canada's Inuit: Political Opportunities, Demographic Realities and Socio-Economic Constraints.* Ottawa: RCAP.

Merritt, John, Randy Ames, Terry Fenge, and Peter Jull. 1989. *Nunavut: Political Choices and Manifest Destiny.* Ottawa: Canadian Arctic Resources Committee.

Merritt, John, and Terry Fenge. 1990. "The Nunavut Land Claims Settlement: Emerging Issues in Law and Public Administration." *Queen's Law Journal* 15 (2): 255-77.

Michael, Simonie. 1966. Letter to NWT Commissioner Stuart Hodgson, 10 June.

Milbrath, Lester. 1965. *Political Participation: How and Why Do People Get Involved in Politics?* Chicago: Rand McNally.

Minogue, Sara. 2005. "Imperfect Subsidies Keep Food Prices Reasonable." *Nunatsiaq News*, 7 October.

Minor, Tina. 2002. "Political Participation of Inuit Women in the Government of Nunavut." *Wicazo Sa Review* 12 (1): 65-90.

Mocellin, J.S.P., and P. Suedfeld. 1991. "Voices from the Ice: Diaries of Polar Explorers." *Environment and Behavior* 23: 704-22.

Mowat, Farley. 1959. *The Desperate People.* Toronto: McClelland Stewart.

Murphy, F.H. 1966. Personal correspondence to Harry Walker, CBC Northern Service. 22 July.

Neumann, Sigmund. 1956. "Towards a Comparative Study of Political Parties." In *Modern Political Parties,* ed. Sigmund Neumann, 395-421. Chicago: University of Chicago Press.

Neve, David. 1966. Letter to Peter Kamingoak. 26 August.

Nevitte, Neil. 1996. *The Decline of Deference: Canadian Value Change in Cross-National Perspective.* Peterborough: Broadview Press.

Northern Administrative Branch. 1963. Extracts from the debates (or votes and proceedings) of the Council of the Northwest Territories referring to the subjects dealt with in Bill C146 – An Act to amend the Northwest Territories Act.

Northwest Territories. N.d. State of Policy Regarding Municipal Development in the Northwest Territories. Yellowknife.

Northwest Territories. Department of Information. 1977. "News Release: Baffin Region Council Makes History." 18 April.

Northwest Territories. Legislative Assembly. 1979. Position of the Legislature on the Constitutional Development in the NWT. Yellowknife.

Nunatsiaq News. 1999. "A Directly Elected Nunavut Premier?" (editorial), 25 June.

–. 2001. "Defining Inuit Qaujimajatuqangit" (editorial), 30 November.

–. 2003. "Praise the Law" (editorial). 14 November.

–. 2004a. "Let the Public See and Hear" (editorial). 27 February.

–. 2004b. "The GN: A Haven of Racism and Incompetence" (editorial). 5 November.

Nunavut. 1999. *Bathurst Mandate Pinasuaqtavut: That Which We've Set Out to Do*. Iqaluit: Government of Nunavut.

–. 2004. *Pinasuaqtavut*. Iqaluit: Government of Nunavut.

Nunavut. Department of Culture, Language, Elders and Youth (CLEY). 2000. *Report from the September Inuit Qaujimjatuqangit Workshop 1999*. Iqaluit: CLEY.

Nunavut. Department of Human Resources, Inuit Employment Planning. 2006. *Towards a Representative Public Service. Statistics as of June 30th*. Iqaluit: Department of Human Resources.

Nunavut. IQ Task Force. 2002. *The First Annual Report of the Inuit Qaujimajatuqanginnut Task Force*. Iqaluit: CLEY.

Nunavut Constitutional Forum. 1983. *Building Nunavut: A Working Document with a Proposal for an Arctic Constitution*. Iqaluit: Nunavut Constitutional Forum.

Nunavut Implementation Commission (NIC). 1994. *Discussion Paper Concerning the Development of Principles to Govern the Design and Operation of the Nunavut Government*. Iqaluit: NIC.

–. 1995. *Footprints in New Snow: A Comprehensive Report from the Nunavut Implementation Commission to the Department of Indian Affairs and Northern Development, Government of the Northwest Territories and Nunavut Tunngavik Incorporated Concerning the Establishment of the Nunavut Government*. Iqaluit: NIC.

–. 1996a. *Footprints 2: A Second Comprehensive Report from the Nunavut Implementation Commission to the Department of Indian Affairs and Northern Development, Government of the Northwest Territories and Nunavut Tunngavik Incorporated Concerning the Establishment of the Nunavut Government*. Iqaluit: NIC.

–. 1996b. *Selection of a Premier in Nunavut*. Iqaluit: NIC.

–. 1996c. *Nunavut's Legislature, Premier and First Election*. Iqaluit: NIC.

–. 1998. *Direct Election of the Nunavut Premier: Schemes for Legislative Enactment*. Iqaluit: NIC.

Nunavut Social Development Council. 1998. *Report of the Nunavut Traditional Knowledge Conference*. Igloolik: NSDC.

NWT Council. 1966. Review of 1966 Operations. Northern Administrative Branch Files 269-5.

O'Brien, Kevin. 2003. "Some Thoughts on Consensus Government in Nunavut." *Canadian Parliamentary Review* 26 (4): 6-10.
Office of the Administrator of the Arctic. 1959. *Annual Report 1958-59.*
Oosten, Jarich, and Frédéric Laugrand, eds. 2000. *The Transition to Christianity, Inuit Perspectives on the 20th Century.* Iqaluit: Nunavut Arctic College.
Pammett, J.H., and L. Leduc. 2004. "Four Vicious Circles of Turnout: Competitiveness, Regionalism, Culture and Participation in Canada." Paper presented at the Joint Sessions of Workshops of the European Consortium for Political Research, Uppsala, Sweden.
Parallés, F., and M. Keating. 2003. "Multi-Level Electoral Competition: Regional Elections and Party Systems in Spain." *European Urban and Regional Studies* 10 (3): 239-56.
Parry, G., and G. Moyser. 1984. "Political Participation in Britain: A Research Agenda for a New Study." *Government and Opposition* 19 (1): 68-92.
Pauktuutit. 1991. *The Inuit Way: A Guide to Inuit Culture.* Ottawa: Pauktuutit.
Peter, Charlie. 1982. "The Need to Protect Inuit from Economic Hardships and Create an Inuit Labour Organization." Memorandum to ITC Board of Directors. 16 February.
Phillips, R.A.J. 1958a. Northern Service Officers. Ottawa: Department of Northern Affairs and National Resources.
–. 1958b. "The Changing Eskimo." Paper presented to the Canadian Political Science Association, Ottawa chapter study group on "The Native and the North," February.
Ponting, J. Rick. 2000. "Public Opinion on Canadian Aboriginal Issues, 1976-98: Persistence, Change, and Cohort Analysis." *Canadian Ethnic Studies* 32 (3): 44-75.
–. 2006. *The Nisga'a Treaty: Polling Dynamics and Political Communication in Comparative Context.* Peterborough: Broadview.
Ponting, J. Rick, and Roger Gibbins. 1981a. "English Canadians' and French Quebecers' Reactions to Native Indian Protest." *Canadian Review of Sociology and Anthropology* 18 (2): 222-38.
–. 1981b. "The Effects of Ethnic Characteristics upon Orientations towards Native Indians." *Canadian Journal of Native Studies* 1 (1): 1-31.
Ponting, J. Rick, and T. Langford. 1992. "Canadians' Responses to Aboriginal Issues: The Roles of Group Conflict, Prejudice, Ethnocentrism, and Economic Conservatism." *Canadian Review of Sociology and Anthropology* 29 (2): 140-66.
Porteous, Wendy. 1978. "Report: Constitutional Options." Memo to Jim Mackenzie. 22 September.
–. 1979. Report of February 8 meeting with [name withheld] settlement council. 13 March.
Putnam, Robert, Robert Leondardi, and Raffaella Y. Nanetti. 1993. *Making Democracy Work: Civic Traditions in Modern Italy.* Princeton: Princeton University Press.
Pye, Lucien and Sidney Verba. 1965. *Political Culture and Political Development.* Princeton: Princeton University Press.

QIA (Qikiqtani Inuit Association) and Makivik Corporation. 2006. "RCMP Self-Investigation Does Not Reveal the Truth about the Slaughter of Inuit Sled Dogs in the 1950s and 1960s." Joint press release, Iqaluit and Montreal, 6 December.

Rasmussen, Knud. 1929. Intellectual Culture of the Iglulik Eskimos. Report of the Fifth Thule Expedition, 1921-24. Vol. 7. Copenhagen: Gyldendalske Boghandel, Nordisk Forlag.

–. 1931. The Netsilik Eskimos, Social Life and Spiritual Culture. Report of the Fifth Thule Expedition, 1921-24. Vol. 8. Copenhagen: Gyldendalske Boghandel, Nordisk Forlag.

Reference as to whether the term "Indians" in head 24 of section 91 of the British North America Act, 1867, includes Eskimo inhabitants of the province of Quebec, [1939] S.C.R. 104.

Regina v. Kikkik (1958), (Terr. Ct. NWT). Unrep.

Reif, K. 1985. "Ten Second-Order Elections." In Ten European Elections: Campaigns and Results of the 1979/1981 First Direct Elections to the European Parliament, ed. Karlheinz Reif, 1-36. Aldershot: Gower.

Reif, K., and H. Schmitt. 1980. "Nine Second-Order National Elections: A Conceptual Framework for the Analysis of European Election Results." European Journal of Political Research 8 (1): 3-44.

Remie, Cornelius H.W., and Jarich Oosten. 2002. "The Birth of a Catholic Inuit Community: The Transition to Christianity in Pelly Bay, Nunavut, 1935-1950." Études/Inuit/Studies 26 (1): 109-41.

Requejo, Ferran. 2005. Multinational Federalism and Value Pluralism. London: Routledge.

Robertson, R.G. 1962. The Evolution of Territorial Government in Canada. Ottawa: Northern Administrative Branch Files 132-33.

Rossow, Ingeborg. 2000. "Suicide, Violence and Child Abuse: A Review of the Impact of Alcohol Consumption on Social Problems." Contemporary Drug Problems 27: 397-433.

Rowley, G.W. 1969. "International Scientific Relations in the Arctic." Unpublished paper.

Russell, Dan. 2000. A People's Dream: Aboriginal Self-Government in Canada. Vancouver: UBC Press.

Rynard, Paul. 2000. "'Welcome In, But Check Your Rights at the Door': The James Bay and Nisga'a Agreements in Canada." Canadian Journal of Political Science 33: 211-43.

Sayers, Anthony. 1999. Parties, Candidates, and Constituency Campaigns in Canadian Elections. Vancouver: UBC Press.

Schmitter, Philippe C. 2001. "Parties Are Not What They Once Were." In Political Parties and Democracy, ed. Larry Diamond and Richard Gunther, 67-89. Baltimore: Johns Hopkins University Press.

Simeon, Richard, and David Elkins. 1974. "Regional Political Cultures in Canada." Canadian Journal of Political Science 7 (3): 397-437.

–. 1980. Small Worlds: Provinces and Parties in Canadian Political Life. Toronto: Methuen.

Sison, Marites N. 2005. "Anglican Diocese Bans Gays from Employment." *Anglican Journal*, 1 September, 8.
Sivertz, Ben. 1963. Letter to Arthur Laing, Minister of Northern Affairs and National Resources, 1 November.
Slowey, Gabrielle A. 2001. "Globalization and Self-Government: Impacts and Implications for First Nations in Canada." *American Review of Canadian Studies* 31 (1/2): 265-82.
Smith, David. 1985. "Party Government, Representation and National Integration in Canada." In *Party Government and Regional Representation in Canada*, ed. Peter Aucoin, 1-61. Toronto: University of Toronto Press.
Smith, Rogers M. 1993. "Beyond Tocqueville, Myrdal, and Hartz: The Multiple Traditions in America." *American Political Science Review* 87 (3): 549-66.
Stabler, Jack C. 1989. "Dualism and Development in the Northwest Territories." *Economic Development and Cultural Change* 37 (4): 805-39.
Statistics Canada. 2001. Average Weekly Food Expenditure per Household: Canada and Selected Regions. Ottawa: Statistics Canada.
Steenhoven, Geert van den. 1956. *Research Report on Caribou Eskimo Law*. Ottawa: Department of Northern Affairs and National Resources.
–. 1959. *Legal Concepts among the Netsilik Eskimos of Pelly Bay*. Ottawa: Department of Northern Affairs and National Resources.
–. 1962. *Leadership and Law among the Eskimos of the Keewatin District in the Northwest Territories*. Rijswijk: Excelsior.
Stevenson, Alexander. 1959. *Memo: Eskimos to Attend Committee on Eskimo Affairs*. 24 March.
Stevenson, Marc G. 1993. *Traditional Inuit Decision-Making Structures and the Administration of Nunavut*. Ottawa: RCAP.
–. 1996. *Inuit Suicide and Economic Reality*. Ottawa: Inuit Tapirisat of Canada.
–. 1997. *Inuit, Whalers, and Cultural Persistence: Structure in Cumberland Sound and Central Inuit Social Organization*. Toronto: Oxford University Press.
Stewart, Donald. 1967. "Election Pledge." *Hay River News*, 28 June.
Stewart, Ian. 1994. *Roasting Chestnuts: The Mythology of Maritime Political Culture*. Vancouver: UBC Press.
Stout, Madeleine Dion, and Gregory D. Kipling. 1999. *Emerging Priorities for the Health of First Nations and Inuit Children and Youth*. Ottawa: Health Canada.
Studlar, D. 2001. "Canadian Exceptionalism: Explaining Differences over Time in Provincial and Federal Voter Turnout." *Canadian Journal of Political Science* 34 (2): 299-319.
Tester, Frank J. 2006. *Iglutaq: The Implications of Homelessness for Inuit – A Case Study of Housing and Homelessness in Kinngait*. Cape Dorset: Harvest Society.
Tester, Frank J., and Peter Kulchyski. 1994. *Tammarniit (Mistakes): Inuit Relocation in the Eastern Arctic, 1939-63*. Vancouver: UBC Press.

Tierney, Stephen. 2004. *Constitutional Law and National Pluralism*. Oxford: Oxford University Press.
Timpson, Annis May. 2006a. "'Hey, That's No Way to Say Goodbye': Territorial Officials' Perspectives on the Division of the Northwest Territories." *Canadian Public Administration* 49 (1): 80-101.
–. 2006b. "Stretching the Concept of Representative Bureaucracy: The Case of Nunavut." *International Review of Administrative Sciences* 72 (4): 517-30.
Trott, Christopher G. 2001. "The Dialectics of 'Us' and 'Other': Anglican Missionary Photographs of the Inuit." *American Review of Canadian Studies* 31 (1/2): 171-90.
Tully, James. 1995a. "Cultural Demands for Constitutional Recognition." *Journal of Political Philosophy* 3 (2): 111-32.
–. 1995b. *Strange Multiplicity: Constitutionalism in an Age of Diversity*. Cambridge: Cambridge University Press.
–. 1999. "Aboriginal Peoples: Negotiating Reconciliation." In *Canadian Politics*, 3rd ed., ed. James Bickerton and Alain-G Gagnon, 413-41. Peterborough: Broadview.
Tungavik Federation of Nunavut. 1989. "An Inuit Response." *Northern Perspectives* 17 (1): 15-18.
Turcotte, Martin. 2005. "Social Engagement and Civic Participation: Are Rural and Small Town Populations Really at an Advantage?" *Rural and Small Town Canada Analysis Bulletin* 6 (4): 1-24.
Usher, Peter, Gérard Duhaime, and Edmund Searles. 2003. "The Household as an Economic Unit in Arctic Aboriginal Communities and Its Measurement by Means of a Comprehensive Survey." *Social Indicators Research* 61 (2): 175-202.
Verba, Sidney, Norman Nie, and Jae-On Kim. 1978. *Participation and Political Equality: A Seven-Nation Comparison*. New York: Cambridge University Press.
Western Constitutional Forum and Nunavut Constitutional Forum. 1987. *Boundary and Constitutional Agreement for the Implementation of Division of the Northwest Territories between the Western Constitutional Forum and the Nunavut Constitutional Forum*. Iqaluit: Canadian Arctic Resources Committee.
Whitbread, Canon. 1967. Letter to Commissioner Stuart Hodgson, 16 May.
White, Graham. 1991. "Westminster in the Arctic: The Adaptation of British Parliamentarism in the Northwest Territories." *Canadian Journal of Political Science* 24 (3): 499-523.
–. 1993. "Structure and Culture in a Non-Partisan Westminster Parliament: Canada's Northwest Territories." *Australian Journal of Political Science* 28: 322-39.
–. 1999a. "Nunavut: Challenges and Opportunities of Creating a New Government." *Public Sector Management* 9 (3): 3-7.
–. 1999b. "The Tundra's Always Greener: A Response to Widdowson and Howard." *Policy Options*, May, 59-63.
–. 2000. "Public Service in Nunavut and the Northwest Territories: Challenges of the

Northern Frontier." In *Government Restructuring and Career Public Service,* ed. Evert Lindquist, 112-47. Toronto: IPAC.

–. 2005. "Culture Clash: Traditional Knowledge and Eurocanadian Governance Processes in Northern Claims Boards." Paper presented at the "First Nations, First Thoughts" Conference, Edinburgh. May.

–. 2006. "Traditional Aboriginal Values in a Westminster Parliament: The Legislative Assembly of Nunavut." *Journal of Legislative Studies* 12 (1): 8-31.

Whittington, Michael S., ed. 1985. *The North.* Toronto: University of Toronto Press, in cooperation with the Royal Commission on the Economic Union and Development Prospects for Canada and the Canadian Government Publishing Centre.

Widdowson, Frances, and Albert Howard. 1999a. "Corruption North of 60." *Policy Options* (January/February): 37-40.

–. 1999b. "Duplicity in the North: A Reply to Graham White." *Policy Options* (September): 66-68.

–. 2002. "The Aboriginal Industry's New Clothes." *Policy Options* (March): 30-34.

Wildavsky, Aaron. 1987. "Choosing Preferences by Constructing Institutions: A Cultural Theory of Preference Formation." *American Political Science Review* 81 (1): 3-21.

Wilson, John, and Robert J. Williams. 1998. "The Itinerant Voter: Another Look at Theories and Methods Used in the Examination of Federal-Provincial Voting Variation in Canada." Paper presented to the New York State Political Science Association, Albany.

Wilson, John. 1974. "The Canadian Political Cultures: Towards a Redefinition of the Nature of the Canadian Political System." *Canadian Journal of Political Science* 7: 438-83.

Wotherspoon, Terry, and Vic Satzewich. 2000. *First Nations: Race, Class and Gender Relations,* 2nd ed. Saskatoon: Canadian Plains Research Center.

Young, Lisa. 1997. "Gender-Equal Legislatures: Evaluating the Proposed Nunavut Electoral System." *Canadian Public Policy* 23 (3): 306-15.

–. 1998. "Party, State and Political Competition in Canada: The Cartel Argument Revisited." *Canadian Journal of Political Science* 31: 339-58.

Younger-Lewis, Greg. 2004. "Gossip Leads to Firing of GN Worker: 'Nunavut Is the Most Racist Place I've Been To.'" *Nunatsiaq News,* 5 November.

Index

Notes: GN stands for Government of Nunavut; IQ, for Inuit Qaujimajatuqangit; ITC, for Inuit Tapirisat of Canada; NLCA, for Nunavut Land Claims Agreement; NRI, for Nunavut Research Institute

Aboriginal affairs, 110-11; departments responsible for, 110-11
Aboriginal peoples, 5-6, 103, 113, 140; Canadian public opinion of, 200; discrimination against, 8; federal approach to, 24, 59, 80-81, 84, 88, 90, 99, 179; First Nations, 11; land claims, 200-1; organizations representing, 81; research on, 5; self-government, 4, 6, 25; status Indians, 59; survey data on, 10; territorial approach to, 83-84, 191-92; title to land, 24, 96; wards of state, 88; white paper on, 96
Aboriginal Peoples Survey, 11
Administrator of the Arctic, 61, 68. *See also* Office of the Administrator of the Arctic
Advisory Commission on the Development of Government in the Northwest Territories (Carrothers Commission), 12, 62, 66, 76, 85, 94-95, 103; reaction to, 95, 103
Advisory Committee on Northern Development, 21

age, 29, 44-45, 121, 140, 142, 152-53, 157-60, 163, 175, 181, 185, 187, 205-6, 211; as predictor of post-materialism, 175; as predictor of support for NLCA and Nunavut, 205-6, 211; as predictor of turnout, 152-53, 157-60, 163
Aklavik, 62, 79
Alaska, 18, 19, 87, 177
Alberta, 56, 58, 87, 90, 172; creation of, 56
alcohol, 30-31, 54, 78, 81; consumption, 30-31, 198, 200; education committee, 54
Alia, Valerie, 24, 141
Alliance Party, 153, 226n6
Allmand, Warren, 93
Amagoalik, John, 98-99, 106
Amitturmiut, 13
Anawak, Jack, 127, 130, 132, 134-35, 196-97; removal from cabinet, 130, 132, 196-97
Anglican church, 20-21, 23, 51, 68, 74, 132, 182, 195; control of residential schools, 23; and IQ, 195, 227n1;

missionaries of, 20-21, 51, 68, 74, 132
anxiety, 42
Apex, 74, 78. *See also* Iqaluit
apology. *See* Government of Canada
Arctic Bay, 25
Article 23, 35, 124, 180
Arviat, 77
Atagotaaluk, Andrew, 195
Australia, 87
Ayaruark, 84

Baffin, 13, 25, 27, 31, 33, 48, 71, 82, 91, 120, 130-32, 141, 145, 164, 167, 177, 179, 183, 185, 187, 224n1, 226n2; and ideological clusters, 185, 187; island, 19-20, 23, 25, 62, 177; regional council, 81, 104; regional Eskimo council, 77
Baffin Regional Inuit Association, 104, 144, 167
Baker Lake, 19, 21, 60, 62, 69-70, 74-75, 77, 82, 130, 196
Bathurst Inlet, 147
Berger, Thomas, 103, 199-200; conciliation report, 199-200; Berger inquiry, 103
bilingualism, 66, 96, 128, 145, 180-81, 187-88, 197
Bloc Québécois, 118
Boy Scouts, 80
Breton, Raymond, 217
Briggs, Jean, 39, 42, 45, 49, 143, 224n2
British Columbia, 172
British North America (BNA) Act, 103. *See also* Constitution Act (1867)
brokerage politics, 118-19, 127, 137, 179

cabinet solidarity, 127, 130, 137, 196-97, 218

Calder decision. *See* Supreme Court
Cambridge Bay, 27, 60, 74-76, 78; housing association, 77
Canadian Broadcasting Corporation (CBC), 125, 142
Canadian Election Study, 10, 136, 170-74
Canadian Opinion Research Archive (CORA), 10-11
Canadian public opinion of Nunavut, 200
Cape Dorset, 74-75, 211
capitalism, 18, 22, 31, 51, 55, 214
Caribou Inuit, 19-20
Carrothers Commission. *See* Advisory Commission on the Development of Government in the Northwest Territories
Centre for Research and Information on Canada (CRIC), 10-11
Charlottetown Accord, 146
Charter of Rights and Freedoms, 7, 195
Chrétien, Jean, 83, 97, 99
Christianity, 15, 20, 31, 44, 46, 51-55, 76, 132-33, 181-82, 187-88, 214, 217, 219; and IQ, 195; atonement, 52; conversion to, 15, 20, 31, 51-55, 76, 132, 214, 217, 219; emphasis on rules, 51-5, 76-77, 219. *See also* siqitiqtut
Chukotka, 177
Churchill, 23, 77
collision of cultures, 3, 7, 188, 223n1
Commissioner of the Northwest Territories, 60, 62, 74-57, 77, 91-93, 95, 100, 102, 110-11; Ben Sivertz, 93; list of, 110-11; Robert Robertson, 67, 87, 90-91, 93; Stuart Hodgson, 64-65, 70-72, 82-83, 91, 95, 98, 100, 102
Committee for Original Peoples' Entitlement (COPE), 81, 96

communities, 25-27
community councils, 73-77, 79, 82-83, 102, 104, 187; role of Inuit on, 74. *See also* Eskimo community councils
community development fund, 76
consensus politics, 8, 16, 33, 112-37; agenda setting and, 121, 125; articulation of interests and, 116, 123, 136; assessments of, 114; citizen integration and, 116, 128, 136; costs of participation, 136; election campaigns and, 119-26; focus on local issues and, 121; legislative behaviour and, 126-36; perceived benefits of, 115; perceived criticisms of, 115-16; reasons for, 112-13; role of media in, 136
Conservative Party of Canada. *See* Progressive Conservative Party of Canada
consociational methods of integrating Inuit, 69, 72
Constitution Act (1867), 56-57
Copper Inuit, 19, 20, 39, 45; and egalitarianism, 45
Coppermine, 69-70. *See also* Kugluktuk
Coral Harbour, 77, 178
cost of living, 27-28
country food, 19, 160, 187, 192, 199, 205-6, 211
Cournoyea, Nellie, 83
credentialism, 192, 196, 198
Cree, 1
cultural change, 31, 144, 174
cultural pluralism, 9
cultural renaissance, 205
cultural trajectory, 175-76, 181, 188
cynicism, 12, 115-16, 160, 170, 172, 183, 185, 188, 221

Dacks, Gurston, 25, 29, 38, 96, 103, 105, 114, 127

decentralization. *See* Government of Nunavut, decentralization
decentralized communities, 178, 180
deference, 6, 12, 45, 51, 140, 160, 162, 170-72, 183, 214, 218-19
Dene, 1, 114, 131
Department of Community and Government Services, 135
Department of Environment, 135
Department of Indian Affairs and Northern Development, 70, 75, 82, 92, 95, 99; change in policy under Chrétien, 99; Hugh Faulkner (minister), 101-2; Jean Chrétien (minister), 83; John MacDonald (deputy minister), 70, 95; list of ministers, 110-12; ministers of, 99, 102; view of Inuit, 100; Warren Allmand (minister), 93
Department of Mines and Resources, 92
Department of Northern Affairs and National Resources, 73-74, 92, 99; Arthur Laing (minister), 91, 93, 95, 99, 224n2; Walter Dinsdale (minister), 60, 71-72, 91
Dinsdale, Walter, 60, 71-72, 91
Distant Early Warning (DEW) line, 22
District of Assiniboia, 88
division of the Northwest Territories, 72, 85-86, 90-91, 99, 101, 103-4, 109, 112-13; Carrothers Commission's view of, 62; federal views of, 97; ITC calls for, 24, 96-97; territorial views of, 92, 97-98
Drury, Bud, 98-100
Drury Commission. *See* Office of the Special Representative
dwelling condition, 159, 206, 211; importance of, 206, 211

E numbers. *See* Inuit, naming
ecological fallacy, 156

economic emancipation, 206
economic well-being, 27-28. *See also* poverty
Edmonton (AB), 178
education, 5, 8, 15, 84, 152, 183, 206; levels of attainment, 138; as predictor of attitudes and behaviour, 206
Education Act, 135
efficacy, 6, 12, 140, 170, 172, 178, 183, 214
elders, 12, 42, 49, 181, 191-92; NRI interviews, 12, 14, 38-54, 143, 198, 224n3
elections in the Northwest Territories, 33, 61-63, 67, 142; electoral system, 33, 67; federal election (1962), 61, 142; territorial (1979), 105. *See also* elections in the Northwest Territories (1966); elections in the Northwest Territories (1967)
elections in the Northwest Territories (1966), 62-65, 142; Central Arctic constituency, 63, 65; and commissioner, 64-65; communication with Canadian chief electoral officer, 63; confusion re nomination process, 65; deposit, 63; Duncan Pryde, 65; eastern Arctic constituency, 63; Gordon Rennie, 65; Keewatin constituency, 63, 65; materials not available in Inuktitut, 64; Peter Kamingoak, 63-64; Robert Williamson, 65; Simonie Michael, 65; Waldy Phipps, 65
elections in the Northwest Territories (1967), 65; and commissioner, 65; Duncan Pryde, 66; materials not available in Inuktitut, 65; Milton Freeman, 65; Northern Administrative Branch, 65-66; Rankin Inlet, 65; Robert Williamson, 65-66; Simonie Michael, 66; turnout, 66; Whale Cove, 65
elections in Nunavut, 120, 123, 147, 152-55; birthright organizations, 150; campaign deposit, 120; federal elections, 147, 152; first-order vs second-order, 154-55; frequency of, 153; local elections, 141; municipal election (2002), 164; territorial election (1999), 120; territorial election (2004), 123; turnout, 147-63
electoral campaigns in Nunavut, 120, 123-25, 141; burger poll, 125; costs, 120; most important issue, 123-24
electoral candidates, 120-23; attention to local issues, 123; motivations for running, 121-22
elites, 3, 9, 35, 138
Elkins, David, 8, 140, 169, 172
Elks, 144, 226n1
Ennadai Lake, 42
Environics, 10-11, 200
environment, 3, 5, 7-8, 18-22, 24, 29, 33, 40-42, 45, 47, 172, 176, 196
Eskimo Affairs committee, 68-70, 79, 84, 179; formation of, 68; Inuit membership of, 69-70
Eskimo community councils, 74-75, 144; topics discussed, 75
Eskimo regional councils, 77-79, 81, 144; efforts to contact council, 77-78; expectations of influence, 79; topics discussed, 77;
evaluations of Nunavut, 200-11; differences over time, 211; ethnic differences, 204; predictors of, 207-10
expectations of Nunavut, 200-2; ethnic differences in, 202

Fair Practices Act, 194

family, 18, 23, 24, 27-29, 39, 43, 170, 193-94
Faulkner, Hugh, 101-2
federal government. *See* Government of Canada
federal-territorial relations, 95
fiscal autonomy, 57, 100
food sharing, 4, 42, 144
Fort Providence, 79
Fort Simpson, 79
freedom of speech, 174
Freeman, Milton, 65
Frobisher Bay, 17, 59-60, 65, 74-75, 78, 80, 92, 94; territorial council visit to, 59. *See also* Iqaluit

gender, 5, 15, 40-41, 44, 67, 108, 159, 176, 185, 187-88, 205-6, 211
gender parity, 34, 108, 138, 146-47; Inuit leadership and, 147
Girl Guides, 80, 144
Gjoa Haven, 19
Government of Canada, 2, 23, 58; apology for relocations, 23; view of Inuit, 58, 101. *See also* Department of Indian Affairs and Northern Development
Government of Nunavut, 107-8, 178, 192, 196, 199, 203; decentralization, 4, 34, 107-8, 130, 178, 180, 196; employment with, 178, 203; Inuktitut and, 192; IQ task force, 193; relationship with Aboriginal organizations, 4
grassroots organizations, 139
Great Whale River, 69-70
Green Party, 153
Greenland, 1, 13, 18, 19, 87, 102, 177, 223n8
Grise Fiord, 21-23, 177

Hall Beach, 13
health indicators, 29-30
hierarchy of needs, 40 173, 215
hierarchy of political activity, 139, 164
high arctic relocations, 3, 21-23, 84, 143, 177, 223n3; compensation package, 23
Hobbes, Thomas, 46; view of human nature, 46
Hodgson, Stuart, 62, 64-65, 70-72, 82-83, 91, 95, 98, 100, 102; as deputy commissioner, 62. *See also* Commissioner of the Northwest Territories
Horowitz, Gad, 7, 113, 216
Hudson's Bay Company (HBC), 20, 68, 74, 88, 223n2
human rights bill (Nunavut), 182, 194-95
hunter and trapper organizations, 75, 138, 144, 163, 167

identity attachment, 155-56; differences between Inuit and Qallunaat, 155-56
ideological clusters, 183-88
Igloolik, 12-14, 17, 19, 38, 48, 79, 148, 190-91
Iglulingmiut, 19, 39, 48
imagined community, 125, 136
incumbency, 129
Indian Act (1876), 21, 56, 59
Indian Brotherhood of the Northwest Territories, 81
information shortcuts, 117, 121, 141; absence of, 121
Inglehart, Ronald, 173
institutions, 3, 34, 85; creation of, 3; design of, 85, 201; innovation in, 34; lessons of development elsewhere, 89-90; public support for reform of, 34, 106; reform of, 106

intergenerational relationships, 29, 42, 44, 48, 96, 180-83; language differences, 181; value differences, 181
Inuinnaqtun, 27, 129, 131, 177, 180, 205
Inuit, 18-21, 38, 42, 58, 72, 78, 92, 94, 97, 101, 177, 197-98; federal responsibility for, 72, 92; federal views of, 101; influence over political institutions, 97; –miut groups, 19, 177; naming, 24; outside Canada, 18; political integration of, 78, 94; recognition as federal responsibility, 21; relocation (*see* High Arctic relocations); reputation for pragmatism, 38, 42; stereotypes, 15, 58, 72, 197-98; territorial views of, 101
Inuit Circumpolar Conference, 163
Inuit Land Claims Commission, 81, 96, 98, 144; view of Drury commission, 98
Inuit Land Claims Committee, 81
Inuit political culture, 3, 12, 14, 37-55, 143, 170, 214-15, 218; absence of institutions, 218; altruism, 143; collective decision making, 39; definitions of politics used in measurement, 39; emphasis on rules, 47, 51-56, 61; impact of capitalism on, 51, 55; impact of Christianity on, 44, 51, 55; inevitability of dissent, 218; leadership, 45; mechanisms of control, 46-48, 54; moralizing, 49-50; punishment, 53-54; resource distribution, 39; sharing and borrowing, 43; social capital, 143; visions of the good life, 39, 55
Inuit Qaujimajatuqangit (IQ), 16, 35, 132, 190-95, 197-99, 214, 219; cabinet solidarity and, 197; challenges to implementation, 194; definitions of, 191, 194; departmental committees of, 193; functional role of, 193; GN approaches to, 191-93; homosexuality and, 194; implementation of, 191; and Nunavut human rights bill, 195; opposition to GN working culture, 192, 194; as personal versus collective, 199; symbolic role of, 193, 198; and traditional knowledge, 194
Inuit Tapiriit Kanatami. *See* Inuit Tapirisat of Canada
Inuit Tapirisat of Canada (ITC), 24, 81, 83, 96-97, 101-2, 104, 108, 144, 167, 190; creation of, 24; Office of Constitutional Development, 98
Inuit traditional culture, 4, 42-50; approaches to knowledge, 45; conservation of resources, 43-44; food sharing, 44; games, 4; gender relations, 44; intergenerational relations, 44; Norse and, 20; private property, 42; songs, 4; treatment of children, 47; treatment of elders, 42-43, 49-50; treatment of violence, 50; whalers and, 20
Inuit values, 190-97, 202; Christianity and, 195; contested definitions of, 194; decision making, 196; identification of, 195-96; individual rights and, 194-95; in legislature, 197; relationships, 196
Inuktitut, 1, 17, 27-28, 63, 65-66, 77-78, 97, 121, 129, 142, 157-58, 160, 163, 170, 180-81, 183, 187, 191-94, 199, 205-6, 212; and election materials, 64-66
Inuvialuit, 1, 18, 23, 81, 96; land claim, 96
Iqaluit, 17, 25, 27-28, 65, 74, 106-7, 125, 128-32, 148-49, 152, 162,

178, 180, 183-87, 206, 211-12; residents less satisfied, 186; selection as capital, 34
Irwin Report, 199

judiciary, 32

Kamingoak, Peter, 63-64
Keewatin region, 18, 19, 27, 33, 59, 62, 71, 76, 82, 91, 177; creation of constituency, 59; regional council, 77-79; regional Eskimo council, 76-79
Keewatin territory, 56, 88-89
Kimmirut, 17, 164
Kitikmeot, 19, 25, 27-28, 120, 130, 131, 141, 164, 177, 187
Kitikmeot Inuit Association, 33, 144, 150, 167
Kivalliq, 13, 25, 27-28, 130-33, 164, 177, 179, 185
Kivalliq Inuit Association, 33, 144, 150
Kugaaruk, 17, 19
Kugluktuk, 17, 27, 62, 150. *See also* Coppermine
Kuujjuaq, 74

Laing, Arthur, 91, 93, 95, 99, 224n2
language, 97, 145, 180-81, 183, 187, 201
Laurier Institute for the Study of Public Opinion and Policy (LISPOP), 10
Legislative Assembly of Nunavut, 1, 31, 126-35; Committee of the Whole, 33; coverage of, 128; defeat of executive, 128, 135; division among members, 131-32; imbalance of political expertise, 129; IQ and, 132; legislative process, 32; partisan behaviour in, 130; Qallunaat members, 132; regional representation in executive, 130; scrutiny of the executive, 32; selection of cabinet members, 127; selection of premier, 127; selection of speaker, 33, 126-27; standing committees, 33. *See also* regular members
Legislative Assembly of the Northwest Territories, 102, 129-30; regional representation in executive, 129-30; view of Drury Commission, 102; view of local democracy, 102
Liberal Party of Canada, 24, 93, 95, 97, 113-14, 118, 134, 153; dominance in Nunavut, 134
life expectancy, 29-30
Lipset, Seymour Martin, 7, 113, 216

MacDonald, John A., 70-71, 95
Makivik Corporation, 22
Manitoba, 27, 87-88, 155; creation of, 56, 88
Marijuana Party, 153
Maslow, Abraham, 40, 173
mass parties, 118
Massachusetts Bay, 87
Mead, Margaret, 44
media, 51, 116, 120, 125, 135, 136, 142, 153
Members of the Legislative Assembly, 131-32, 165-69; division among, 131-32, 169; experience of elected office, 167; incumbency and, 165; professions of, 165-66
Métis, 1
Michael, Simonie, 65, 66
Milbrath, Lester, 139, 164
missionaries, 2, 4, 12, 15, 20-21, 39, 51, 54-56, 68, 74, 132, 182, 198, 216-17, 219; views of cultural change, 54
mobility, 12, 28, 135, 179
moral traditionalism, 171

Nanisivik, 25, 147

Netsilingmiut, 19, 39, 48
New Democratic Party, 114, 118, 226n8
Newfoundland, 172
Ng, Kelvin, 134
Northern Administrative Branch, 12, 60-61, 77, 79-80, 87, 92; models of political development, 87; view of Inuit, 60
Northern Service Officers, 58, 73-75, 77-79, 216
Northwest Passage, 20
Northwest Territories, 85-109; Aboriginal political exclusion from, 90; changes to borders, 88; debates about division, 92-94; political development of, 85-109; settlers to, 90
Nova Scotia, 172
Nunatsiaq News, 25, 28, 34, 108, 128, 130, 135, 142, 191, 194-95, 199, 226n6
Nunavummi Nangminiqaqtunik Ikajuuti (NNI) policy, 35, 136, 180
Nunavut as primary political community, 145, 154-57
Nunavut Constitutional Forum, 96, 144
Nunavut Household Survey, 11-12, 115, 123, 128, 136, 156, 158-59, 170-72, 201-2, 204
Nunavut Impact Review Board, 33
Nunavut Implementation Commission, 4, 34-35, 86, 105-9, 114, 141, 147, 190, 201, 225n6; decentralization, 107; gender parity, 108; mandate of, 34, 105; membership of, 106; public consultations, 106; recommendations of, 107; reports, 106; selection of capital, 34, 107; view of political parties, 107
Nunavut Land Claims Agreement, 1-2, 5, 11, 17, 29, 31, 33, 35, 37, 86, 105, 109, 114, 135, 138, 144, 147-48, 151, 158, 188-91, 190-91, 200-6, 211-12, 219; campaign, 24, 96; evaluations of, 25, 204; expectations of, 201; importance of resources, 100; organizations campaigning for, 96. *See also* Article 23
Nunavut Land Claims Project, 96
Nunavut Planning Commission, 33
Nunavut Political Accord, 1-2, 5, 31-32, 34-35, 105, 109, 114, 141, 145, 147, 162
Nunavut Social Development Council, 191; meeting in Igloolik, 191
Nunavut Status of Women Council, 144
Nunavut Tunngavik Incorporated, 33, 35, 135-36, 138, 144-45, 150-51, 154, 156, 159-60, 162-63, 165, 226n9; shadow cabinet, 136
Nunavut Water Board, 33
Nunavut Wildlife Management Board, 33

Office of Native Claims, 24
Office of the Administrator of the Arctic, 12, 74, 79
Office of the Special Representative, 12, 86, 98-103; attention to political culture, 103; innovation and, 101; Inuit reaction to, 98-99, 103; report of, 103; view of Berger Inquiry, 103; view of Carrothers commission, 103; view of political institutions, 103; view of political parties, 103; view of regional government, 102
Okalik, Paul, 194
Okpik, Abe, 24, 62, 79

Pangnirtung, 13, 18, 20, 31
party identification, 141
Patterson, Dennis, 134
Pauktuutit, 31, 144
Pembroke, 164

Phillips, R.A.J., 82
Phipps, Waldy, 65
Picco, Ed, 125
plebiscites, 24-25, 34, 78, 138, 146-47; on boundary (1992), 25; on capital (1995), 138, 146-47; on division (1982), 24, 146; on gender parity (1997), 34, 138, 146-47; on NLCA (1992), 25, 138, 146; turnout, 146
political attitudes, 168-89; comparisons with provinces, 172
political cleavages, 176-83; among MLAs, 131-32; demographic, 183; ethnic, 131, 179-80; generational, 180-82; geographic, 131, 177-79; spiritual, 182-83
political congealment, 215-58; as congruence of institutions and attitudes, 217-18; and institutions, 216-17
political culture, 1-17, 35, 38, 85, 103, 108-9, 112-13, 139-40, 168-73, 177, 179, 188, 190-206, 211-20; benefits of blending, 188; in Communist states, 216; cultural fragments, 2, 7, 113, 215; definitions, 1-2, 6; diversity within, 2, 9; federal political culture, 8, 113; impact of, 6; impact of institutions on, 4, 7; institutions and, 103, 108, 169, 193; measurement of, 38; Nunavut as separate, 140; provincial variations, 140, 169
political development, 57, 85, 101-2, 104, 110-11, 169; departments responsible for, 110-11; priority of local democracy, 101; public vs ethnic, 102, 104; vs local concerns, 104
political participation, 138-67; amount, 139; apathetics, 139; avenues of, 139; gladiators, 139, 163; spectators, 139; unconventional forms, 140

political parties, 114, 116-19, 139, 141; in Canada, 118; development of, 114; perceived necessity of, 116; roles of during campaigns, 117; shortcuts, 141; in US, 119
Pond Inlet, 13, 18, 20-21, 23, 28, 43, 177
postmaterialism, 12, 173-76, 181, 183-89, 215, 222; age, 175-76; applicability in Nunavut, 175; ethnicity, 175-76
poverty, 27-28. *See also* cost of living
Premier of Nunavut, 33; direct election, 107; selection of, 112
Premier of the Northwest Territories, 110-12, 194; list of, 110-11; selection of, 112
Prince Edward Island, 172
Progressive Conservative Party of Canada, 24, 97, 118, 153
Project Surname. *See* Inuit, naming
provincial status, 57, 86, 91, 93-95, 98-99, 101, 105, 109, 218; Inuit views on, 99
Pryde, Duncan, 65, 66
public opinion polls, 125

Qairnirmiut, 19
Qallunaat population, 27, 74, 79, 131, 155, 179, 198-99, 224n2
Qikiqtaaluk region. *See* Baffin
Qikiqtani Inuit Association, 22, 33, 144-45, 151, 167
Qikiqtarjuaq, 17, 31
Quebec, 21-23, 56, 74, 96-97, 155, 172, 177, 180, 223n4

racism, 180
Rankin Inlet, 19, 25, 27, 62, 65-66, 72, 74, 77, 84, 107, 130, 152, 178, 196, 226n4
Red River Colony, 88

Reform Party, 118, 153
regular members, 127, 130-31, 133, 196; caucus, 135; compliance of, 133; division among, 131; incentives for, 133
religion, 182, 188, 193; and regionalism, 183
Rennie, Gordon, 65
representation, 66-67; by geography, 67; of people, 67
Repulse Bay, 13, 177
residential schools, 23, 31, 96, 143, 181, 200, 217; compensation package, 23
Resolute, 21-23, 65, 177
responsible government, 32, 57-58, 67, 71, 86-93, 95, 101-2, 105, 109, 134, 141, 213, 218
Robertson, Robert, 67, 87, 90-91, 93
Roman Catholic church, 20-21, 23, 51-52, 68, 74, 132, 182
Royal Canadian Legion, 144, 226n1
Royal Canadian Mounted Police (RCMP), 21-23, 54, 68, 89; dog slaughter, 22-23
Royal Commission on Aboriginal Peoples (RCAP), 23
Royal Commission on Electoral Reform and Party Financing, 10, 141
rules, 47, 51-56, 61, 81, 217
Rupert's Land, 20, 88

Sanguya, Joelie, 195-96
Saskatchewan, 56, 87, 172
Saskatoon (SK), 72
seal hunt, 31
sexual abuse, 23, 31
shamanism, 44-45, 47, 51-52, 54-55, 182, 217
Simeon, Richard, 8, 140, 169, 172
siqitiqtut, 52-53
Sivertz, Ben, 93

social capital, 36, 140, 142-44, 186
social well-being, 27, 31, 211
Standing Committee on Northern Affairs and National Resources, 78
starvation, 11, 21-22, 41
Statistics Canada, 11, 26, 28
stereotypes of Inuit, 15, 58, 68, 72, 84; by federal officials, 58, 197-98
Stevenson, Alexander, 68
Stevenson, Marc, 31, 39, 45, 48
suicide, 30-32, 198, 223n7
Supreme Court, 21, 24, 56, 92, 96; *Calder* decision, 24, 96; *Re Eskimos* [1939], 21, 56, 92
Survey of Living Conditions in the Arctic (SLiCA), 11
Switzerland, 153

taboos, 4, 44, 46-47, 49, 50, 52-54, 194; confession, 47; gender and, 47; hunters and, 46; risks of breaking, 47
Tagoona, Eric, 81, 101
Taloyoak, 19, 48
Territorial Council of the Northwest Territories, 58, 88, 90, 94, 100, 134; appointment to, 58; arrival in Yellowknife, 93; balance between appointed and elected members, 88; first elections to, 86, 90; meetings of, 60, 62; relations between appointed and elected members, 72; view of resources, 100
territorial identity, 93-94, 109; development of, 93-94
Thompson, Manitok, 134, 153, 225n6
Tootoo, Hunter, 125, 132, 196
traditional knowledge, 35, 78, 132; working groups in NWT, 191
traditionalism, 178, 185, 187
transgenerational grief, 31
Trudeau, Pierre Elliott, 80

Tuktoyaktuk, 69-70, 74
Tungavik Federation of Nunavut (TFN), 24, 33, 96, 100, 144, 190. *See also* Nunavut Tunngavik Incorporated
Tununirmiut, 13

unemployment, 29, 157, 165
Ungava, 56
United States, 22, 87, 89, 119, 142, 153; patterns of institutional design, 89
Upper Canada, 87
Uqqurmiut, 13

voter turnout, 16, 126, 136, 138, 147-63, 213; and age, 160; birthright organizations, 150-51; calculation of, 148-49; community size, 162; comparison of federal and territorial rates, 158; and consensus politics, 153; cynicism, 160, 162; deference, 160, 162; federal elections, 152; income, 159, 162; individual and systemic predictors of, 151-63; Inuktitut speakers and, 148; overreporting in Nunavut, 149-50; overreporting in surveys, 159; political community, 163; territorial election (1999), 148; territorial election (2004), 148, 152; traditional activities and, 160
voters, 127-38; influence over formation of government, 127; system of enumeration, 138
voting pamphlet for Inuit, 61-63, 76; by-elections (1966), 61-63; description of federalism, 76; federal election (1962), 76

Washie, James, 83
Westminster, 2, 32, 56-57, 64, 67, 113, 168, 195, 198
Whale Cove, 25, 65, 77-78
White, Graham, 29, 38, 105, 112, 114, 128, 130-31, 140, 190, 223n1, 223n5
Wildavsky, Aaron, 9
Williamson, Robert, 65-66, 72
Winnipeg (MB), 178
World Values Survey, 10, 12, 173

Yellowknife, 23, 34, 71, 85, 87, 93-94, 106, 113, 129-31, 178, 218; arrival of territorial administration, 94, 109, 113, 115
Yukon, 1, 56, 87, 89-90, 109; commissioner of, 89; creation of, 56, 89
Y'upik, 18

Printed and bound in Canada by Friesens
Set in Giovanni and Scala Sans by Artegraphica Design Co. Ltd.
Copy editor: Joanne Richardson
Proofreader: James Leahy
Cartographer: Eric Leinberger